287 – Part One: "Take Two"

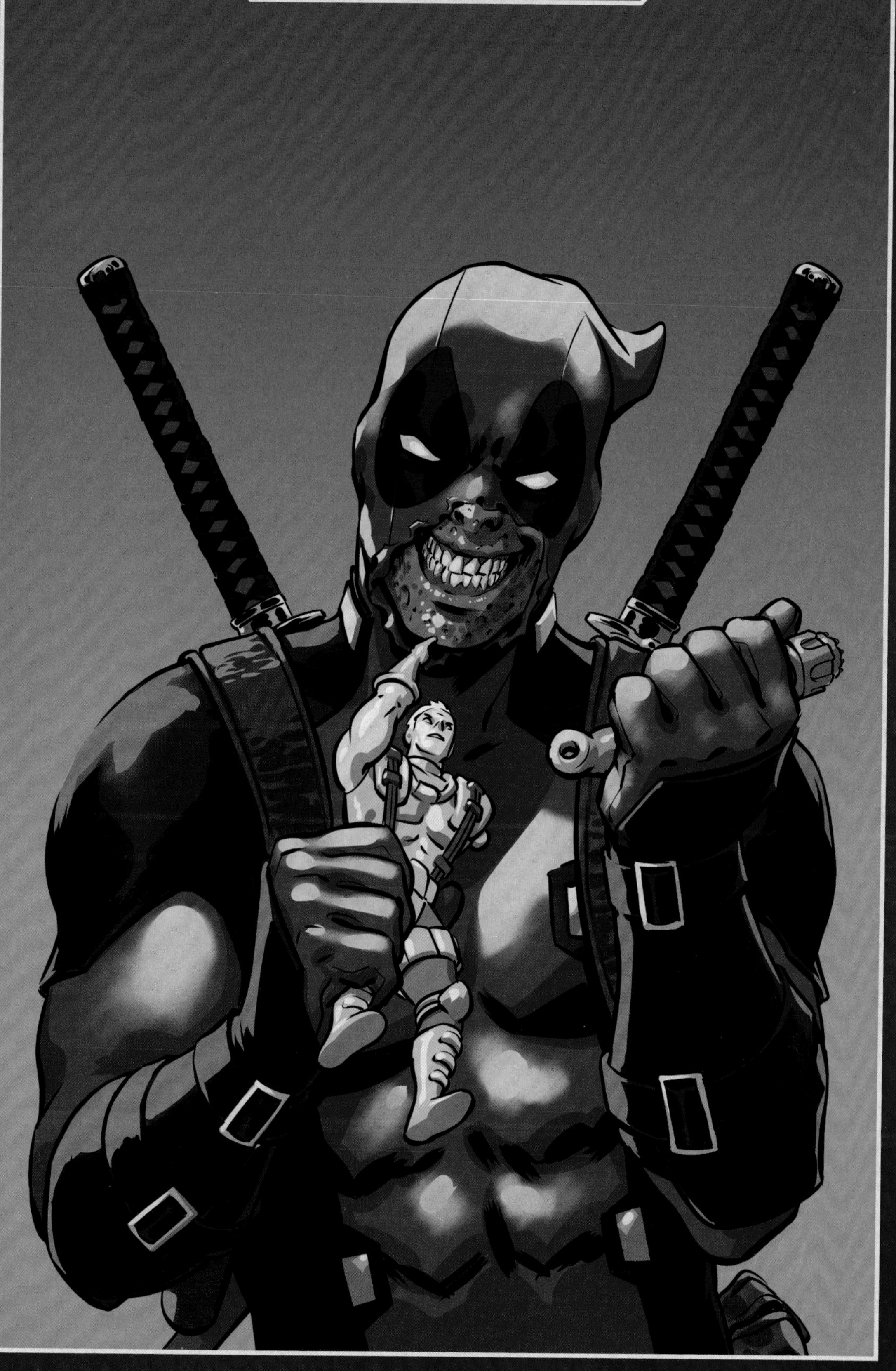

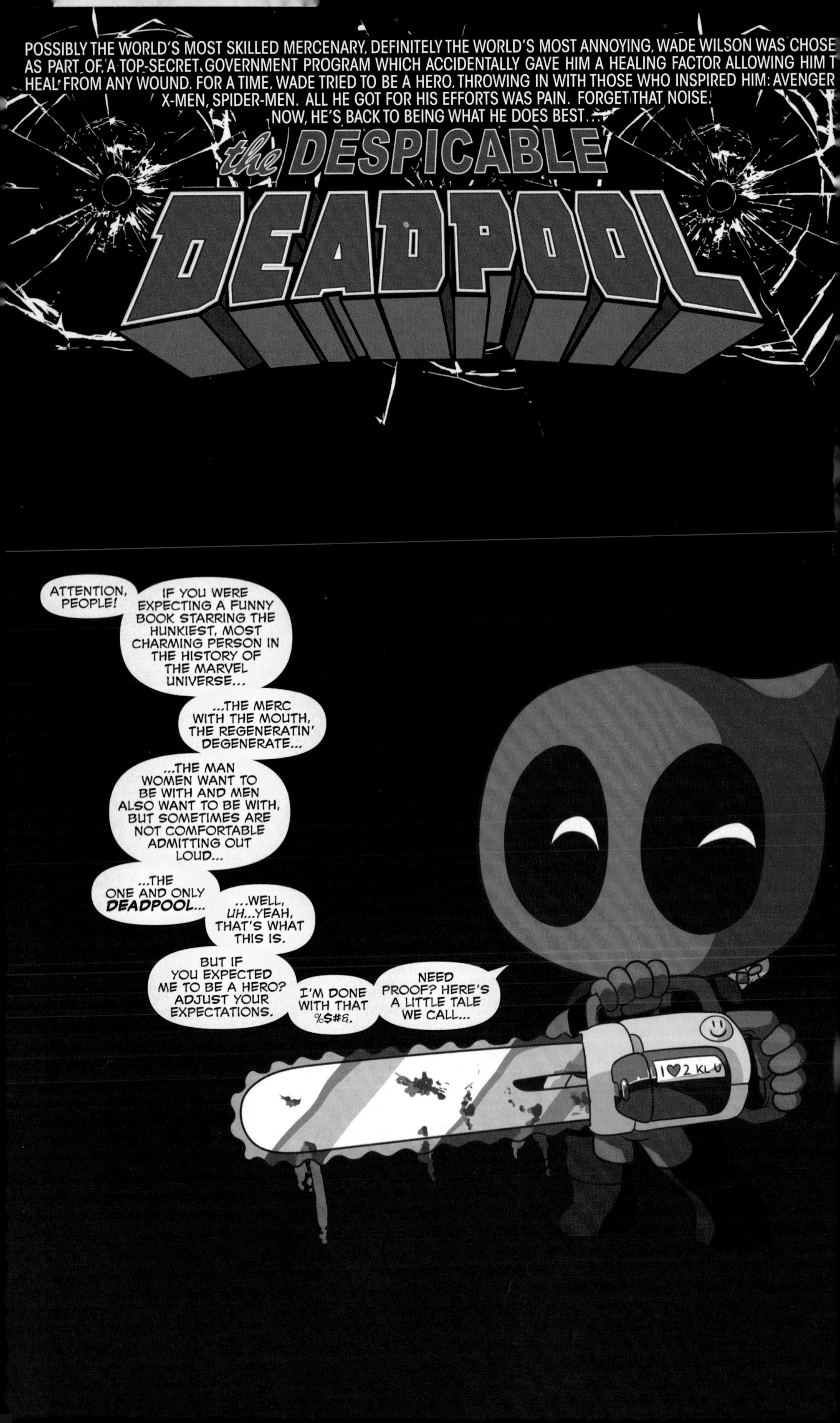
POSSIBLY THE WORLD'S MOST SKILLED MERCENARY, DEFINITELY THE WORLD'S MOST ANNOYING, WADE WILSON WAS CHOSE AS PART OF A TOP-SECRET GOVERNMENT PROGRAM WHICH ACCIDENTALLY GAVE HIM A HEALING FACTOR ALLOWING HIM T HEAL FROM ANY WOUND. FOR A TIME, WADE TRIED TO BE A HERO, THROWING IN WITH THOSE WHO INSPIRED HIM: AVENGER X-MEN, SPIDER-MEN. ALL HE GOT FOR HIS EFFORTS WAS PAIN. FORGET THAT NOISE. NOW, HE'S BACK TO BEING WHAT HE DOES BEST...
the DESPICABLE DEADPOOL
ATTENTION, PEOPLE!
IF YOU WERE EXPECTING A FUNNY BOOK STARRING THE HUNKIEST, MOST CHARMING PERSON IN THE HISTORY OF THE MARVEL UNIVERSE...
...THE MERC WITH THE MOUTH, THE REGENERATIN' DEGENERATE...
...THE MAN WOMEN WANT TO BE WITH AND MEN ALSO WANT TO BE WITH, BUT SOMETIMES ARE NOT COMFORTABLE ADMITTING OUT LOUD...
...THE ONE AND ONLY DEADPOOL...
...WELL, UH...YEAH, THAT'S WHAT THIS IS.
BUT IF YOU EXPECTED ME TO BE A HERO? ADJUST YOUR EXPECTATIONS.
I'M DONE WITH THAT %$#&.
NEED PROOF? HERE'S A LITTLE TALE WE CALL...
I ♥ 2 KL U

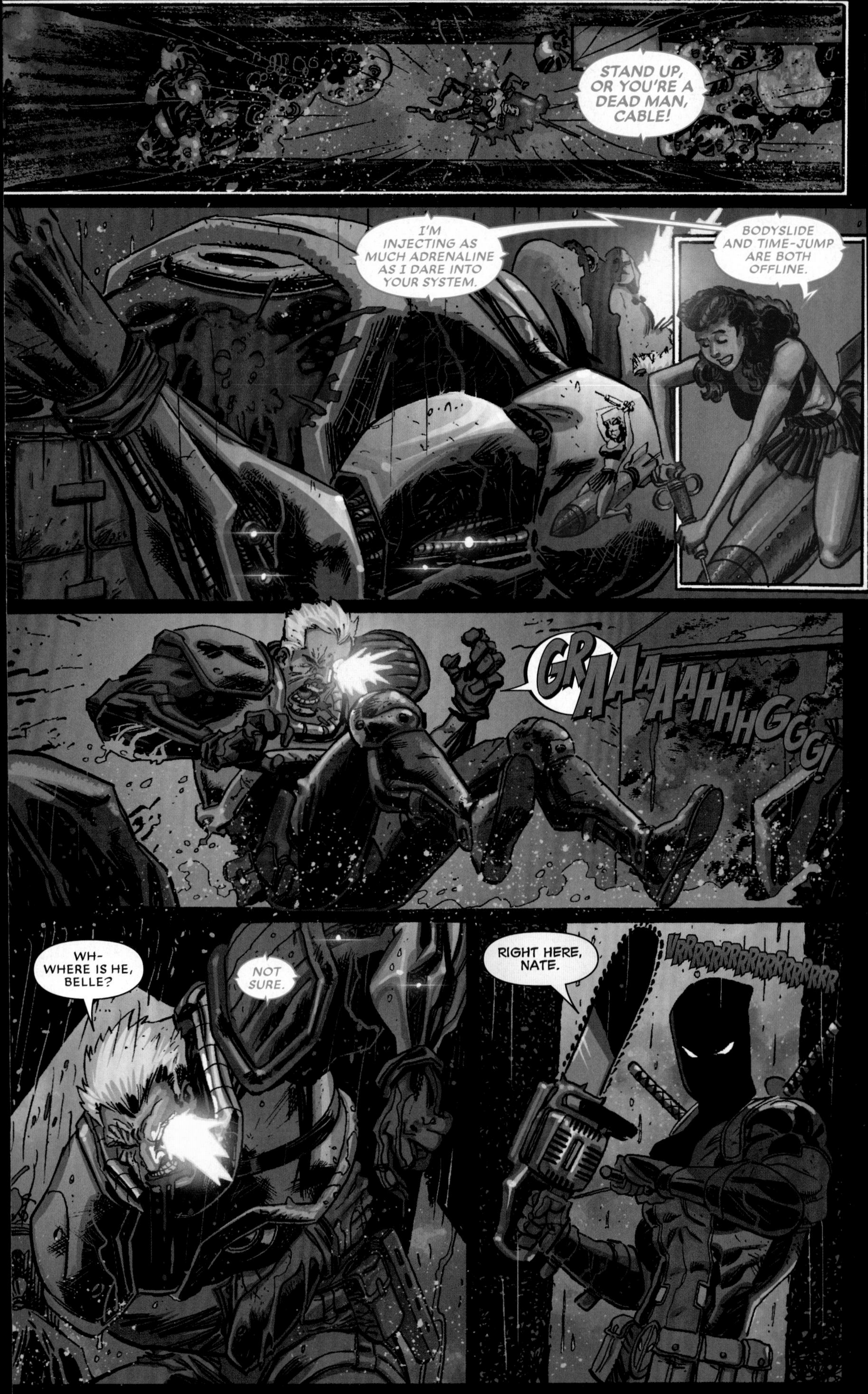
STAND UP, OR YOU'RE A DEAD MAN, CABLE!
I'M INJECTING AS MUCH ADRENALINE AS I DARE INTO YOUR SYSTEM.
BODYSLIDE AND TIME-JUMP ARE BOTH OFFLINE.
GRAAAAAHHHGGG!
WH- WHERE IS HE, BELLE?
NOT SURE.
RIGHT HERE, NATE.
VRRRRRRRRRRRRRRRRR

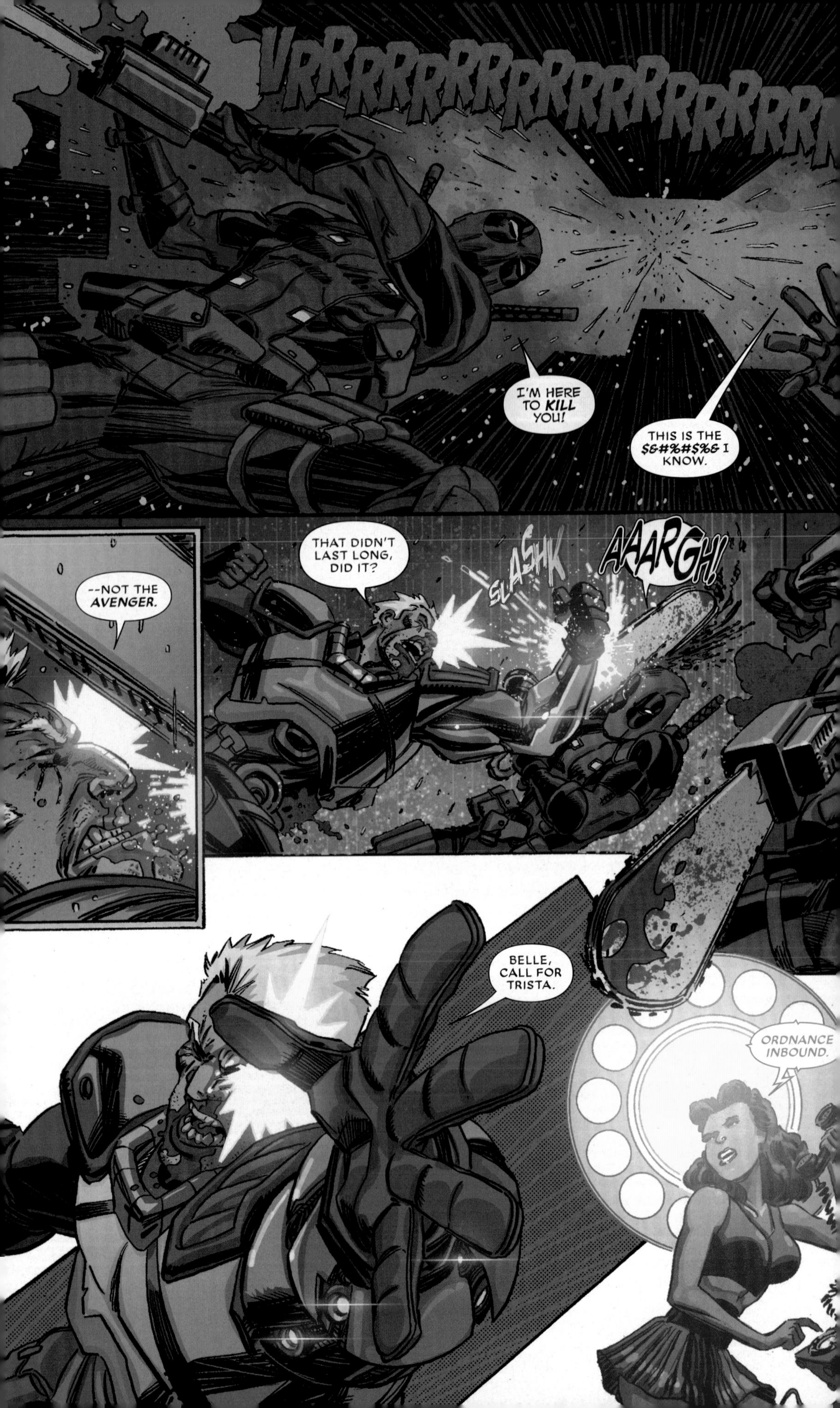
VRRRRRRRRRRRRRRRRRRRRR
I'M HERE TO KILL YOU!
THIS IS THE $&#%#$%& I KNOW.
--NOT THE AVENGER.
THAT DIDN'T LAST LONG, DID IT?
SLASHK
AAARGH!
BELLE, CALL FOR TRISTA.
ORDNANCE INBOUND.

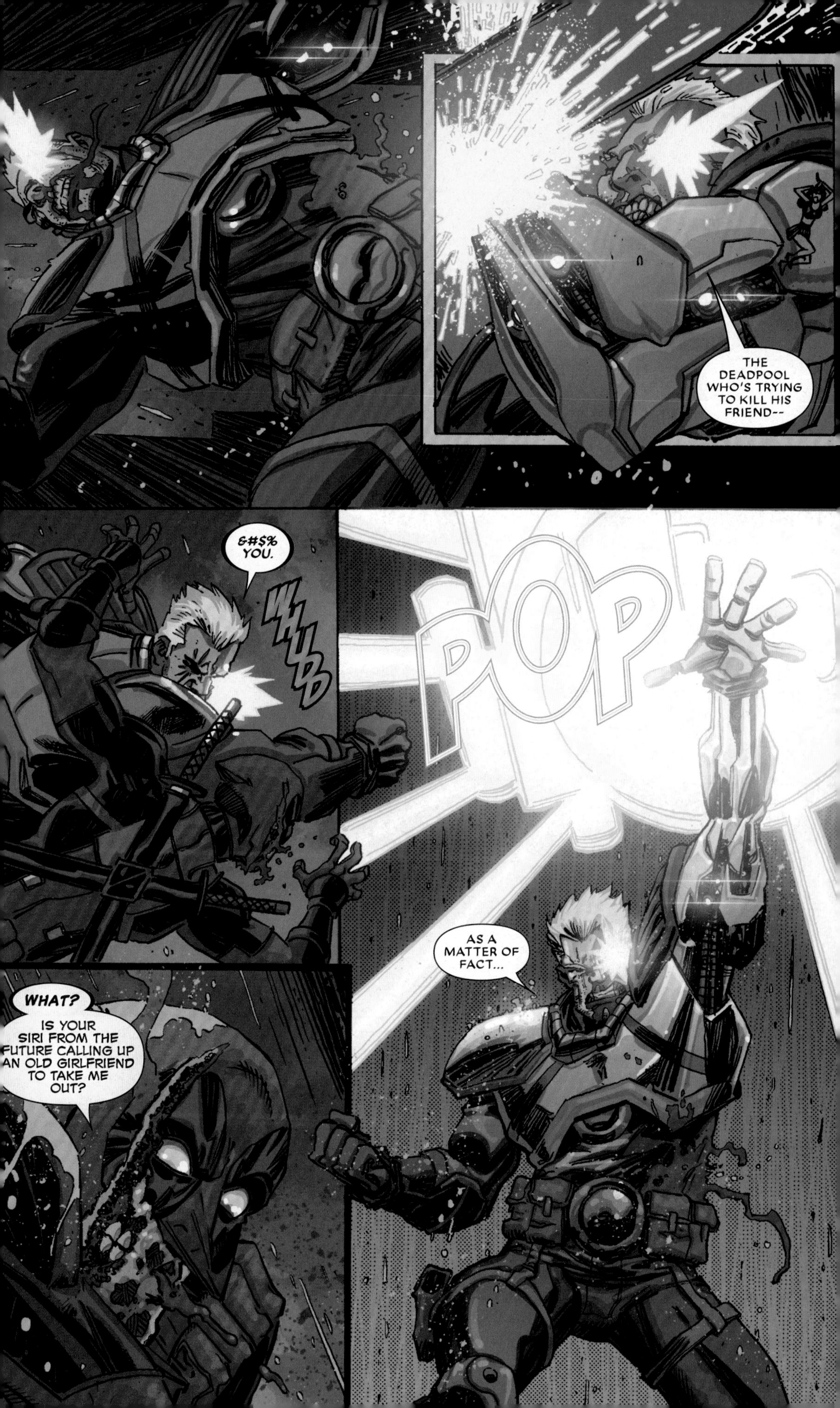

THE DEADPOOL WHO'S TRYING TO KILL HIS FRIEND--
&#$% YOU.
WHUDD
POP
AS A MATTER OF FACT...
WHAT?
IS YOUR SIRI FROM THE FUTURE CALLING UP AN OLD GIRLFRIEND TO TAKE ME OUT?

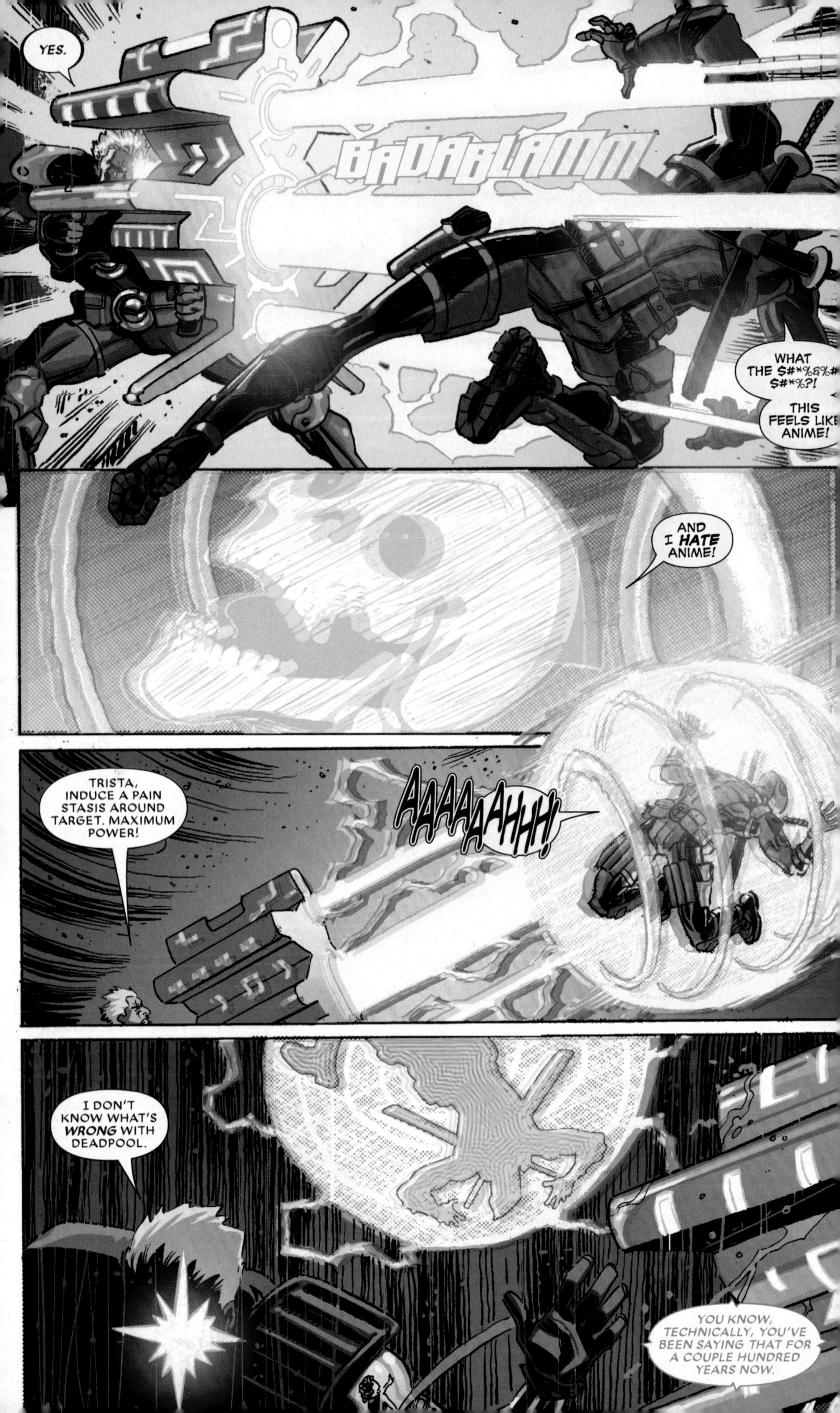
YES.
BADABLAMM
WHAT THE $#*%&%# $#*%?!
THIS FEELS LIKE ANIME!
AND I HATE ANIME!
TRISTA, INDUCE A PAIN STASIS AROUND TARGET. MAXIMUM POWER!
AAAAAAHHH!
I DON'T KNOW WHAT'S WRONG WITH DEADPOOL.
YOU KNOW, TECHNICALLY, YOU'VE BEEN SAYING THAT FOR A COUPLE HUNDRED YEARS NOW.

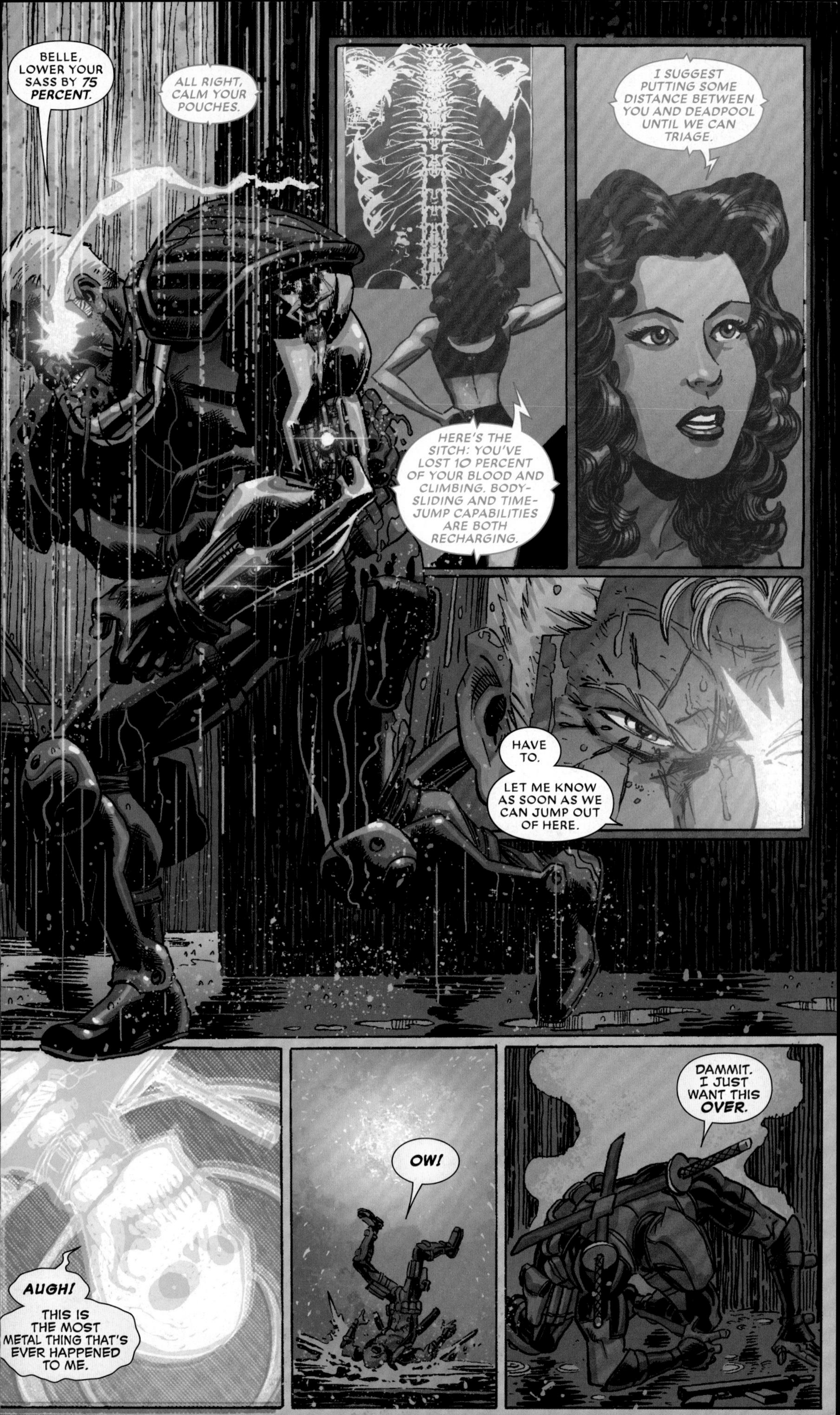

BELLE, LOWER YOUR SASS BY *75 PERCENT.*
ALL RIGHT, CALM YOUR POUCHES.
I SUGGEST PUTTING SOME DISTANCE BETWEEN YOU AND DEADPOOL UNTIL WE CAN TRIAGE.
HERE'S THE SITCH: YOU'VE LOST 10 PERCENT OF YOUR BLOOD AND CLIMBING. BODY-SLIDING AND TIME-JUMP CAPABILITIES ARE BOTH RECHARGING.
HAVE TO.
LET ME KNOW AS SOON AS WE CAN JUMP OUT OF HERE.
AUGH!
THIS IS THE MOST METAL THING THAT'S EVER HAPPENED TO ME.
OW!
DAMMIT. I JUST WANT THIS *OVER.*

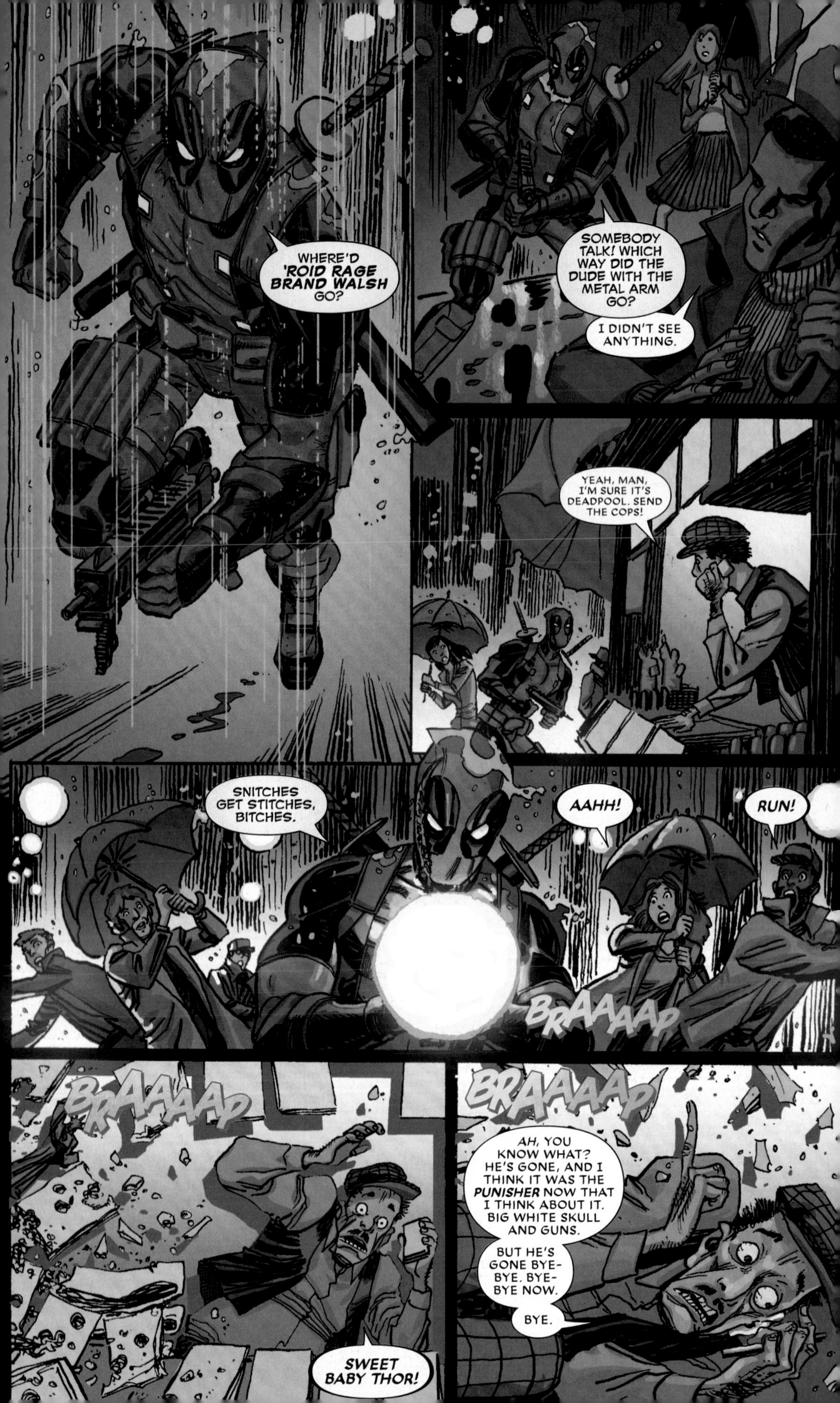

WHERE'D 'ROID RAGE BRAND WALSH GO?
SOMEBODY TALK! WHICH WAY DID THE DUDE WITH THE METAL ARM GO?
I DIDN'T SEE ANYTHING.
YEAH, MAN, I'M SURE IT'S DEADPOOL. SEND THE COPS!
SNITCHES GET STITCHES, BITCHES.
AAHH!
RUN!
BRAAAAAP
BRAAAAAP
SWEET BABY THOR!
BRAAAAAP
AH, YOU KNOW WHAT? HE'S GONE, AND I THINK IT WAS THE PUNISHER NOW THAT I THINK ABOUT IT. BIG WHITE SKULL AND GUNS.
BUT HE'S GONE BYE-BYE. BYE-BYE NOW.
BYE.

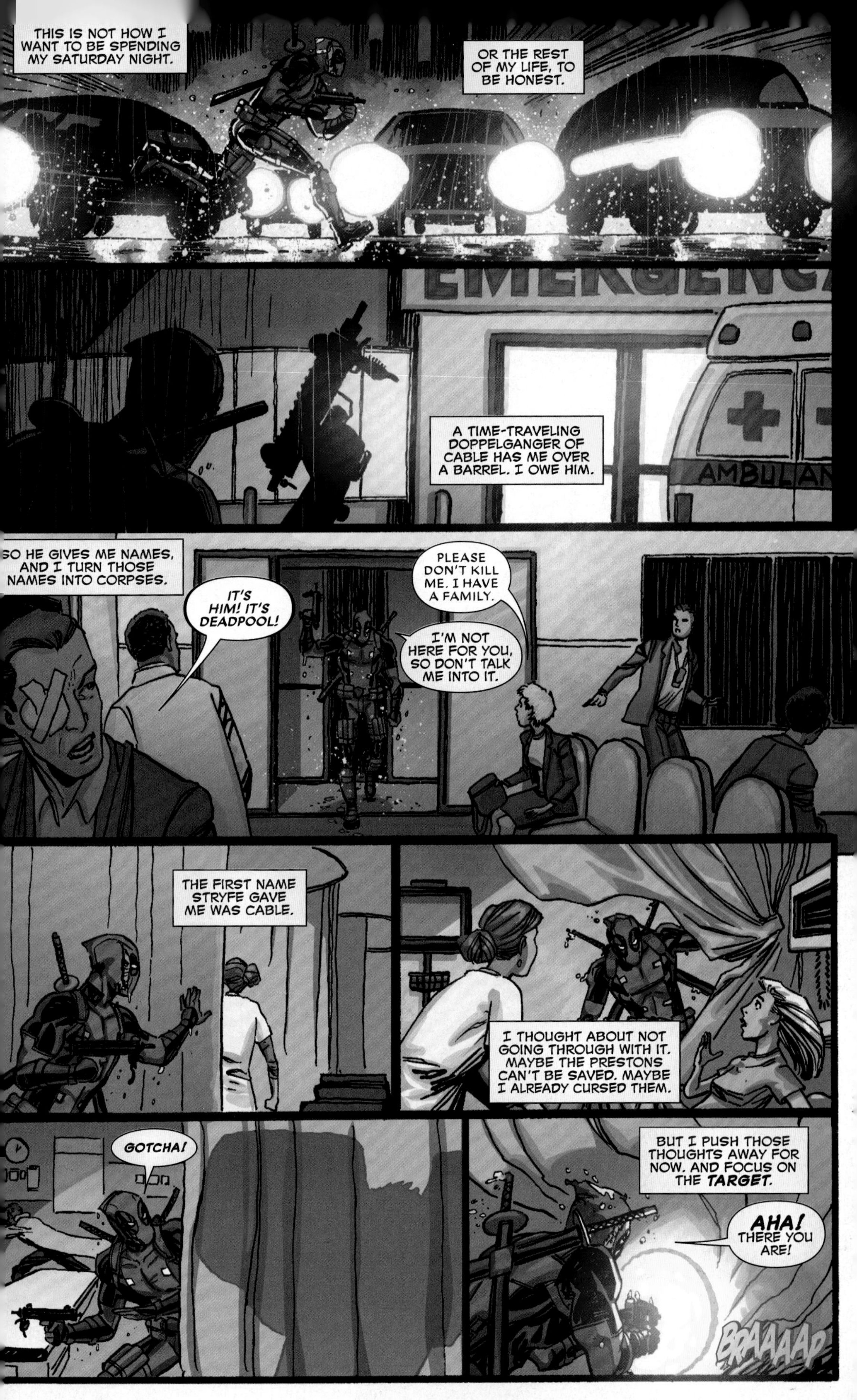
THIS IS NOT HOW I WANT TO BE SPENDING MY SATURDAY NIGHT.
OR THE REST OF MY LIFE, TO BE HONEST.
EMERGENC
A TIME-TRAVELING DOPPELGANGER OF CABLE HAS ME OVER A BARREL. I OWE HIM.
AMBULAN
SO HE GIVES ME NAMES, AND I TURN THOSE NAMES INTO CORPSES.
IT'S HIM! IT'S DEADPOOL!
PLEASE DON'T KILL ME. I HAVE A FAMILY.
I'M NOT HERE FOR YOU, SO DON'T TALK ME INTO IT.
THE FIRST NAME STRYFE GAVE ME WAS CABLE.
I THOUGHT ABOUT NOT GOING THROUGH WITH IT. MAYBE THE PRESTONS CAN'T BE SAVED. MAYBE I ALREADY CURSED THEM.
GOTCHA!
BUT I PUSH THOSE THOUGHTS AWAY FOR NOW. AND FOCUS ON THE TARGET.
AHA! THERE YOU ARE!
BRAAAAP

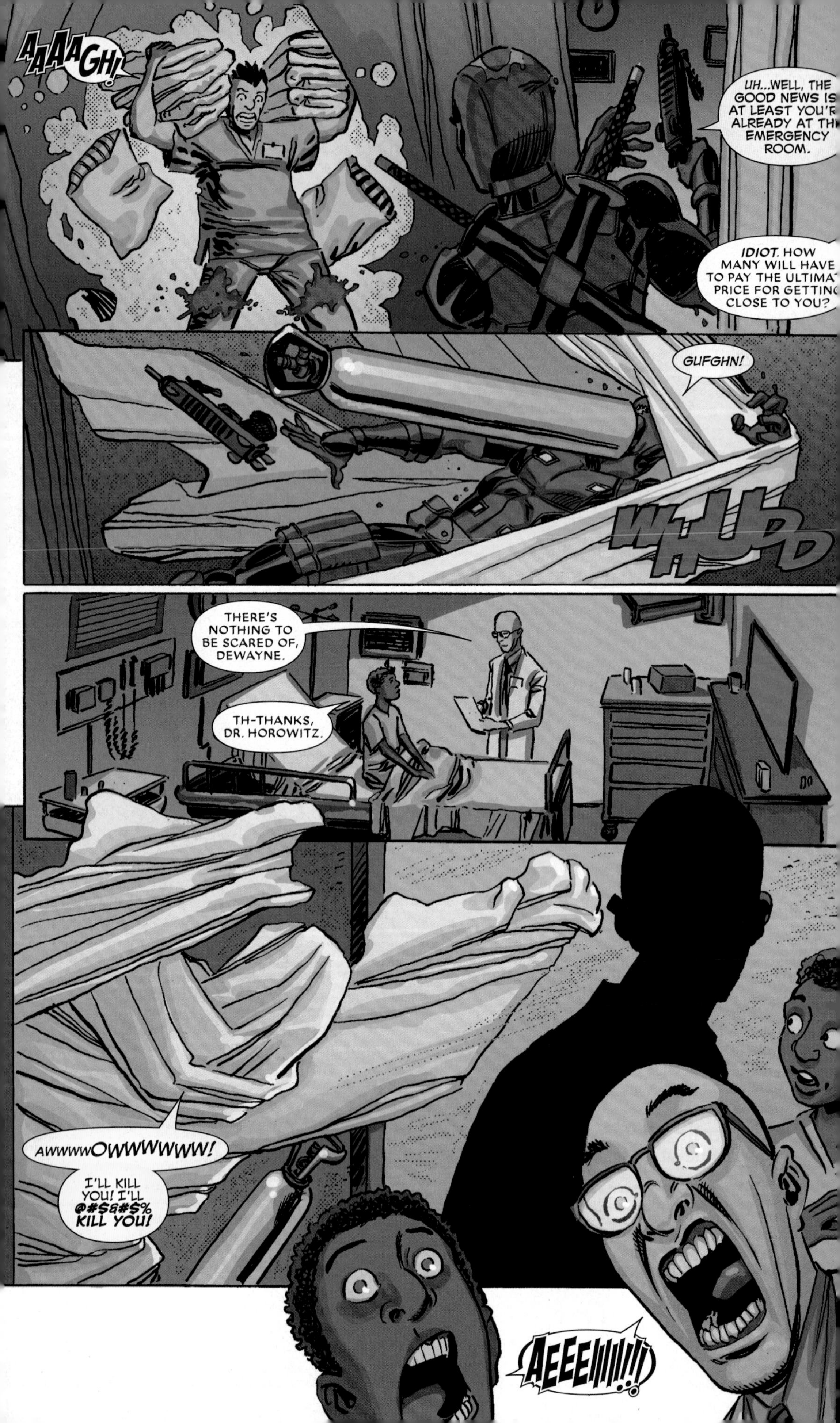
AAAAGH!
UH...WELL, THE GOOD NEWS IS AT LEAST YOU'R ALREADY AT TH EMERGENCY ROOM.
IDIOT. HOW MANY WILL HAVE TO PAY THE ULTIMAT PRICE FOR GETTIN CLOSE TO YOU?
GUFGHN!
WHUDD
THERE'S NOTHING TO BE SCARED OF, DEWAYNE.
TH-THANKS, DR. HOROWITZ.
AWWWWOWWWWWW!
I'LL KILL YOU! I'LL @#$&#$% KILL YOU!
AEEEIIIIII!!!

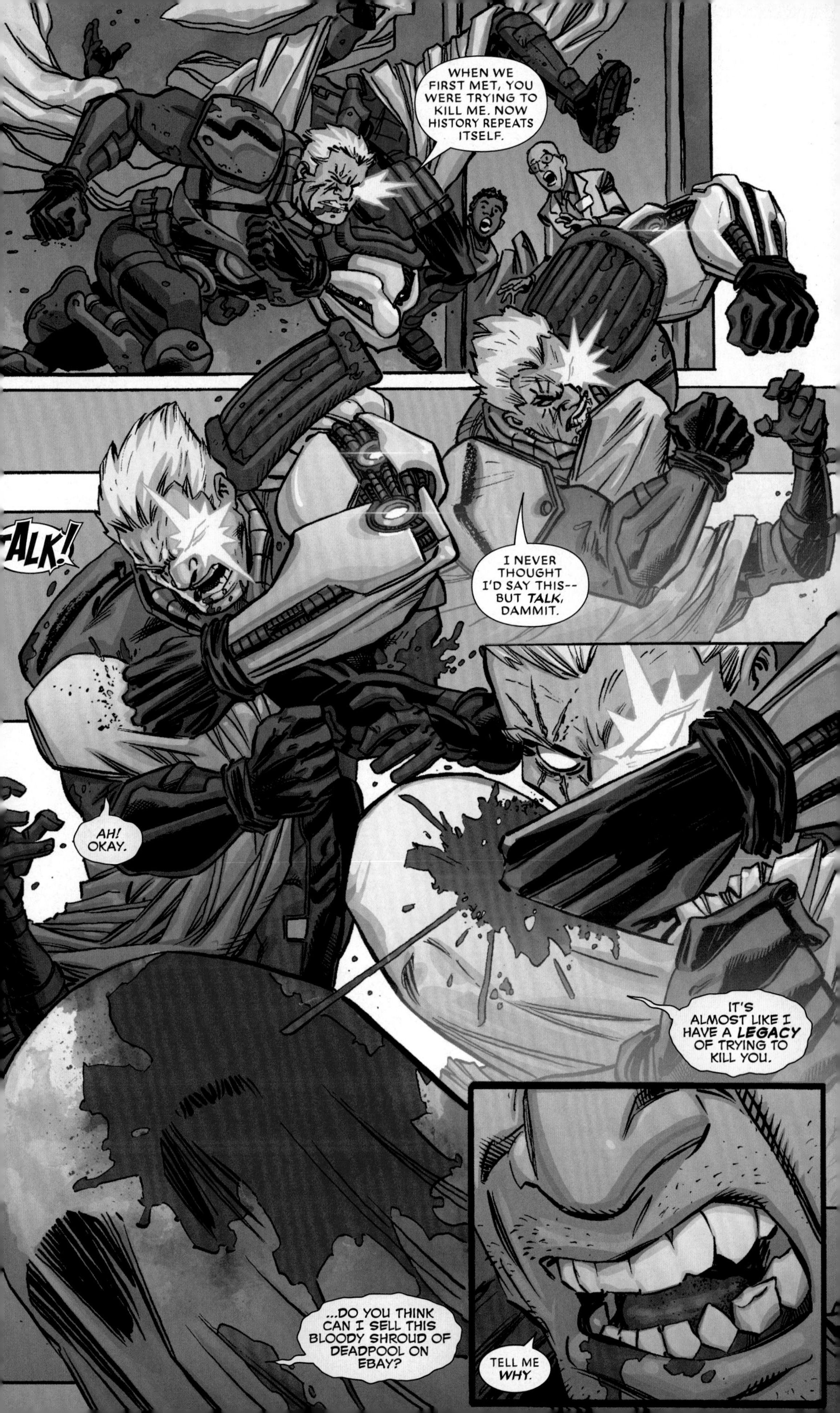
WHEN WE FIRST MET, YOU WERE TRYING TO KILL ME. NOW HISTORY REPEATS ITSELF.
I NEVER THOUGHT I'D SAY THIS-- BUT *TALK*, DAMMIT.
TALK!
AH! OKAY.
IT'S ALMOST LIKE I HAVE A *LEGACY* OF TRYING TO KILL YOU.
...DO YOU THINK CAN I SELL THIS BLOODY SHROUD OF DEADPOOL ON EBAY?
TELL ME *WHY*.

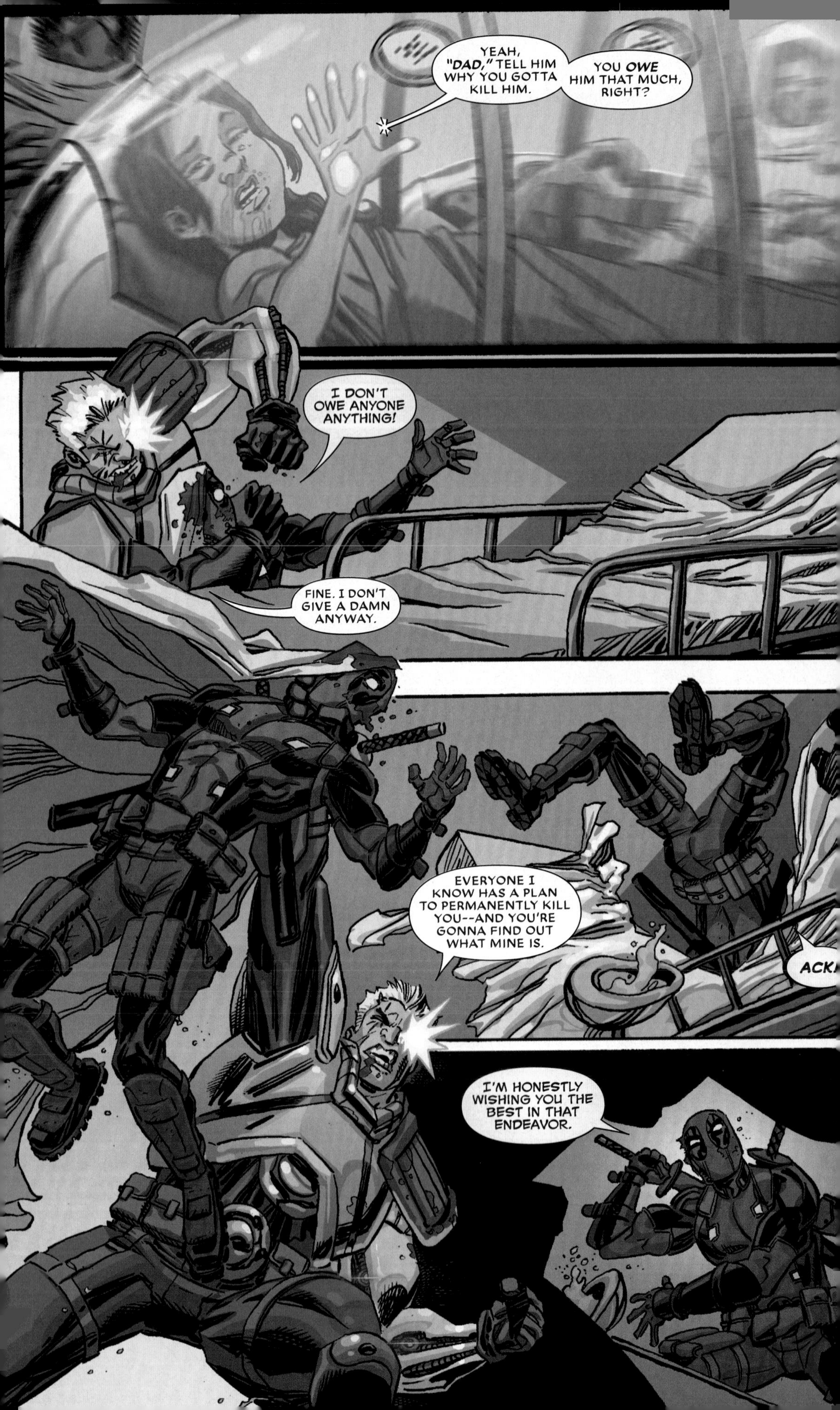
YEAH, "DAD," TELL HIM WHY YOU GOTTA KILL HIM.
YOU OWE HIM THAT MUCH, RIGHT?
I DON'T OWE ANYONE ANYTHING!
FINE. I DON'T GIVE A DAMN ANYWAY.
EVERYONE I KNOW HAS A PLAN TO PERMANENTLY KILL YOU--AND YOU'RE GONNA FIND OUT WHAT MINE IS.
I'M HONESTLY WISHING YOU THE BEST IN THAT ENDEAVOR.

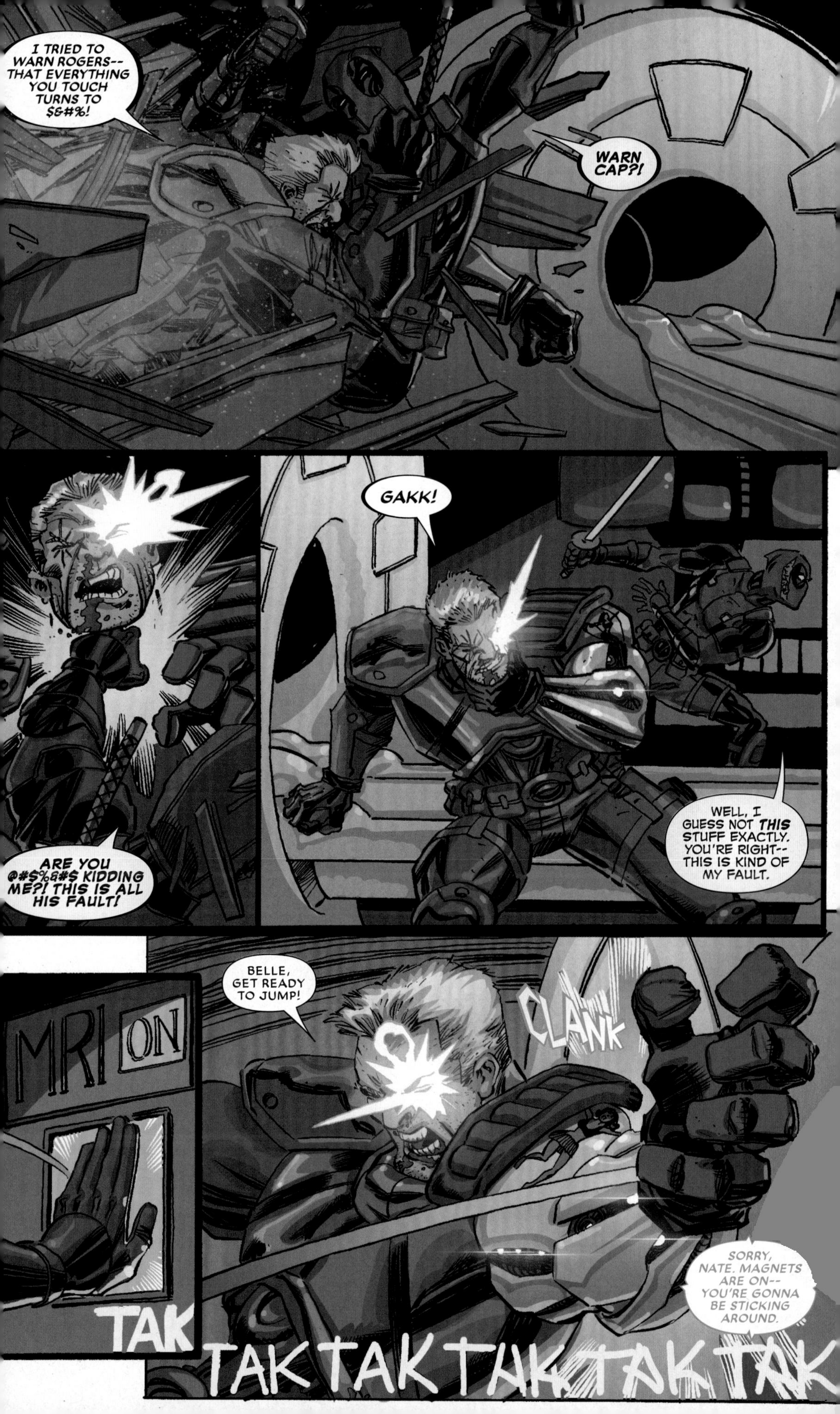
I TRIED TO WARN ROGERS-- THAT EVERYTHING YOU TOUCH TURNS TO $&#%!
WARN CAP?!
ARE YOU @#$%&#$ KIDDING ME?! THIS IS ALL HIS FAULT!
GAKK!
WELL, I GUESS NOT THIS STUFF EXACTLY. YOU'RE RIGHT-- THIS IS KIND OF MY FAULT.
MRI
ON
BELLE, GET READY TO JUMP!
CLANK
SORRY, NATE. MAGNETS ARE ON-- YOU'RE GONNA BE STICKING AROUND.
TAK
TAK TAK TAK TAK TAK

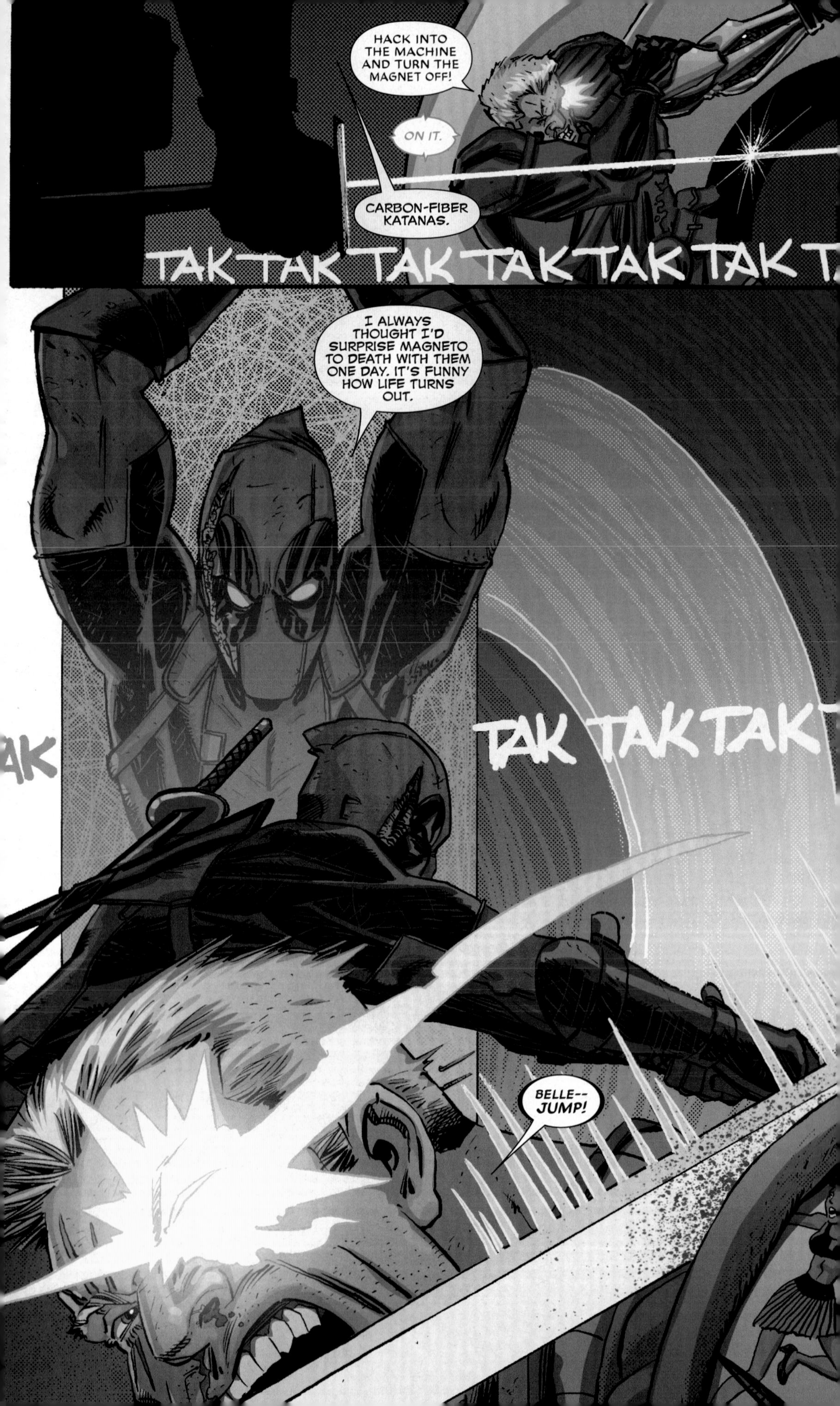

HACK INTO THE MACHINE AND TURN THE MAGNET OFF!
ON IT.
CARBON-FIBER KATANAS.
TAK TAK TAK TAK TAK TAK
I ALWAYS THOUGHT I'D SURPRISE MAGNETO TO DEATH WITH THEM ONE DAY. IT'S FUNNY HOW LIFE TURNS OUT.
TAK TAK TAK
BELLE-- JUMP!

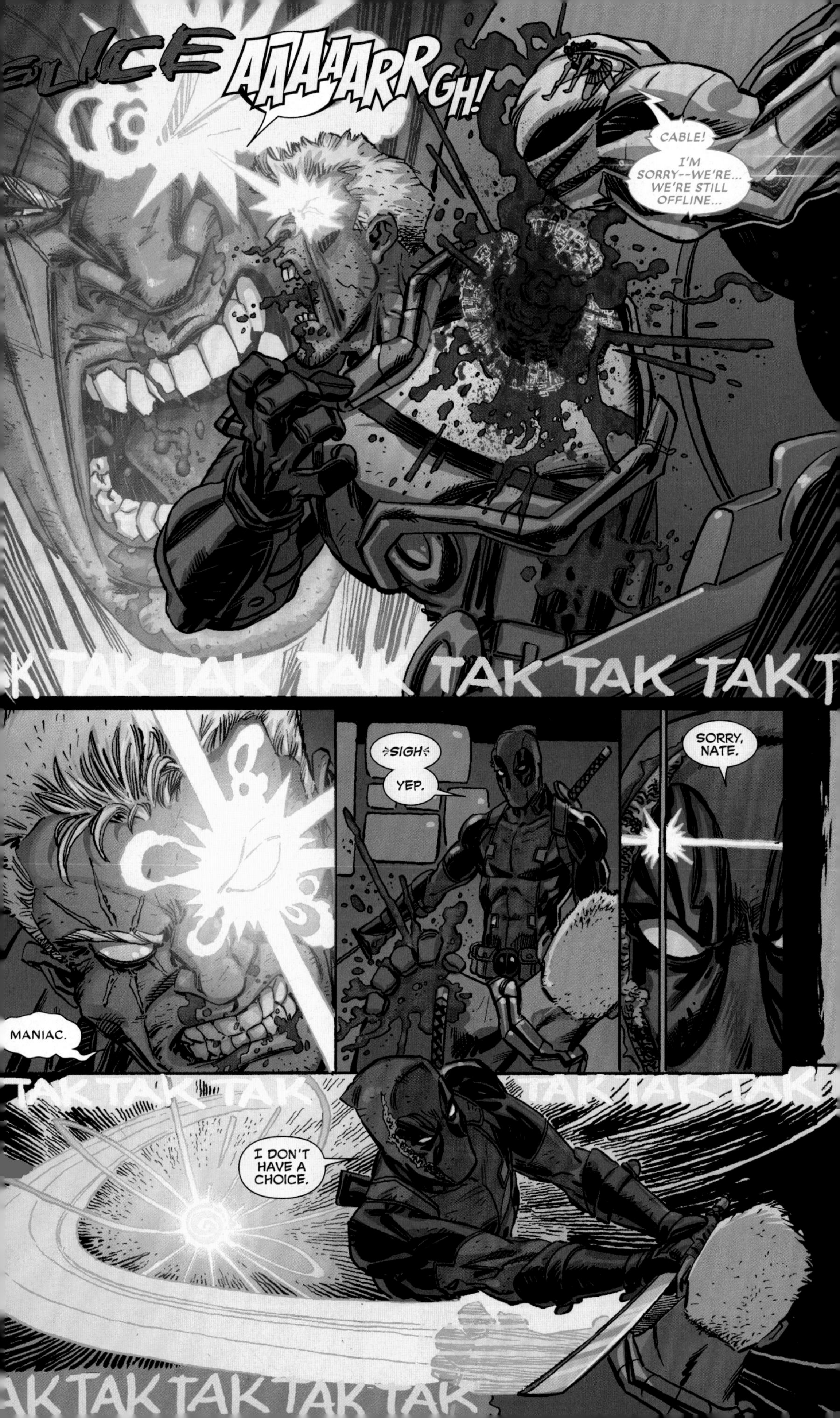
SLICE
AAAAARRRGH!
CABLE!
I'M SORRY--WE'RE... WE'RE STILL OFFLINE...
TAK TAK TAK TAK TAK TAK
SIGH
YEP.
SORRY, NATE.
MANIAC.
TAK TAK TAK
TAK TAK TAK
I DON'T HAVE A CHOICE.
TAK TAK TAK TAK TAK

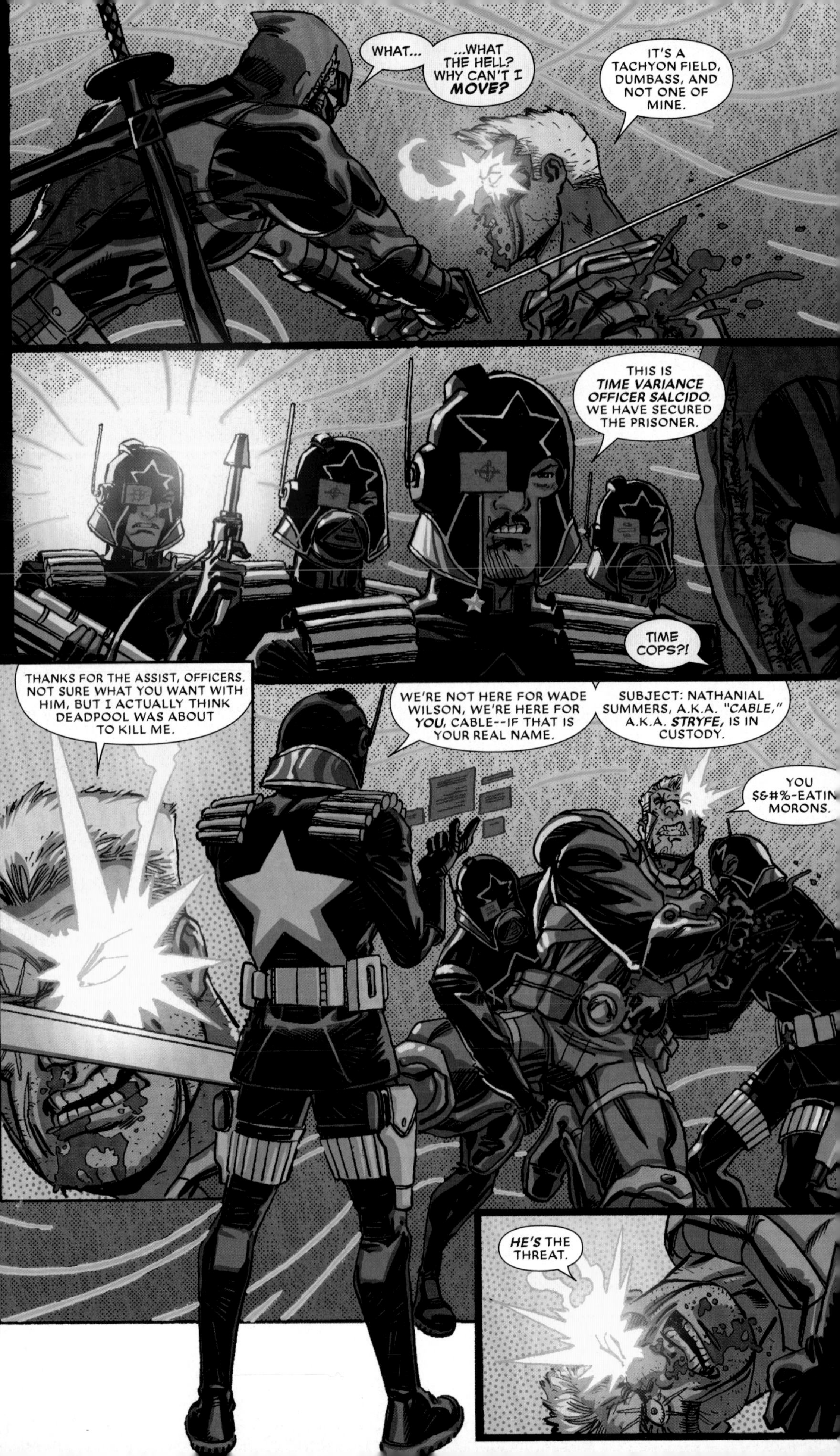
WHAT...
...WHAT THE HELL? WHY CAN'T I MOVE?
IT'S A TACHYON FIELD, DUMBASS, AND NOT ONE OF MINE.
THIS IS TIME VARIANCE OFFICER SALCIDO. WE HAVE SECURED THE PRISONER.
TIME COPS?!
THANKS FOR THE ASSIST, OFFICERS. NOT SURE WHAT YOU WANT WITH HIM, BUT I ACTUALLY THINK DEADPOOL WAS ABOUT TO KILL ME.
WE'RE NOT HERE FOR WADE WILSON, WE'RE HERE FOR YOU, CABLE--IF THAT IS YOUR REAL NAME.
SUBJECT: NATHANIAL SUMMERS, A.K.A. "CABLE," A.K.A. STRYFE, IS IN CUSTODY.
YOU $&#%-EATIN MORONS.
HE'S THE THREAT.

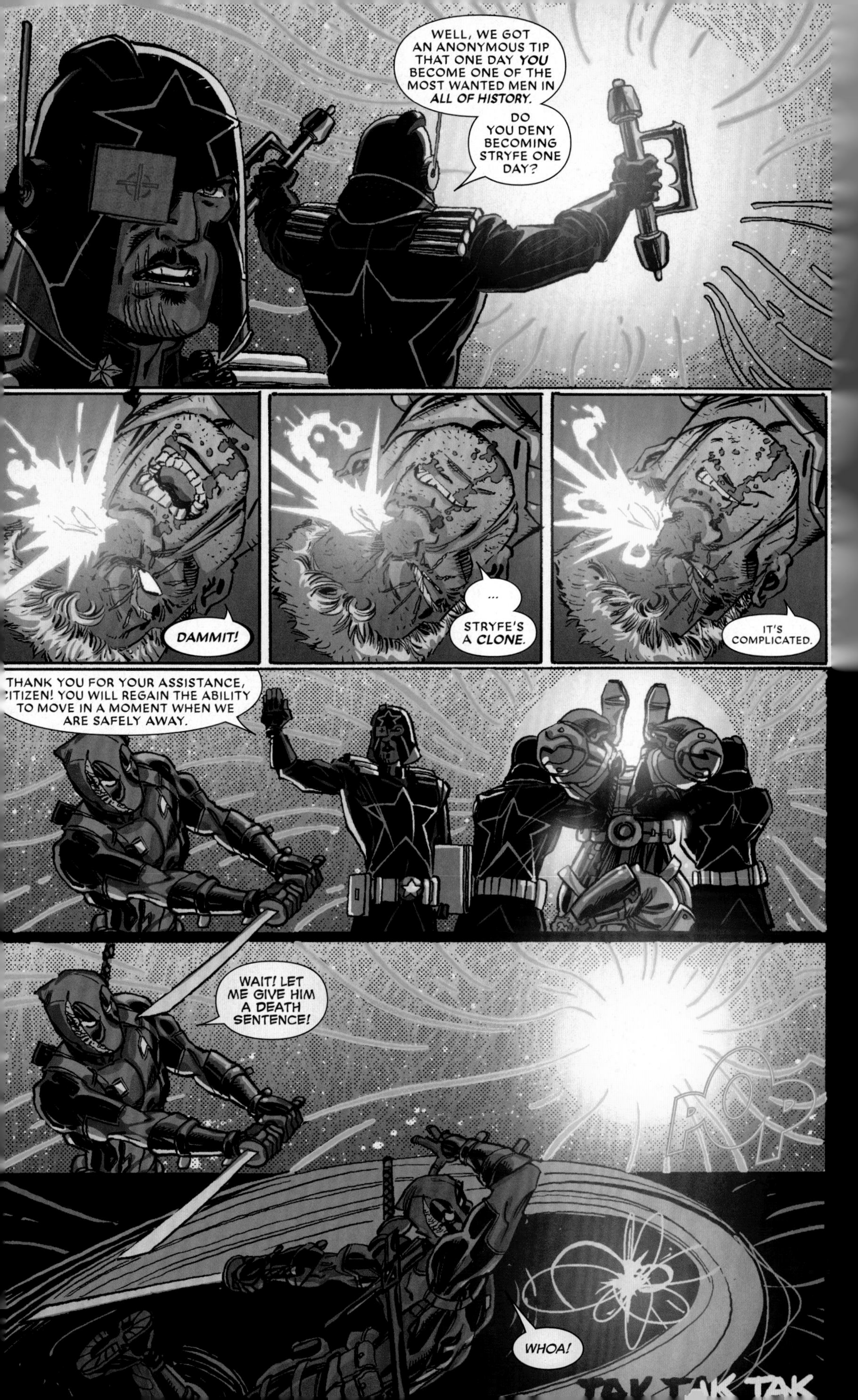
WELL, WE GOT AN ANONYMOUS TIP THAT ONE DAY *YOU* BECOME ONE OF THE MOST WANTED MEN IN ***ALL OF HISTORY.***
DO YOU DENY BECOMING STRYFE ONE DAY?
DAMMIT!
...
STRYFE'S A ***CLONE***.
IT'S COMPLICATED.
THANK YOU FOR YOUR ASSISTANCE, CITIZEN! YOU WILL REGAIN THE ABILITY TO MOVE IN A MOMENT WHEN WE ARE SAFELY AWAY.
WAIT! LET ME GIVE HIM A DEATH SENTENCE!
WHOA!
TAK TAK TAK

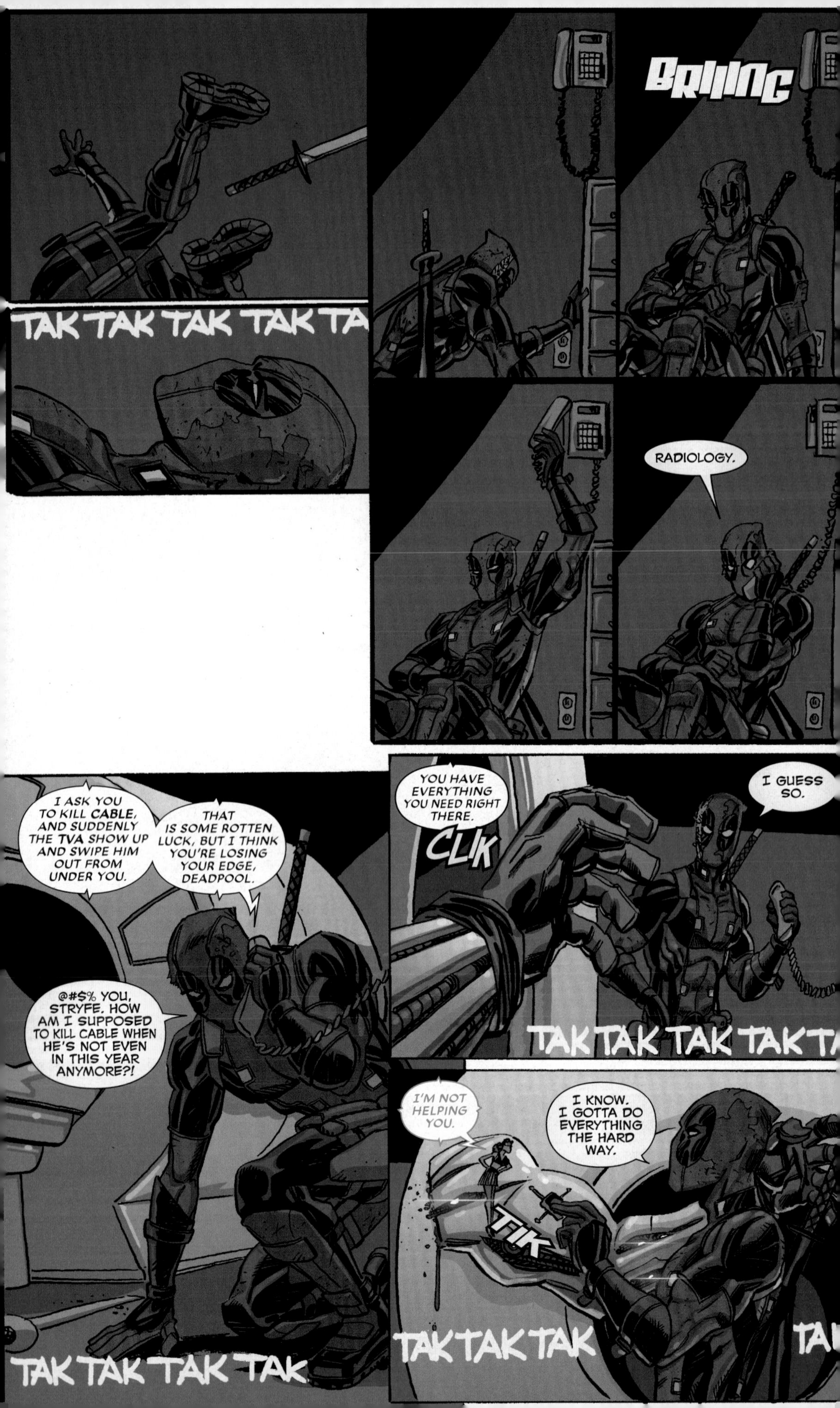

BRIIING
TAK TAK TAK TAK TA
RADIOLOGY.
I ASK YOU TO KILL CABLE, AND SUDDENLY THE TVA SHOW UP AND SWIPE HIM OUT FROM UNDER YOU.
THAT IS SOME ROTTEN LUCK, BUT I THINK YOU'RE LOSING YOUR EDGE, DEADPOOL.
@#$% YOU, STRYFE. HOW AM I SUPPOSED TO KILL CABLE WHEN HE'S NOT EVEN IN THIS YEAR ANYMORE?!
TAK TAK TAK TAK
YOU HAVE EVERYTHING YOU NEED RIGHT THERE.
CLIK
I GUESS SO.
TAK TAK TAK TAK TA
I'M NOT HELPING YOU.
I KNOW. I GOTTA DO EVERYTHING THE HARD WAY.
TIK
TAK TAK TAK
TA

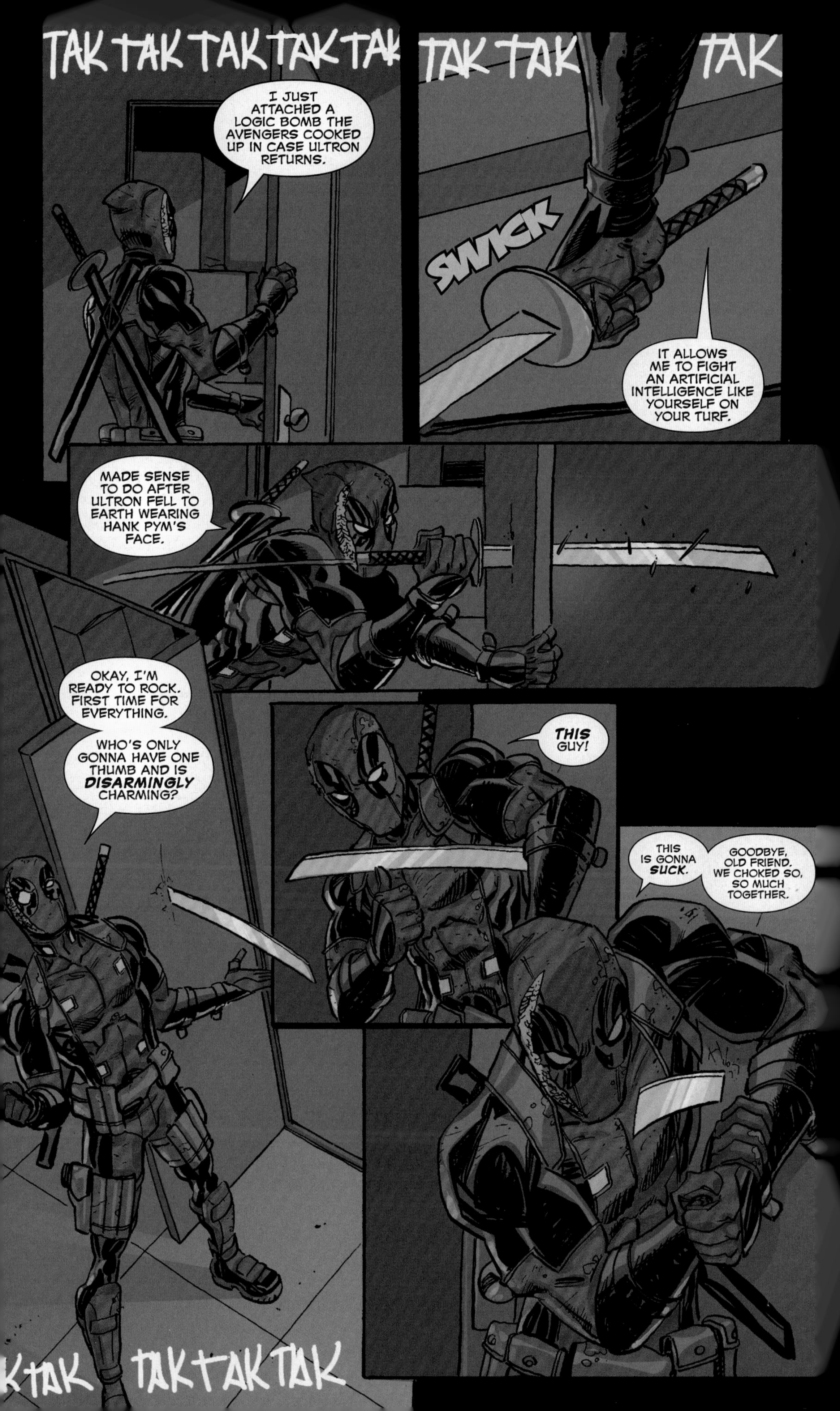
TAK TAK TAK TAK TAK
I JUST ATTACHED A LOGIC BOMB THE AVENGERS COOKED UP IN CASE ULTRON RETURNS.
TAK TAK TAK
SWICK
IT ALLOWS ME TO FIGHT AN ARTIFICIAL INTELLIGENCE LIKE YOURSELF ON YOUR TURF.
MADE SENSE TO DO AFTER ULTRON FELL TO EARTH WEARING HANK PYM'S FACE.
OKAY, I'M READY TO ROCK. FIRST TIME FOR EVERYTHING.
WHO'S ONLY GONNA HAVE ONE THUMB AND IS DISARMINGLY CHARMING?
THIS GUY!
THIS IS GONNA SUCK.
GOODBYE, OLD FRIEND. WE CHOKED SO, SO MUCH TOGETHER.
K TAK TAK TAK TAK

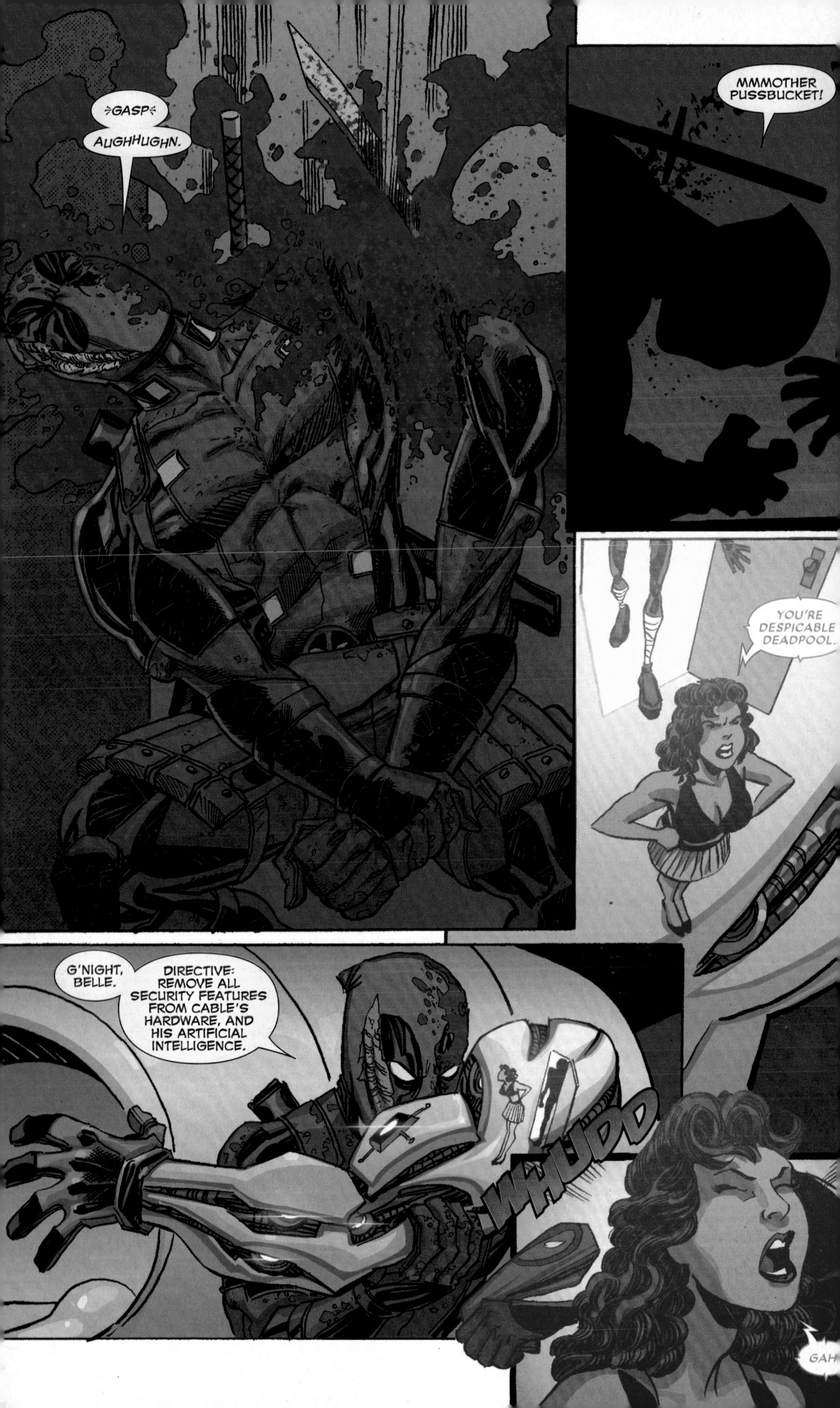

GASP
AUGHHUGHN.
MMMOTHER PUSSBUCKET!
YOU'RE DESPICABLE DEADPOOL.
G'NIGHT, BELLE.
DIRECTIVE: REMOVE ALL SECURITY FEATURES FROM CABLE'S HARDWARE, AND HIS ARTIFICIAL INTELLIGENCE.
WHUDD
GAH

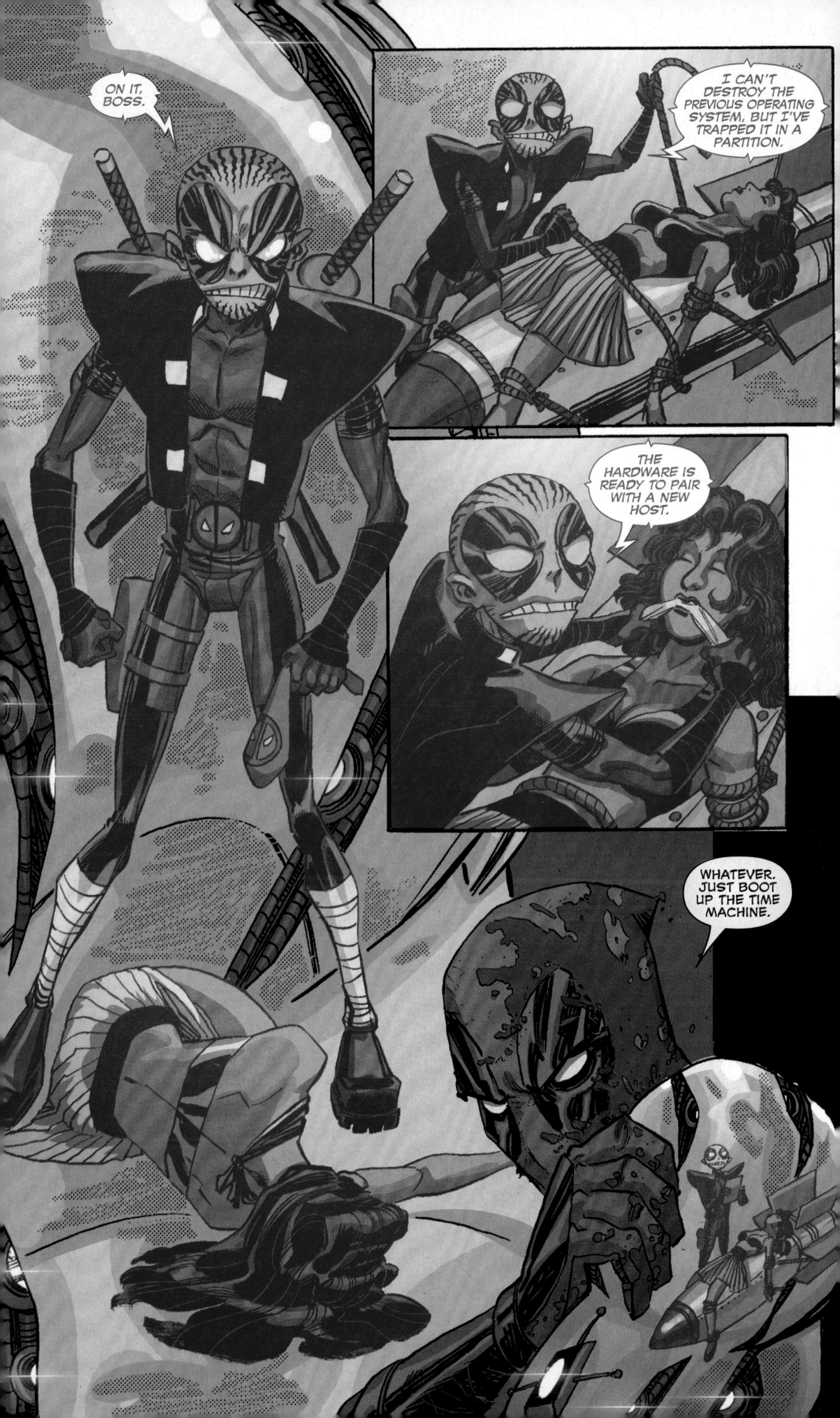
ON IT, BOSS.
I CAN'T DESTROY THE PREVIOUS OPERATING SYSTEM, BUT I'VE TRAPPED IT IN A PARTITION.
THE HARDWARE IS READY TO PAIR WITH A NEW HOST.
WHATEVER. JUST BOOT UP THE TIME MACHINE.

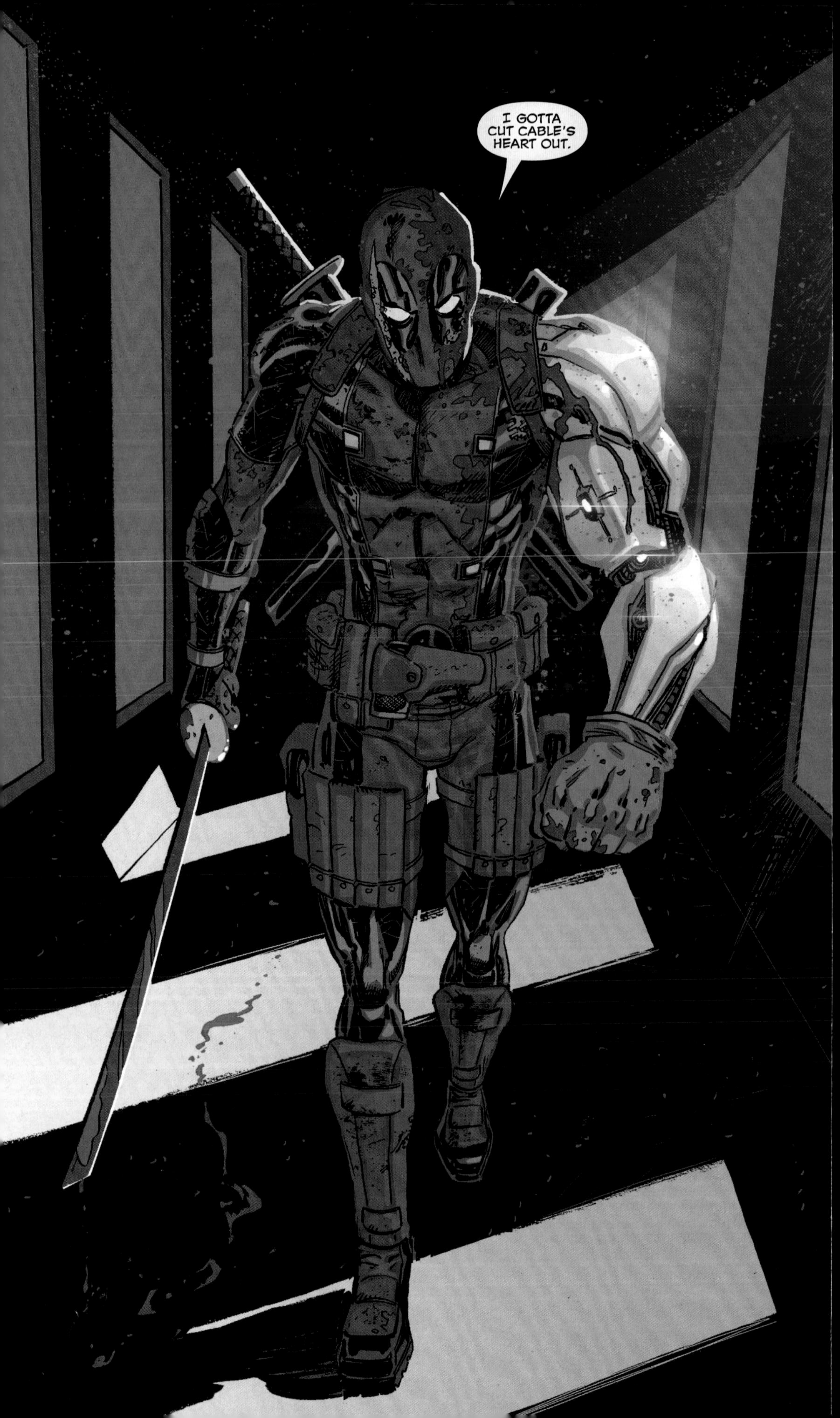
I GOTTA CUT CABLE'S HEART OUT.

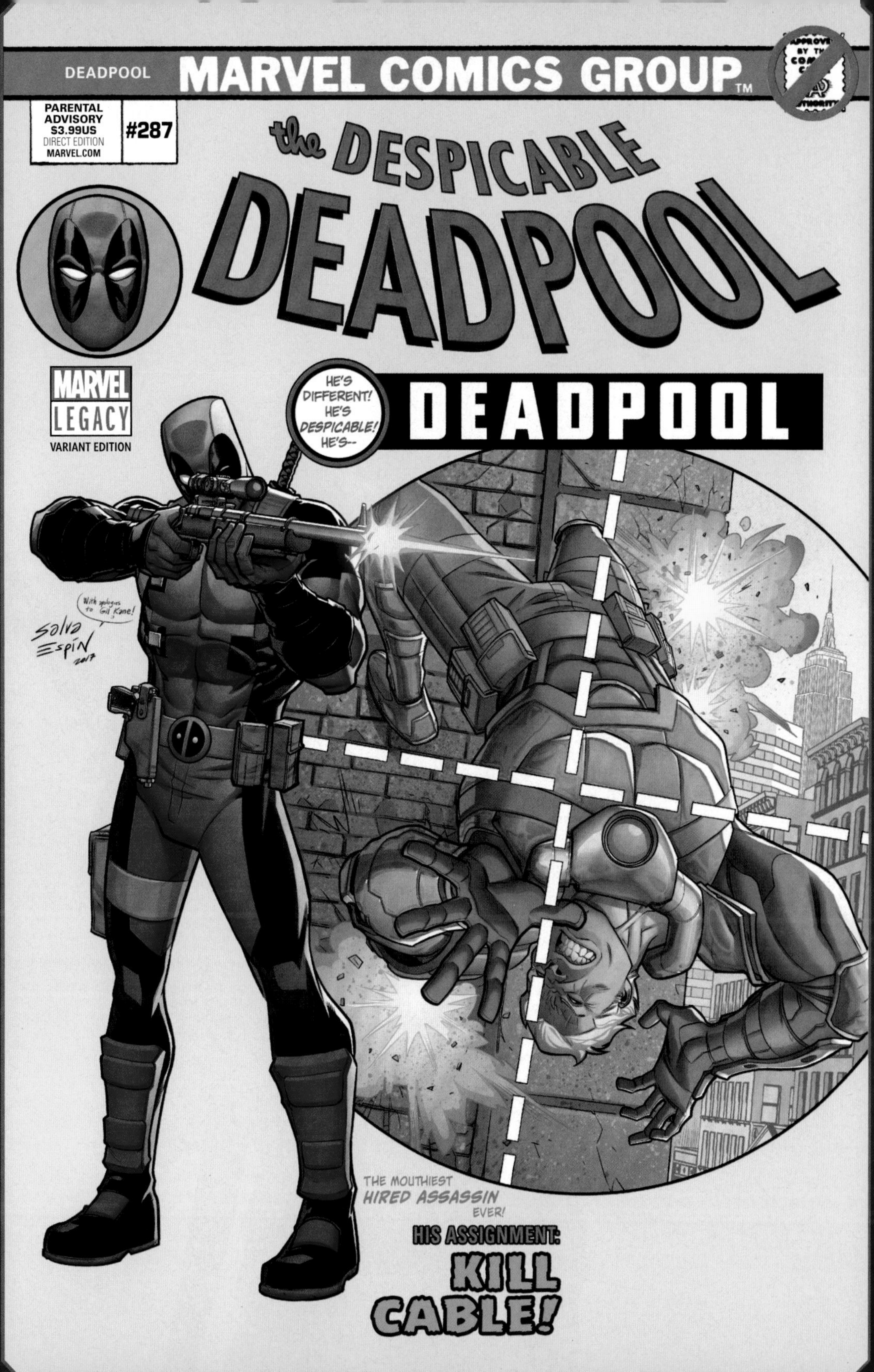

DEADPOOL
MARVEL COMICS GROUP™
PARENTAL ADVISORY
$3.99US
DIRECT EDITION
MARVEL.COM
#287
the DESPICABLE DEADPOOL
MARVEL LEGACY
VARIANT EDITION
HE'S DIFFERENT! HE'S DESPICABLE! HE'S--
DEADPOOL
With apologies to Gil Kane!
Salva Espín 2017
THE MOUTHIEST HIRED ASSASSIN EVER!
HIS ASSIGNMENT: KILL CABLE!

288 – Part Two: "Waiting for Cable Installation"

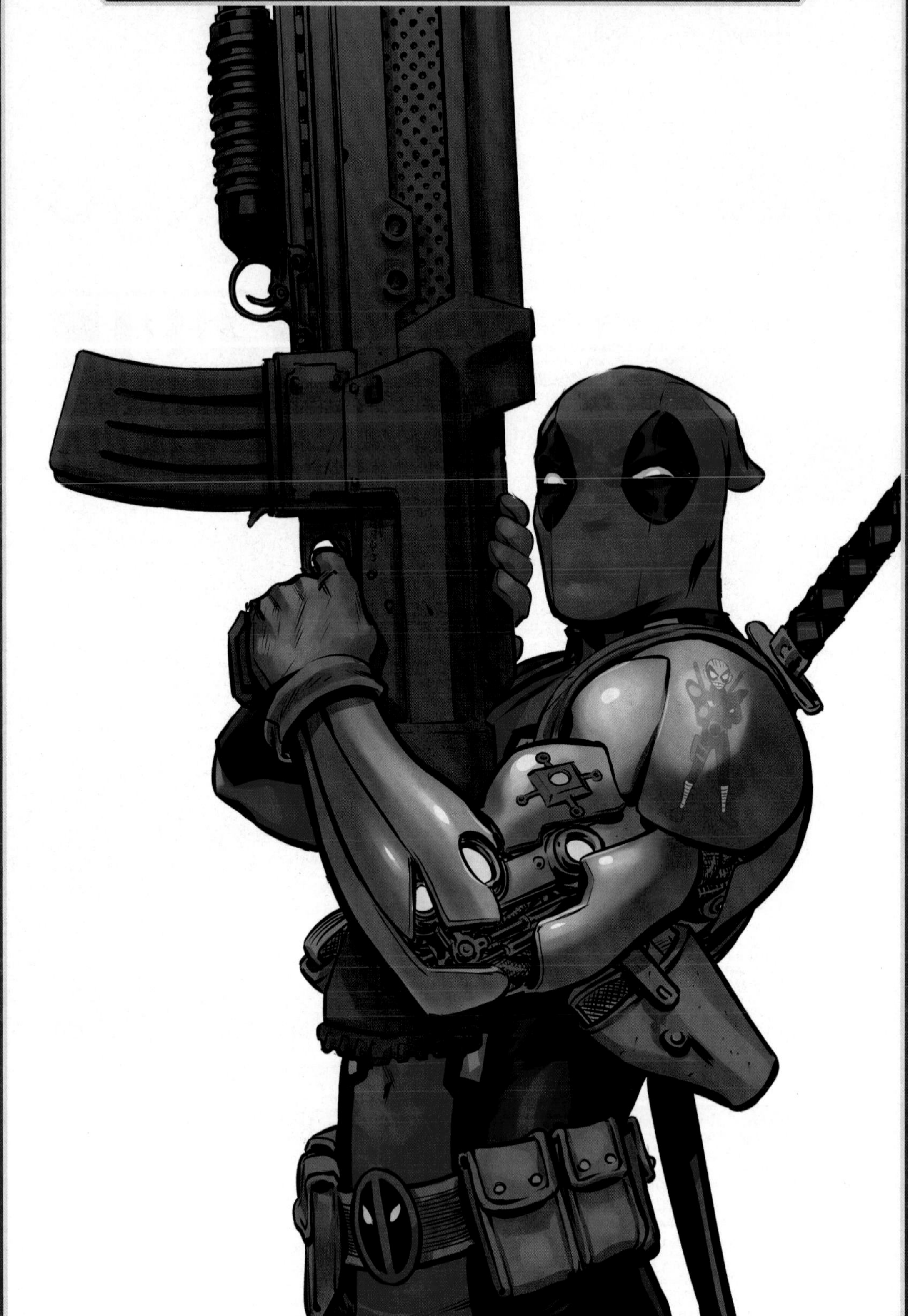

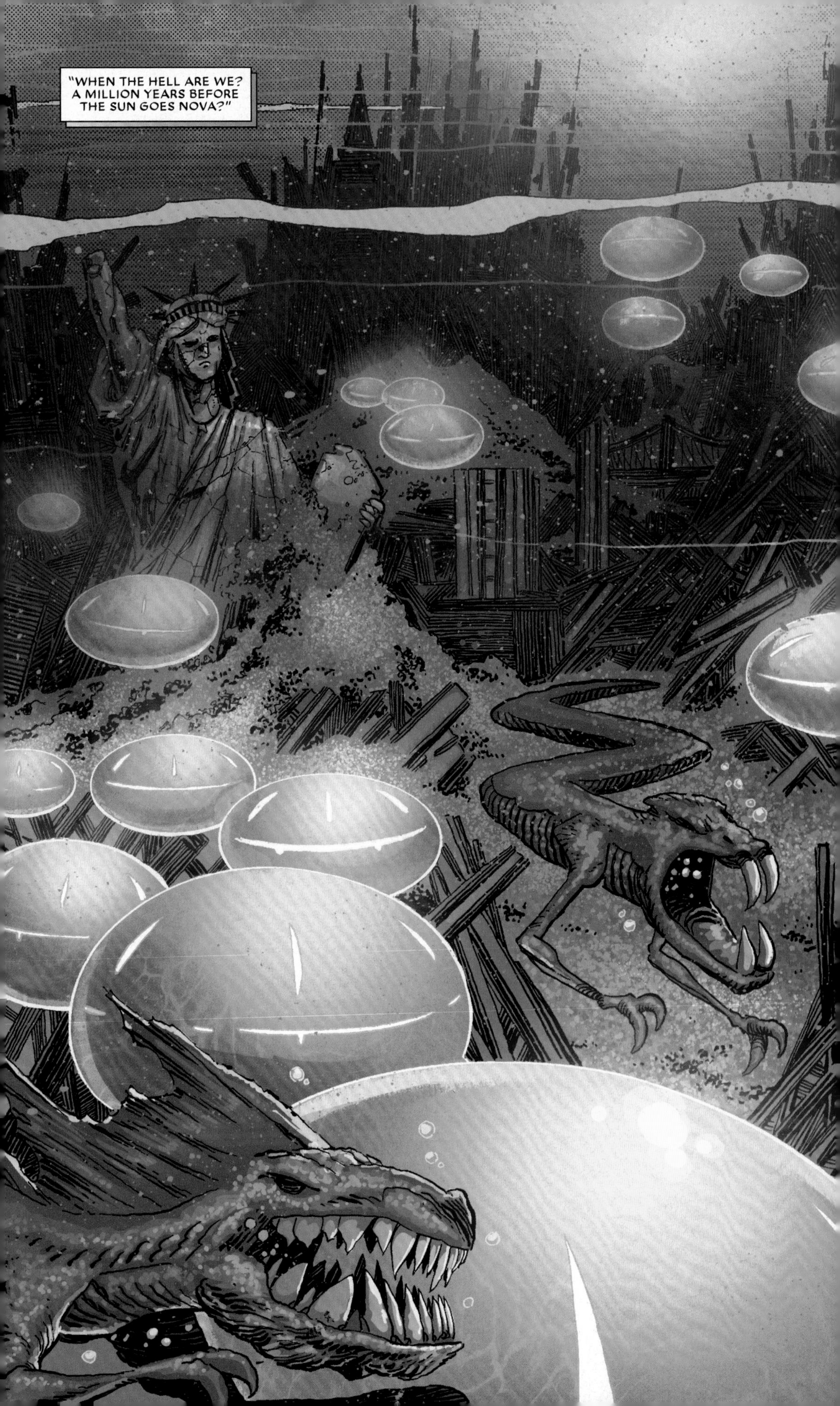
"WHEN THE HELL ARE WE? A MILLION YEARS BEFORE THE SUN GOES NOVA?"

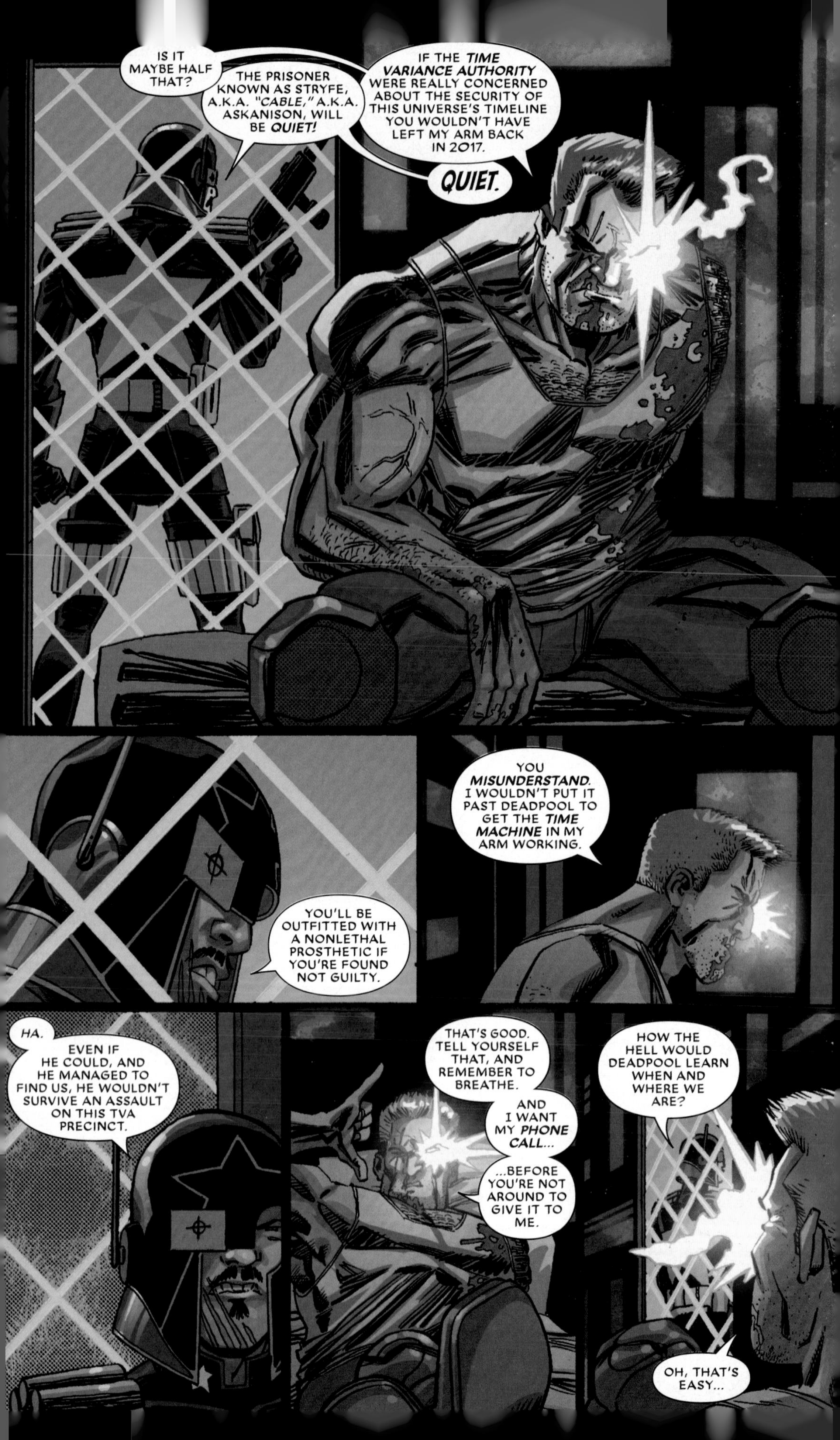

IS IT MAYBE HALF THAT?
THE PRISONER KNOWN AS STRYFE, A.K.A. "CABLE," A.K.A. ASKANISON, WILL BE QUIET!
IF THE TIME VARIANCE AUTHORITY WERE REALLY CONCERNED ABOUT THE SECURITY OF THIS UNIVERSE'S TIMELINE YOU WOULDN'T HAVE LEFT MY ARM BACK IN 2017.
QUIET.
YOU'LL BE OUTFITTED WITH A NONLETHAL PROSTHETIC IF YOU'RE FOUND NOT GUILTY.
YOU MISUNDERSTAND. I WOULDN'T PUT IT PAST DEADPOOL TO GET THE TIME MACHINE IN MY ARM WORKING.
HA.
EVEN IF HE COULD, AND HE MANAGED TO FIND US, HE WOULDN'T SURVIVE AN ASSAULT ON THIS TVA PRECINCT.
THAT'S GOOD. TELL YOURSELF THAT, AND REMEMBER TO BREATHE.
AND I WANT MY PHONE CALL...
...BEFORE YOU'RE NOT AROUND TO GIVE IT TO ME.
HOW THE HELL WOULD DEADPOOL LEARN WHEN AND WHERE WE ARE?
OH, THAT'S EASY...

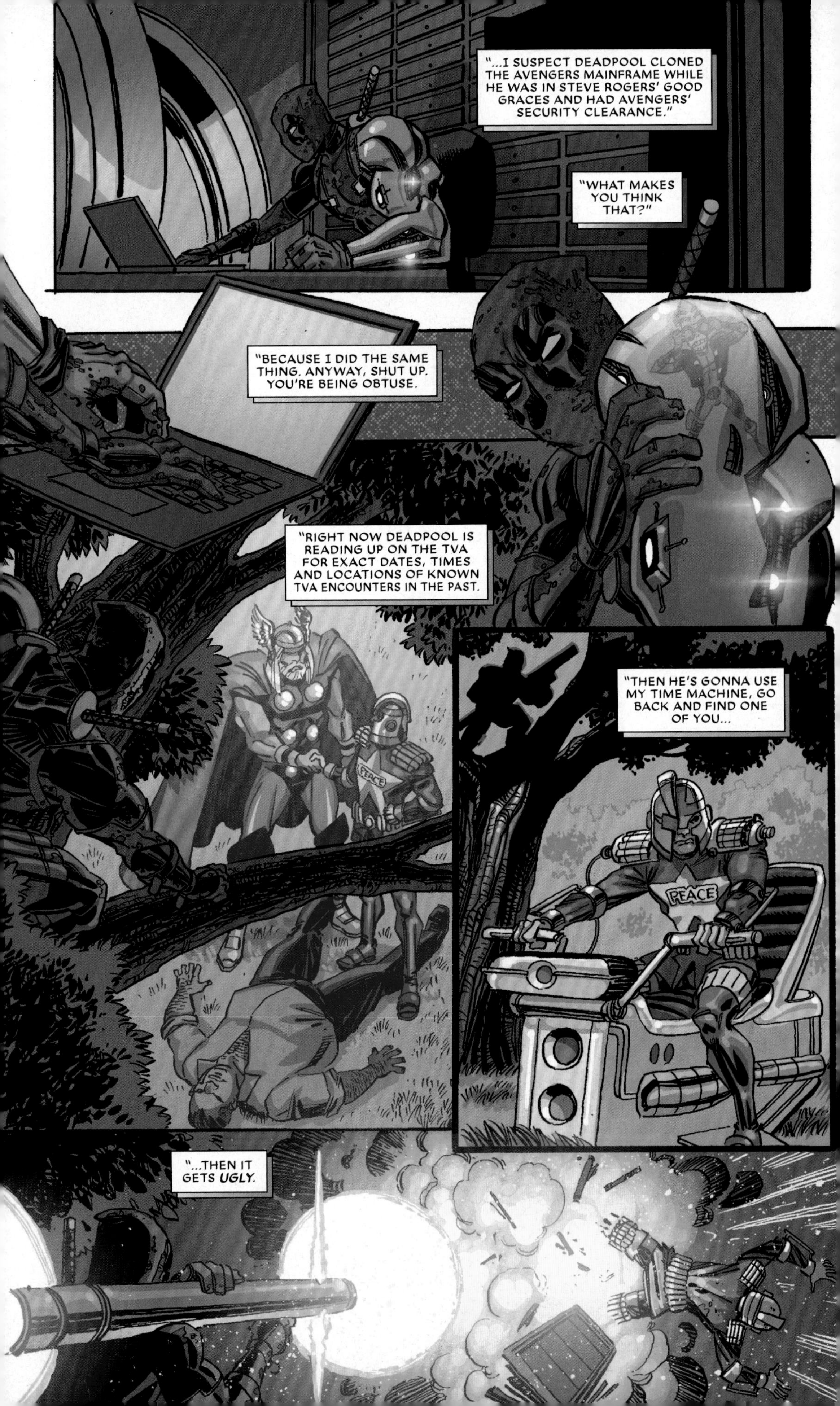
"...I SUSPECT DEADPOOL CLONED THE AVENGERS MAINFRAME WHILE HE WAS IN STEVE ROGERS' GOOD GRACES AND HAD AVENGERS' SECURITY CLEARANCE."
"WHAT MAKES YOU THINK THAT?"
"BECAUSE I DID THE SAME THING. ANYWAY, SHUT UP. YOU'RE BEING OBTUSE.
"RIGHT NOW DEADPOOL IS READING UP ON THE TVA FOR EXACT DATES, TIMES AND LOCATIONS OF KNOWN TVA ENCOUNTERS IN THE PAST.
PEACE
"THEN HE'S GONNA USE MY TIME MACHINE, GO BACK AND FIND ONE OF YOU...
PEACE
"...THEN IT GETS *UGLY*.

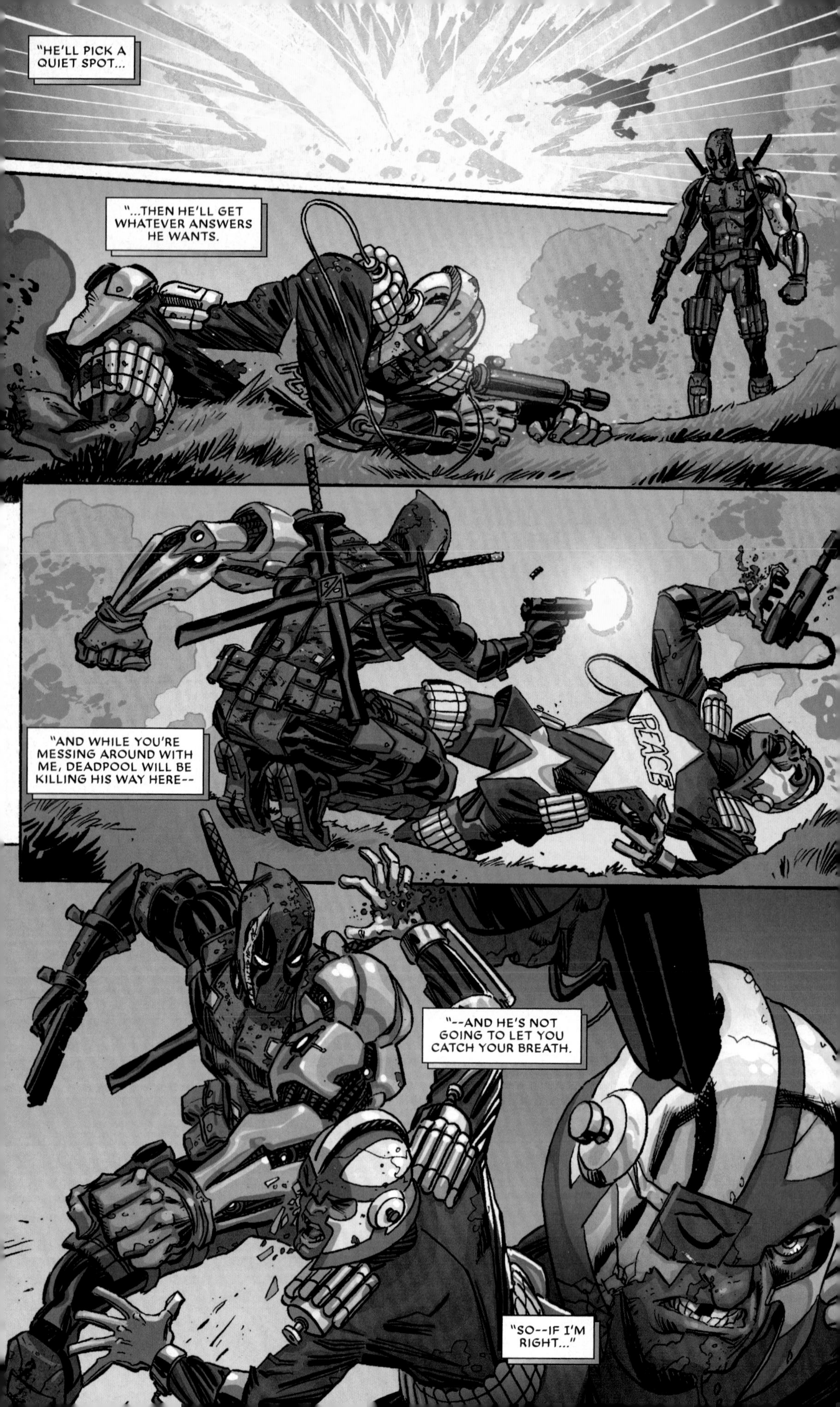
"HE'LL PICK A QUIET SPOT...
"...THEN HE'LL GET WHATEVER ANSWERS HE WANTS.
PEACE
"AND WHILE YOU'RE MESSING AROUND WITH ME, DEADPOOL WILL BE KILLING HIS WAY HERE--
"--AND HE'S NOT GOING TO LET YOU CATCH YOUR BREATH.
"SO--IF I'M RIGHT..."

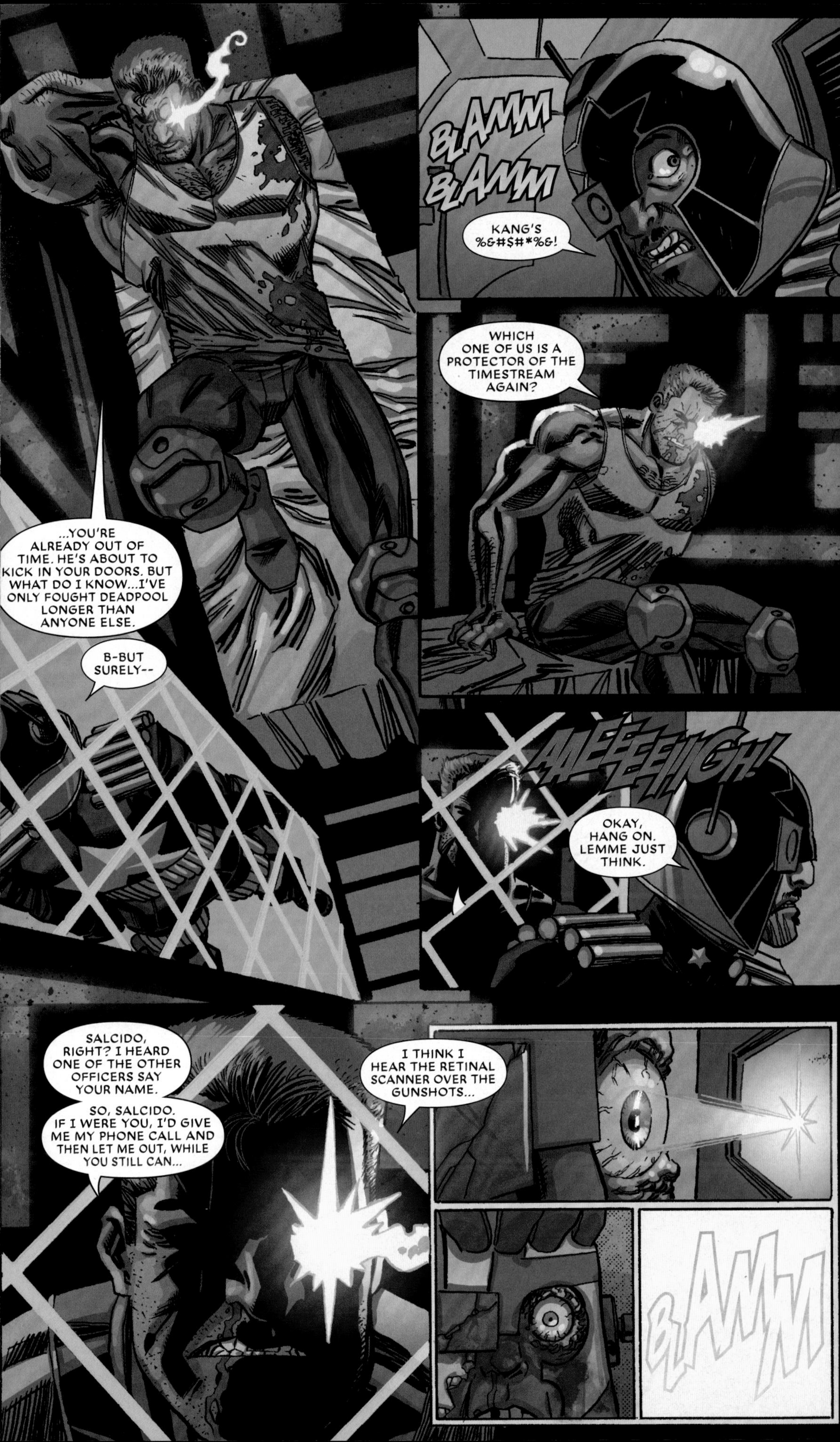
BLAMM BLAMM
KANG'S %&#$#*%&!
WHICH ONE OF US IS A PROTECTOR OF THE TIMESTREAM AGAIN?
...YOU'RE ALREADY OUT OF TIME. HE'S ABOUT TO KICK IN YOUR DOORS. BUT WHAT DO I KNOW...I'VE ONLY FOUGHT DEADPOOL LONGER THAN ANYONE ELSE.
B-BUT SURELY--
AAEEEEEIIGH!
OKAY, HANG ON. LEMME JUST THINK.
SALCIDO, RIGHT? I HEARD ONE OF THE OTHER OFFICERS SAY YOUR NAME.
SO, SALCIDO. IF I WERE YOU, I'D GIVE ME MY PHONE CALL AND THEN LET ME OUT, WHILE YOU STILL CAN...
I THINK I HEAR THE RETINAL SCANNER OVER THE GUNSHOTS...
BLAMM

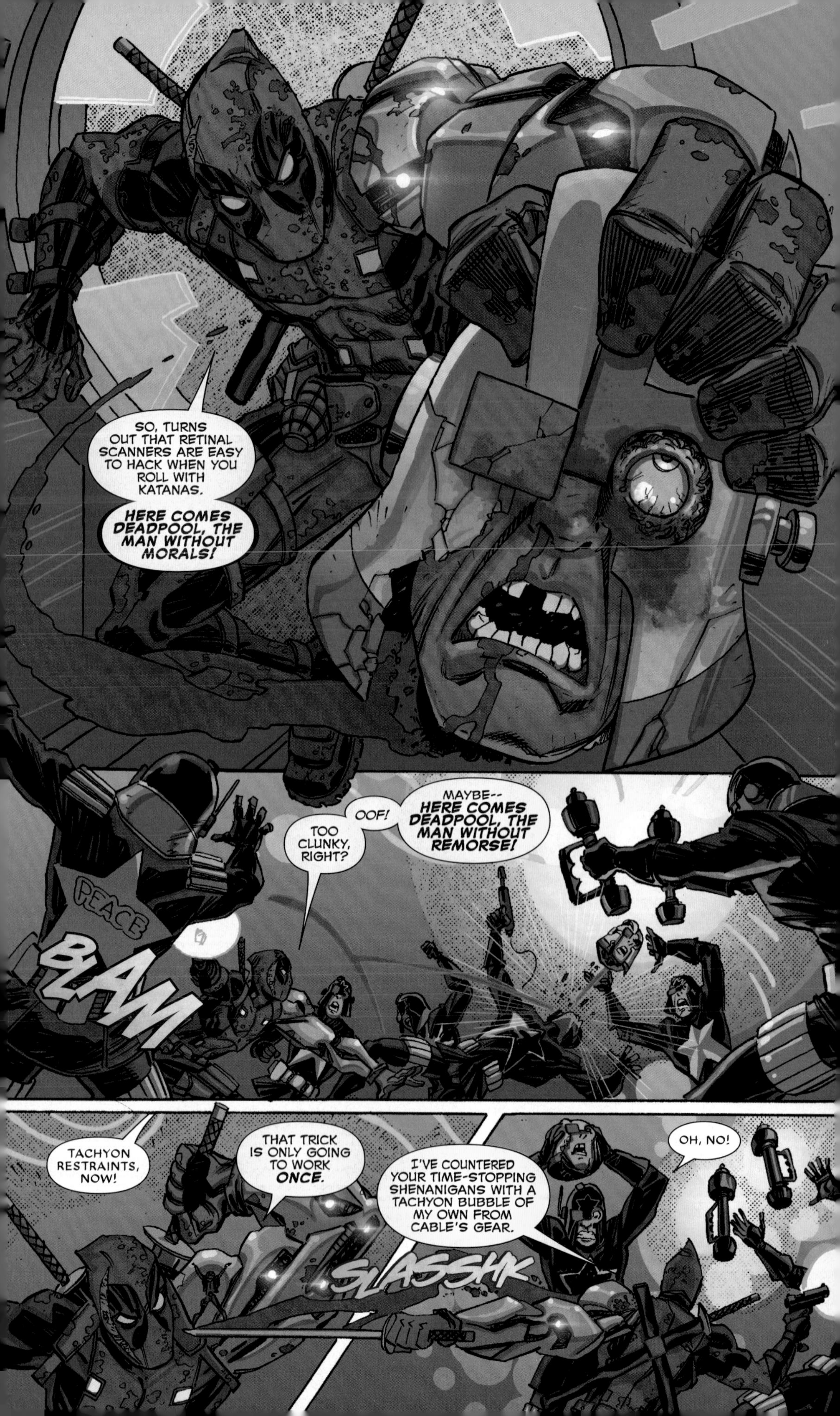

SO, TURNS OUT THAT RETINAL SCANNERS ARE EASY TO HACK WHEN YOU ROLL WITH KATANAS.
HERE COMES DEADPOOL, THE MAN WITHOUT MORALS!
PEACE
BLAM
TOO CLUNKY, RIGHT?
OOF!
MAYBE-- HERE COMES DEADPOOL, THE MAN WITHOUT REMORSE!
TACHYON RESTRAINTS, NOW!
THAT TRICK IS ONLY GOING TO WORK ONCE.
I'VE COUNTERED YOUR TIME-STOPPING SHENANIGANS WITH A TACHYON BUBBLE OF MY OWN FROM CABLE'S GEAR.
SLASSHK
OH, NO!

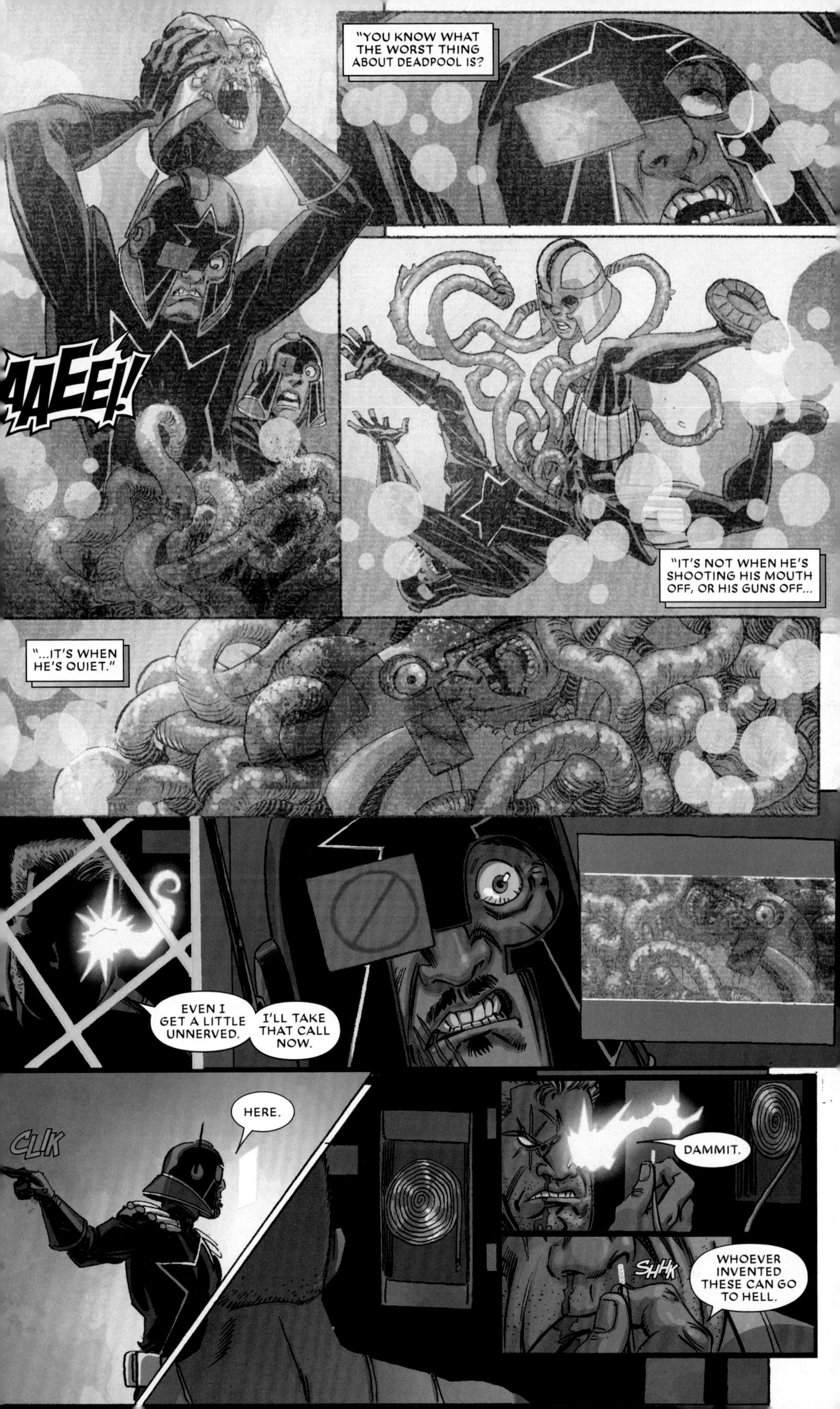
"YOU KNOW WHAT THE WORST THING ABOUT DEADPOOL IS?
AAEE!!
"IT'S NOT WHEN HE'S SHOOTING HIS MOUTH OFF, OR HIS GUNS OFF...
"...IT'S WHEN HE'S QUIET."
EVEN I GET A LITTLE UNNERVED.
I'LL TAKE THAT CALL NOW.
HERE.
CLIK
DAMMIT.
SHHK
WHOEVER INVENTED THESE CAN GO TO HELL.

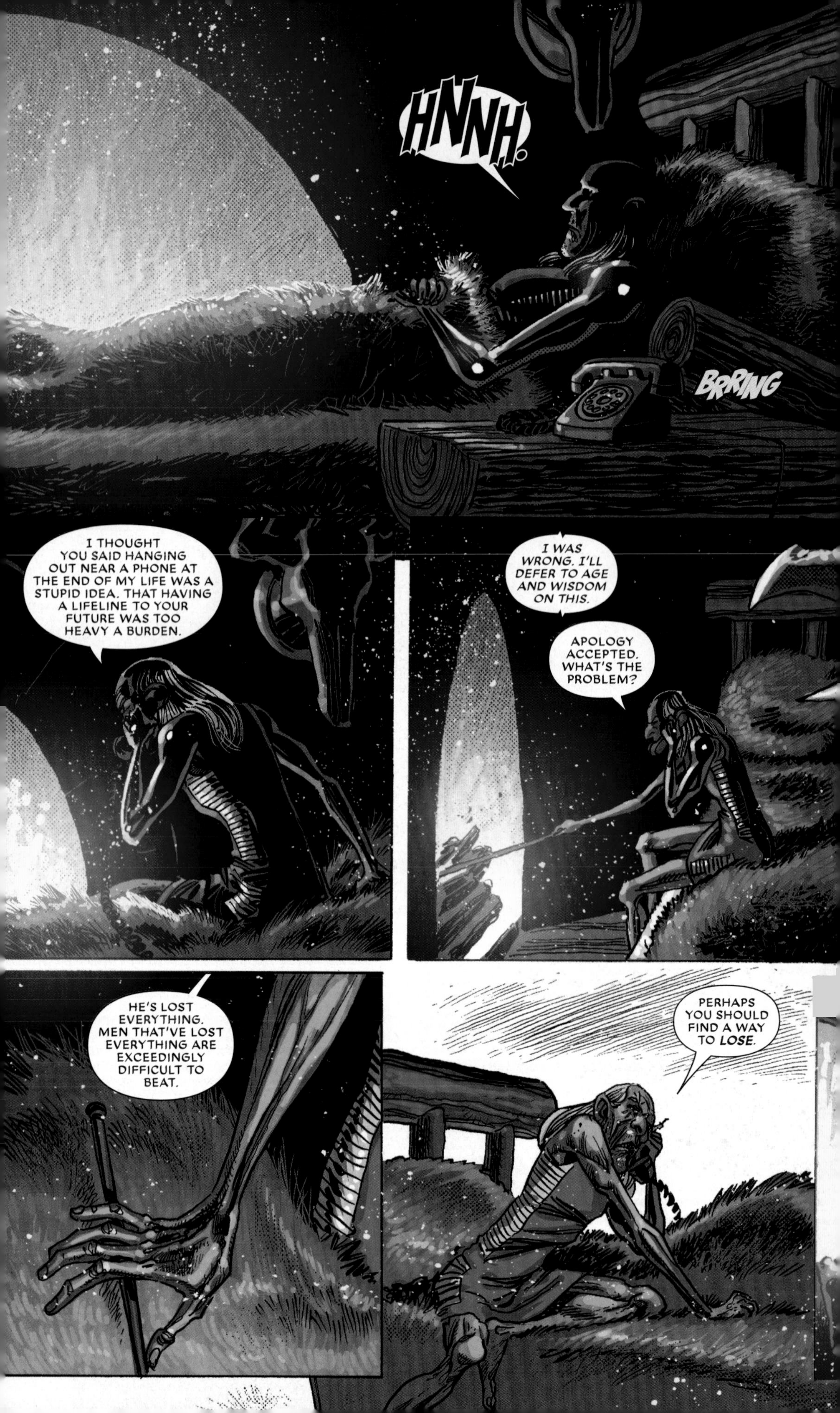
HNNH.
BRRING
I THOUGHT YOU SAID HANGING OUT NEAR A PHONE AT THE END OF MY LIFE WAS A STUPID IDEA. THAT HAVING A LIFELINE TO YOUR FUTURE WAS TOO HEAVY A BURDEN.
I WAS WRONG. I'LL DEFER TO AGE AND WISDOM ON THIS.
APOLOGY ACCEPTED. WHAT'S THE PROBLEM?
HE'S LOST EVERYTHING. MEN THAT'VE LOST EVERYTHING ARE EXCEEDINGLY DIFFICULT TO BEAT.
PERHAPS YOU SHOULD FIND A WAY TO *LOSE*.

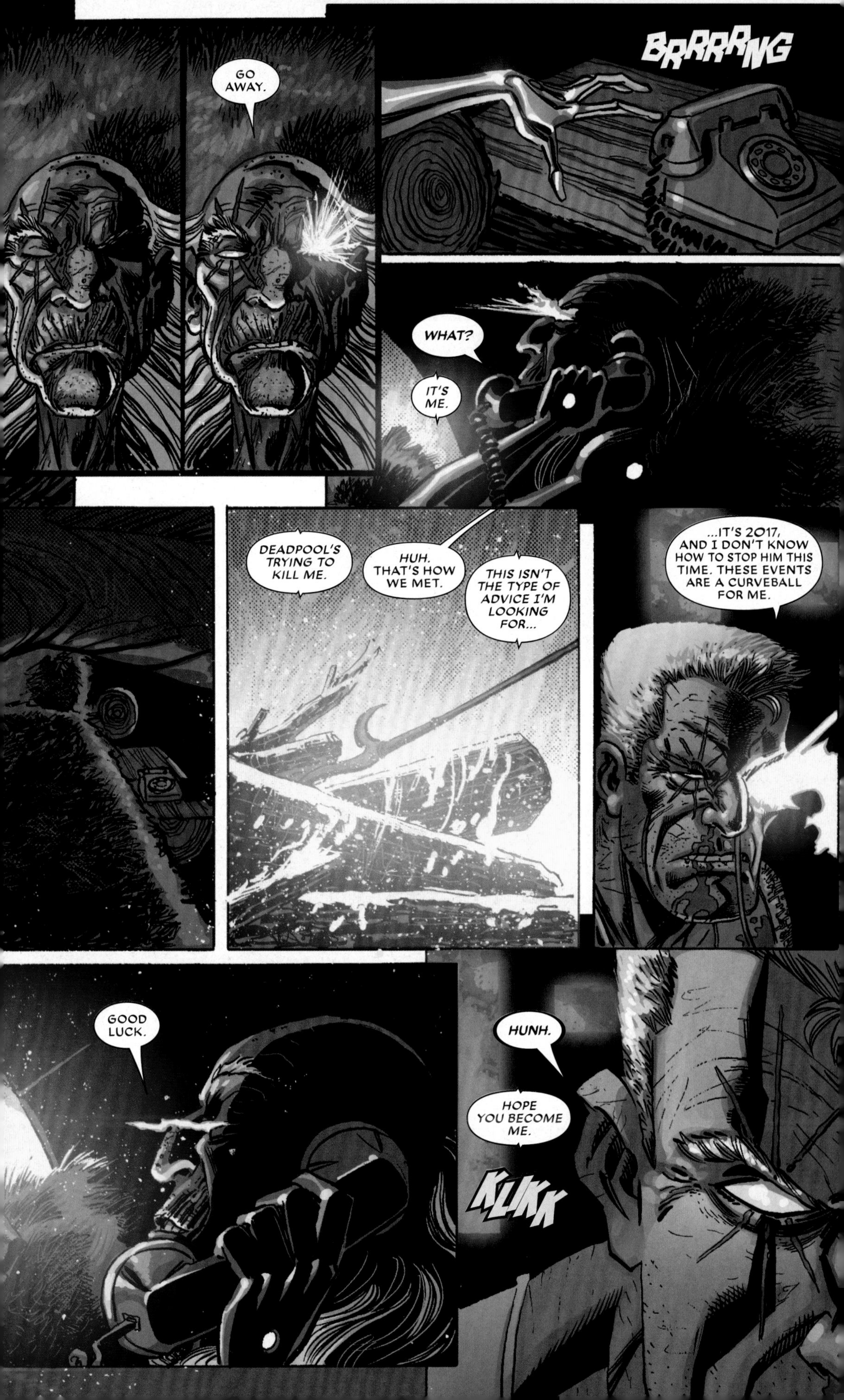
GO AWAY.
BRRRRNG
WHAT?
IT'S ME.
DEADPOOL'S TRYING TO KILL ME.
HUH. THAT'S HOW WE MET.
THIS ISN'T THE TYPE OF ADVICE I'M LOOKING FOR...
...IT'S 2017, AND I DON'T KNOW HOW TO STOP HIM THIS TIME. THESE EVENTS ARE A CURVEBALL FOR ME.
GOOD LUCK.
HUNH.
HOPE YOU BECOME ME.
KLIKK

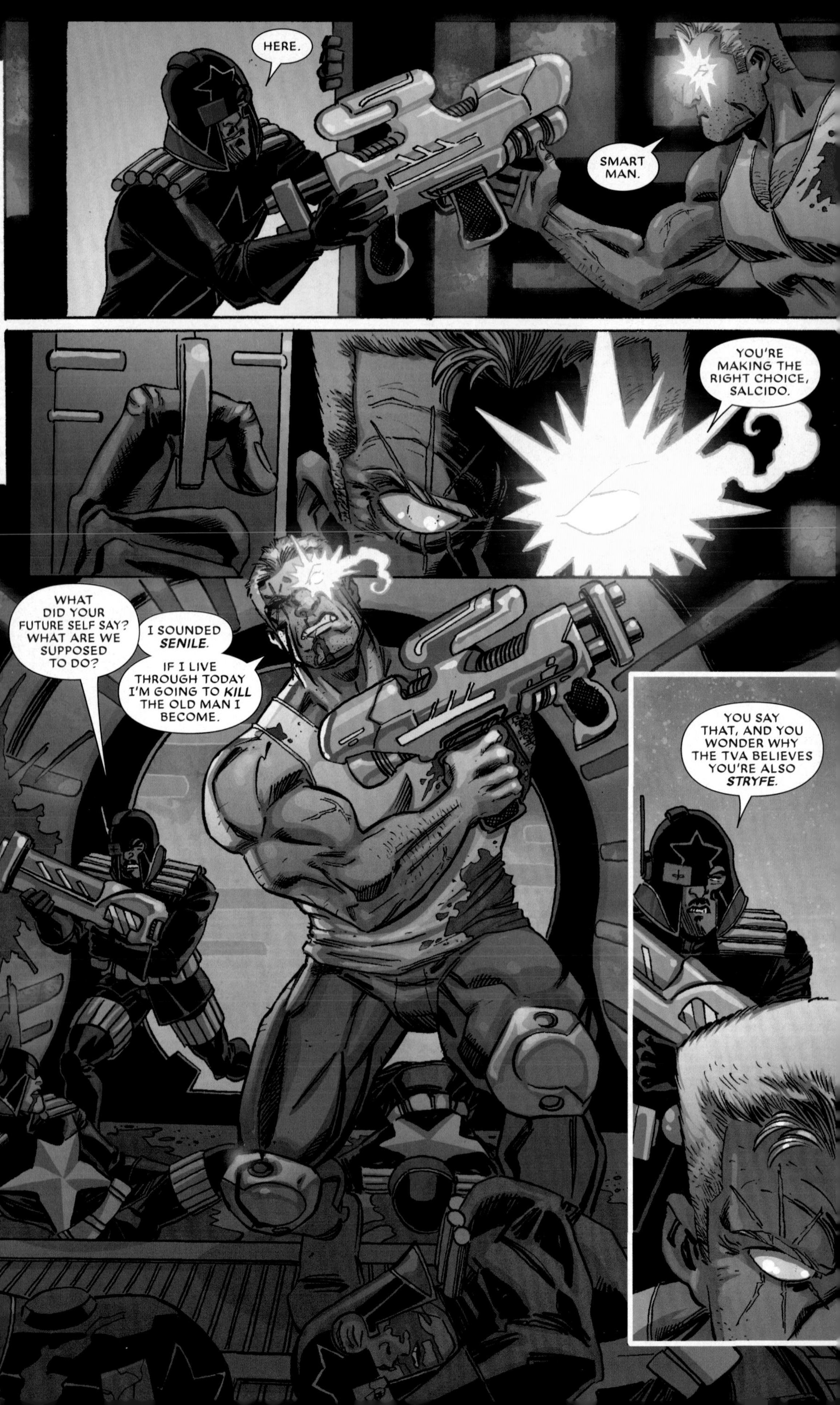
HERE.
SMART MAN.
YOU'RE MAKING THE RIGHT CHOICE, SALCIDO.
WHAT DID YOUR FUTURE SELF SAY? WHAT ARE WE SUPPOSED TO DO?
I SOUNDED *SENILE*.
IF I LIVE THROUGH TODAY I'M GOING TO *KILL* THE OLD MAN I BECOME.
YOU SAY THAT, AND YOU WONDER WHY THE TVA BELIEVES YOU'RE ALSO *STRYFE*.

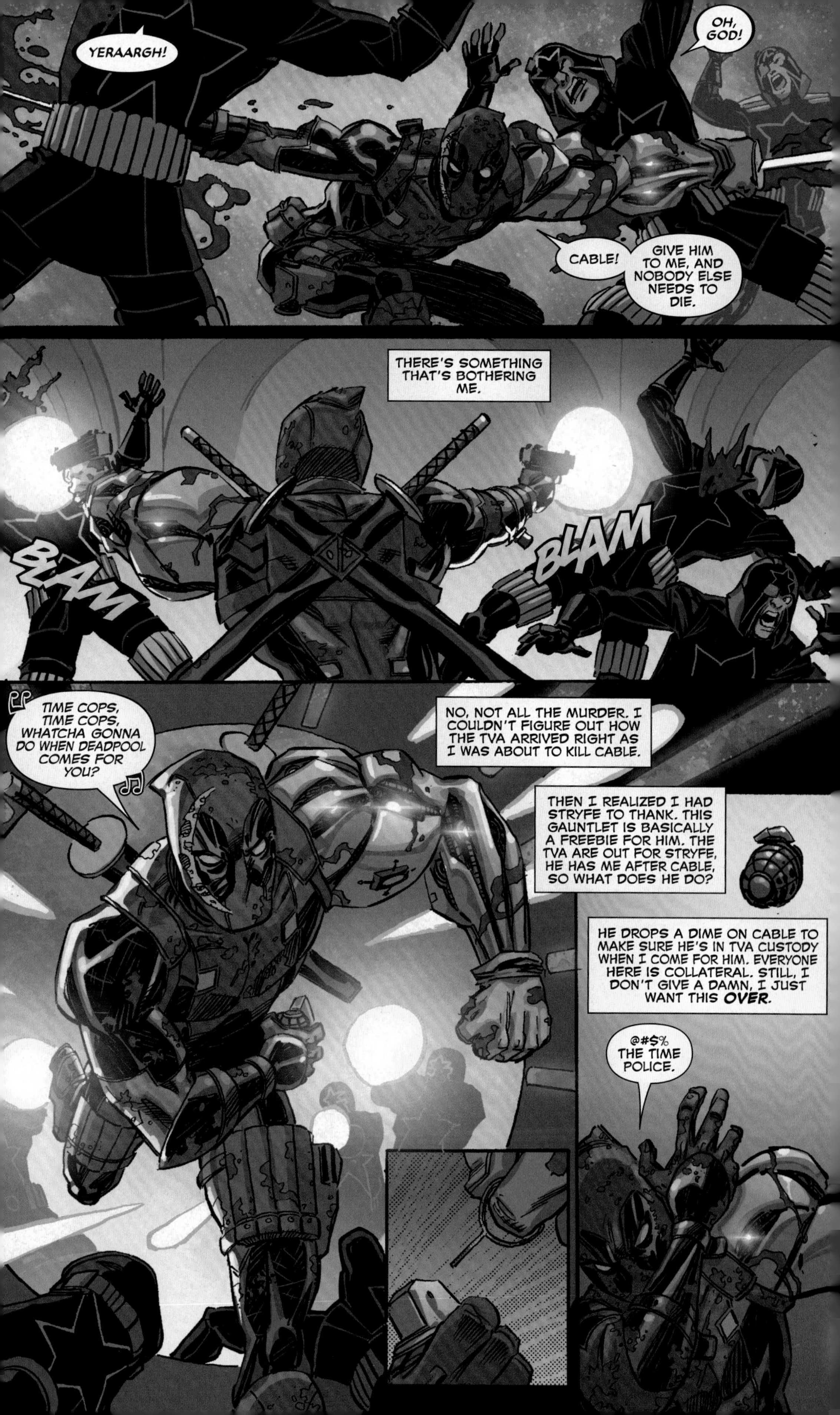
YERAARGH!
OH, GOD!
CABLE!
GIVE HIM TO ME, AND NOBODY ELSE NEEDS TO DIE.
THERE'S SOMETHING THAT'S BOTHERING ME.
BLAM
BLAM
TIME COPS, TIME COPS, WHATCHA GONNA DO WHEN DEADPOOL COMES FOR YOU?
NO, NOT ALL THE MURDER. I COULDN'T FIGURE OUT HOW THE TVA ARRIVED RIGHT AS I WAS ABOUT TO KILL CABLE.
THEN I REALIZED I HAD STRYFE TO THANK. THIS GAUNTLET IS BASICALLY A FREEBIE FOR HIM. THE TVA ARE OUT FOR STRYFE, HE HAS ME AFTER CABLE, SO WHAT DOES HE DO?
HE DROPS A DIME ON CABLE TO MAKE SURE HE'S IN TVA CUSTODY WHEN I COME FOR HIM. EVERYONE HERE IS COLLATERAL. STILL, I DON'T GIVE A DAMN, I JUST WANT THIS OVER.
@#$% THE TIME POLICE.

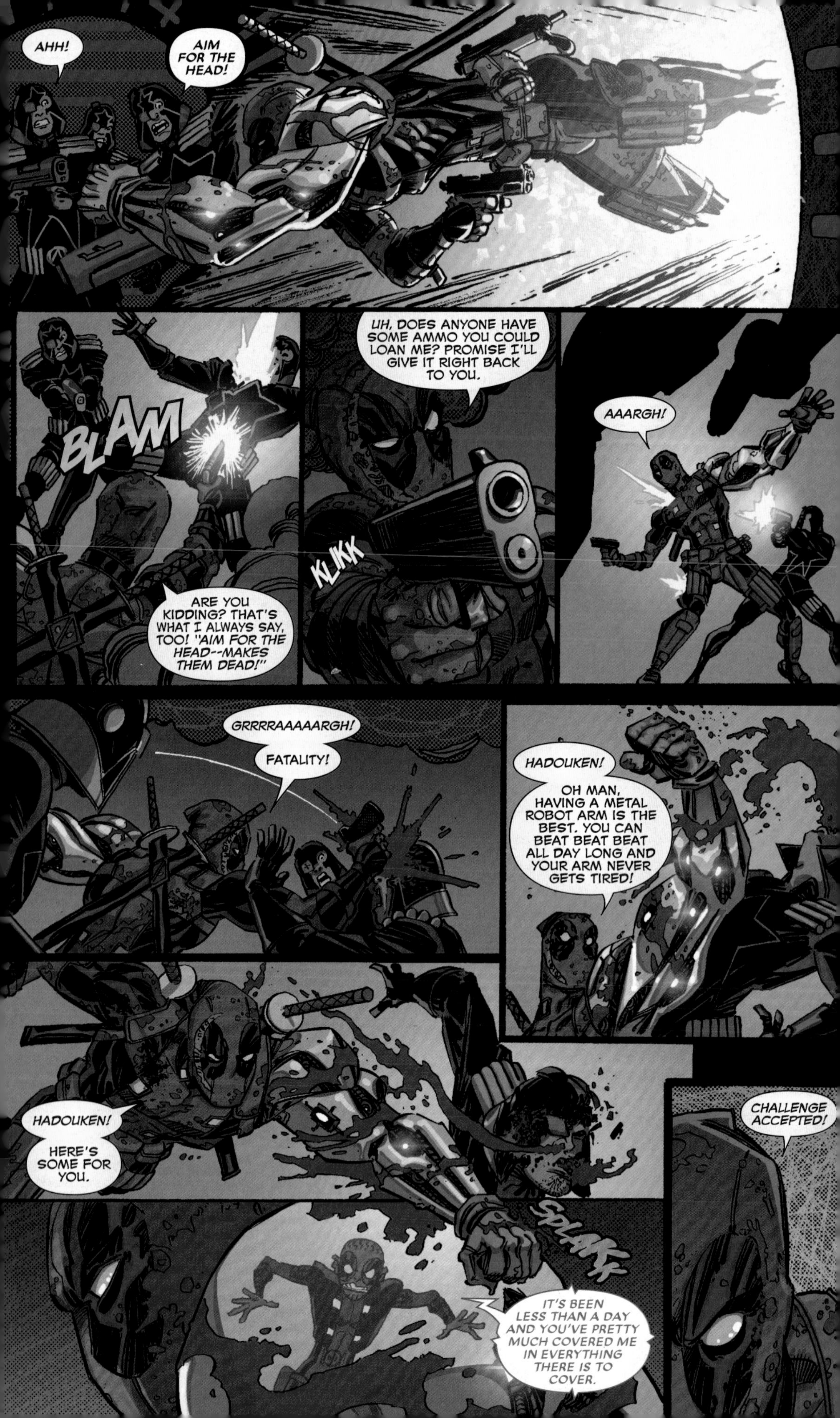

AHH!
AIM FOR THE HEAD!
BLAM
ARE YOU KIDDING? THAT'S WHAT I ALWAYS SAY, TOO! "AIM FOR THE HEAD--MAKES THEM DEAD!"
UH, DOES ANYONE HAVE SOME AMMO YOU COULD LOAN ME? PROMISE I'LL GIVE IT RIGHT BACK TO YOU.
KLIKK
AAARGH!
GRRRRAAAAARGH!
FATALITY!
HADOUKEN!
OH MAN, HAVING A METAL ROBOT ARM IS THE BEST. YOU CAN BEAT BEAT BEAT ALL DAY LONG AND YOUR ARM NEVER GETS TIRED!
HADOUKEN!
HERE'S SOME FOR YOU.
SPLAKKK
CHALLENGE ACCEPTED!
IT'S BEEN LESS THAN A DAY AND YOU'VE PRETTY MUCH COVERED ME IN EVERYTHING THERE IS TO COVER.

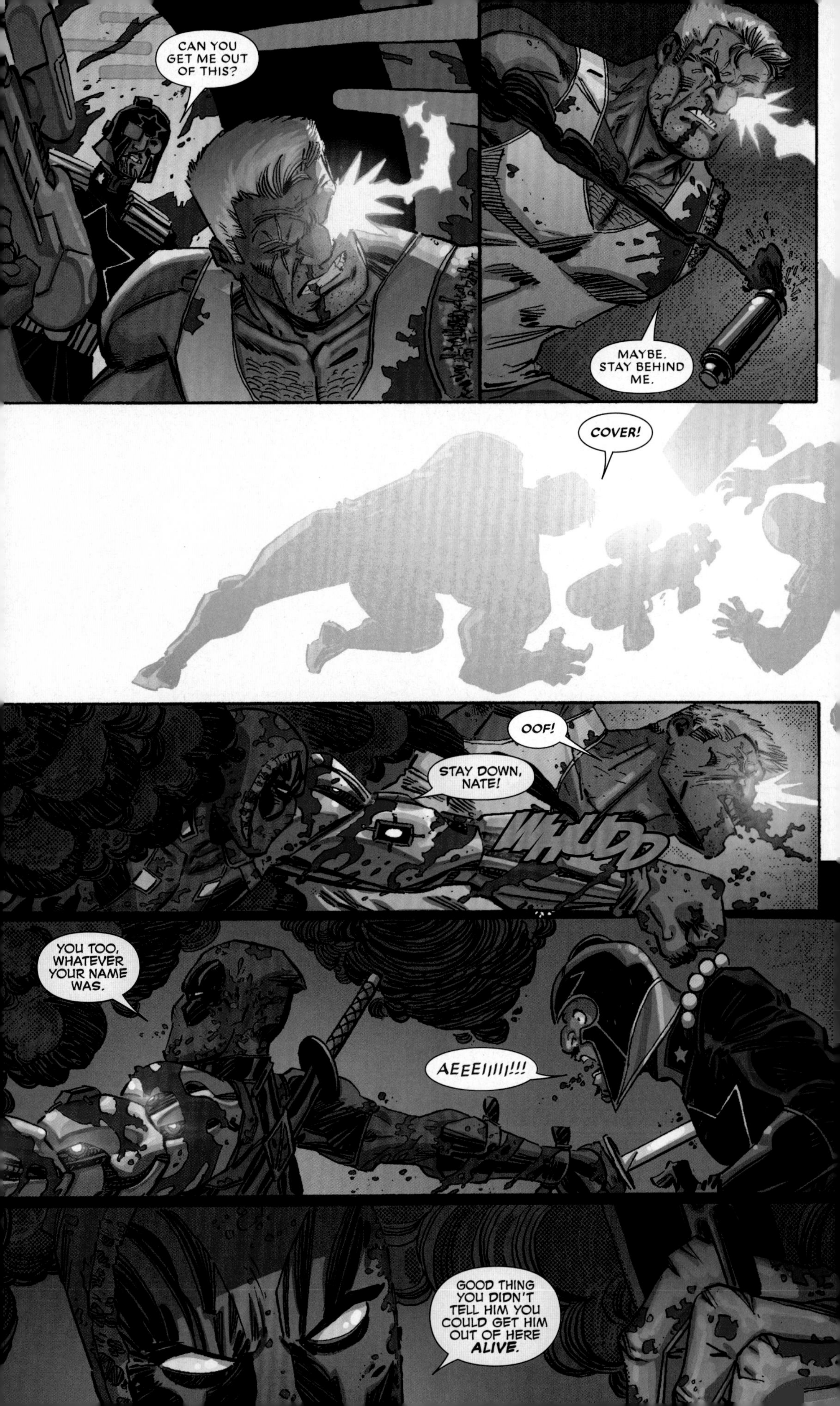
CAN YOU GET ME OUT OF THIS?
MAYBE. STAY BEHIND ME.
COVER!
OOF!
STAY DOWN, NATE!
WHUDD
YOU TOO, WHATEVER YOUR NAME WAS.
AEEEIIIII!!!
GOOD THING YOU DIDN'T TELL HIM YOU COULD GET HIM OUT OF HERE ALIVE.

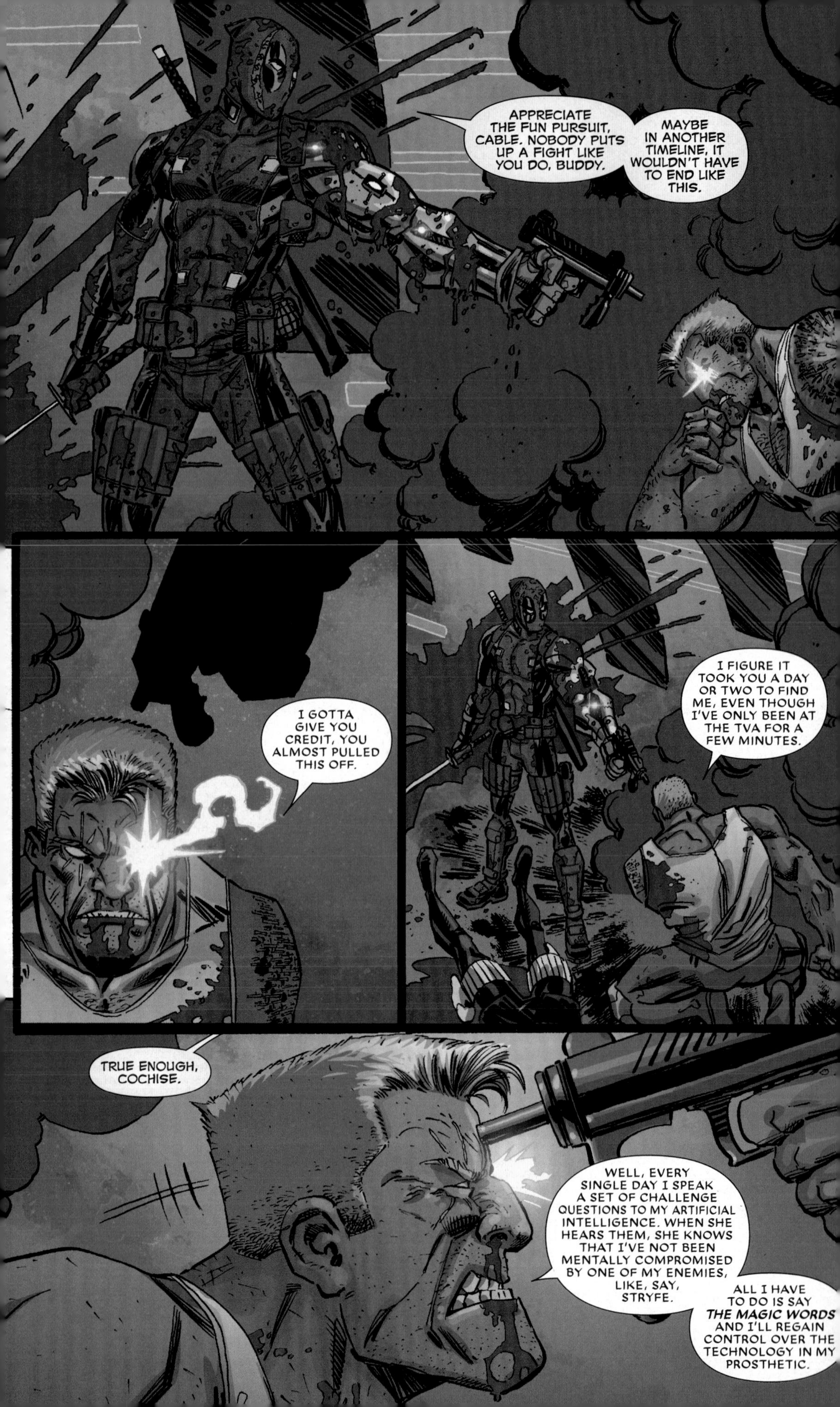
APPRECIATE THE FUN PURSUIT, CABLE. NOBODY PUTS UP A FIGHT LIKE YOU DO, BUDDY.
MAYBE IN ANOTHER TIMELINE, IT WOULDN'T HAVE TO END LIKE THIS.
I GOTTA GIVE YOU CREDIT, YOU ALMOST PULLED THIS OFF.
I FIGURE IT TOOK YOU A DAY OR TWO TO FIND ME, EVEN THOUGH I'VE ONLY BEEN AT THE TVA FOR A FEW MINUTES.
TRUE ENOUGH, COCHISE.
WELL, EVERY SINGLE DAY I SPEAK A SET OF CHALLENGE QUESTIONS TO MY ARTIFICIAL INTELLIGENCE. WHEN SHE HEARS THEM, SHE KNOWS THAT I'VE NOT BEEN MENTALLY COMPROMISED BY ONE OF MY ENEMIES, LIKE, SAY, STRYFE.
ALL I HAVE TO DO IS SAY *THE MAGIC WORDS* AND I'LL REGAIN CONTROL OVER THE TECHNOLOGY IN MY PROSTHETIC.

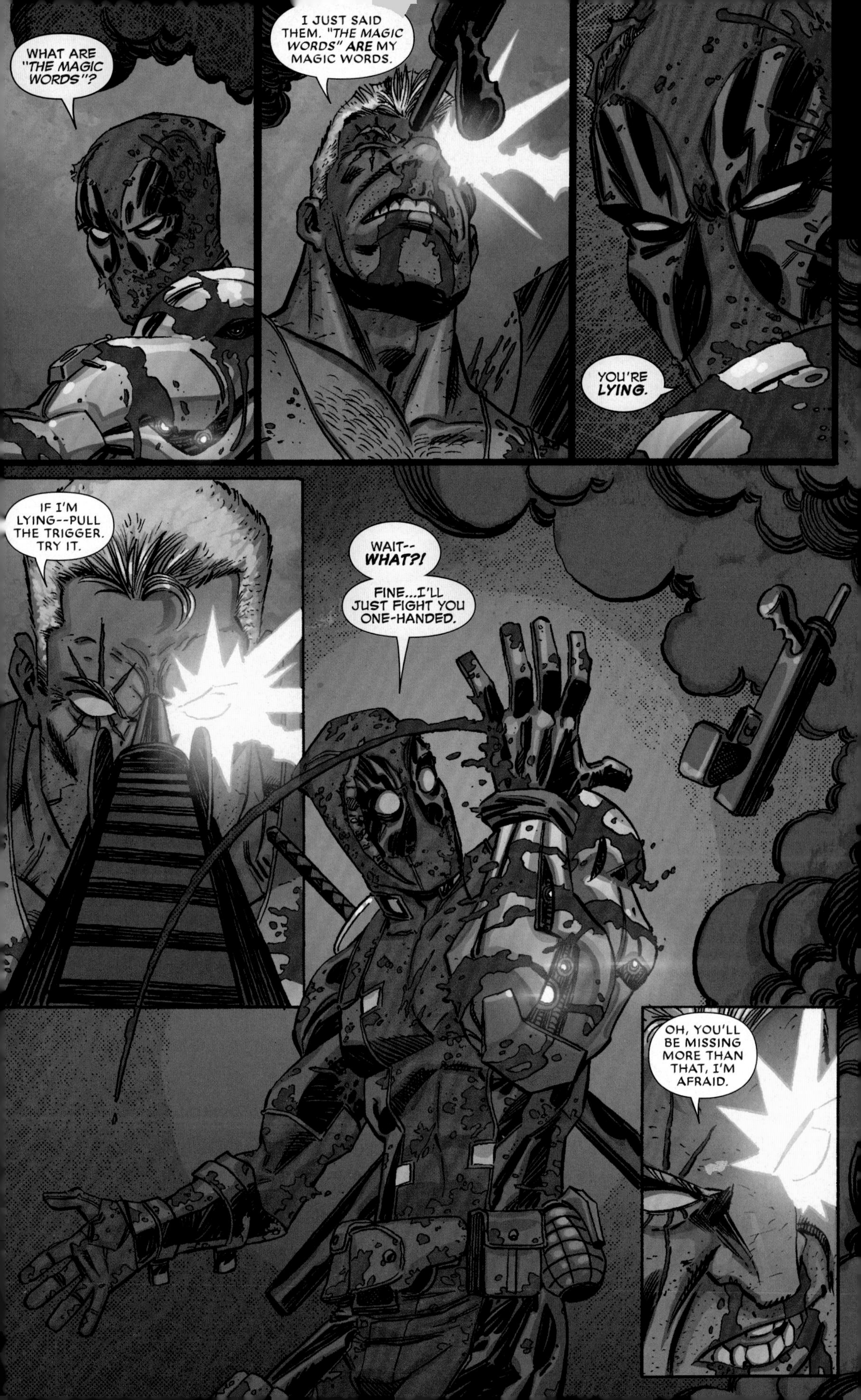
WHAT ARE "THE MAGIC WORDS"?
I JUST SAID THEM. "THE MAGIC WORDS" ARE MY MAGIC WORDS.
YOU'RE LYING.
IF I'M LYING--PULL THE TRIGGER. TRY IT.
WAIT-- WHAT?!
FINE...I'LL JUST FIGHT YOU ONE-HANDED.
OH, YOU'LL BE MISSING MORE THAN THAT, I'M AFRAID.

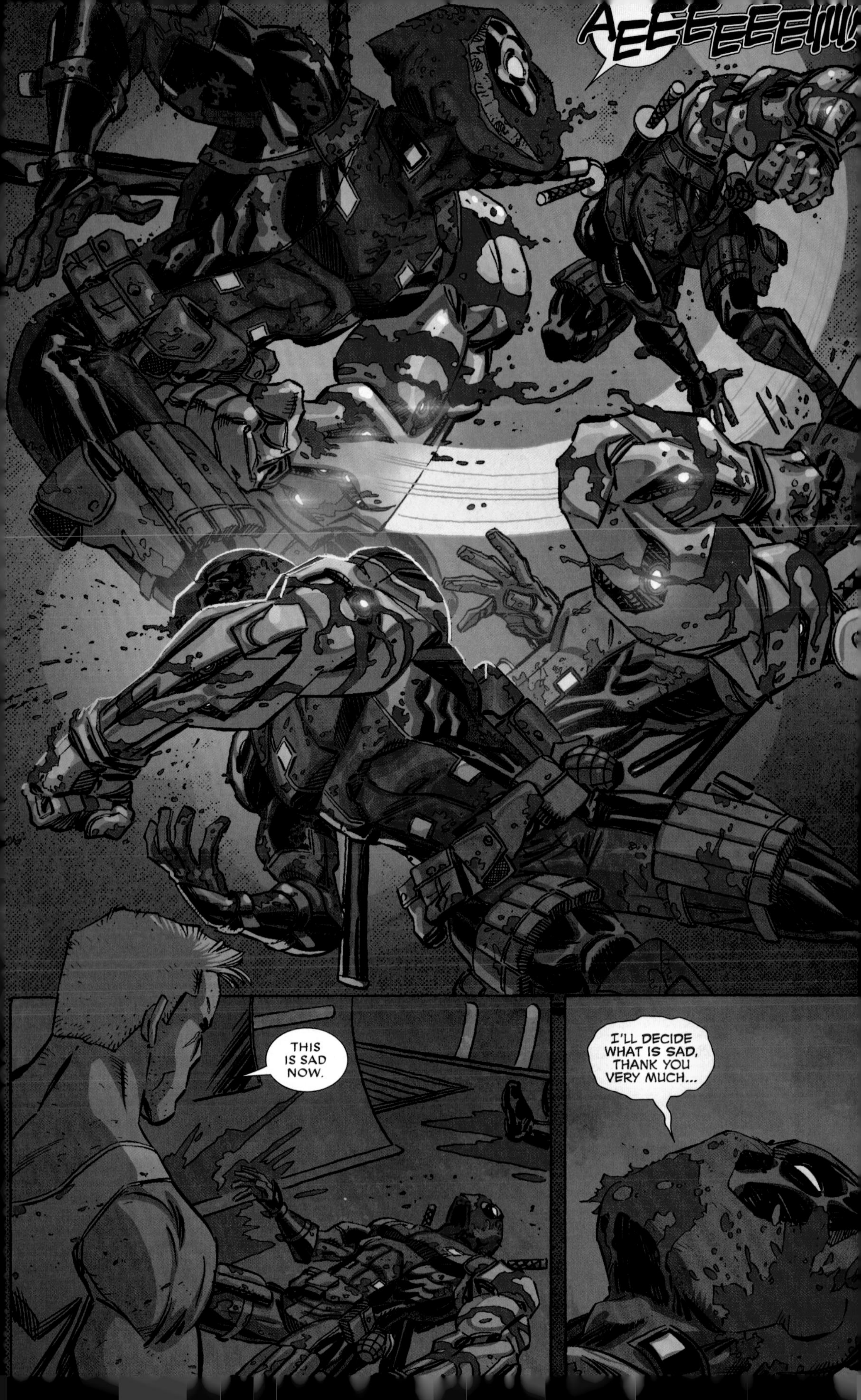
AEEEEEEEE!!!!
THIS IS SAD NOW.
I'LL DECIDE WHAT IS SAD, THANK YOU VERY MUCH...

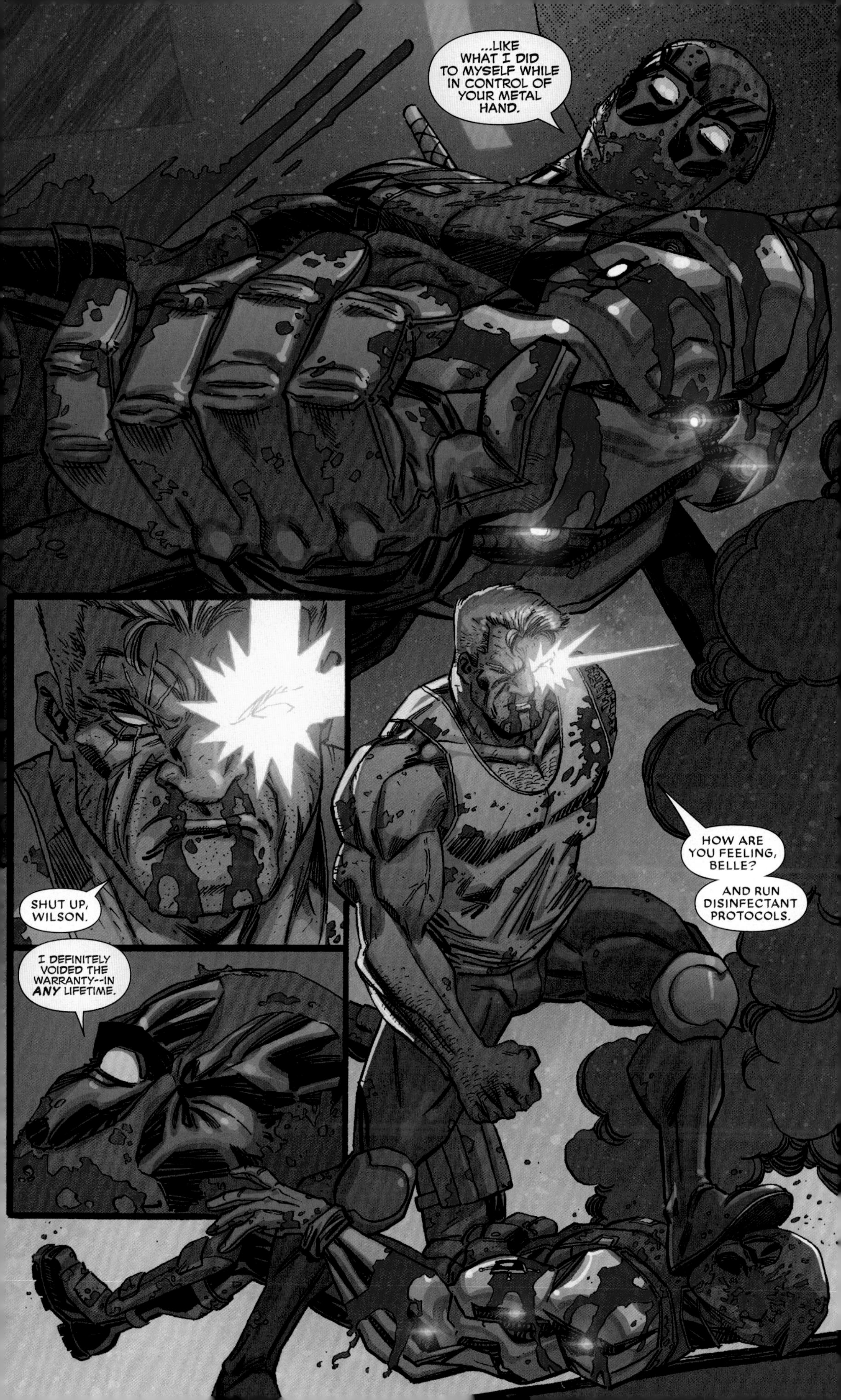
...LIKE WHAT I DID TO MYSELF WHILE IN CONTROL OF YOUR METAL HAND.
SHUT UP, WILSON.
I DEFINITELY VOIDED THE WARRANTY--IN ANY LIFETIME.
HOW ARE YOU FEELING, BELLE?
AND RUN DISINFECTANT PROTOCOLS.

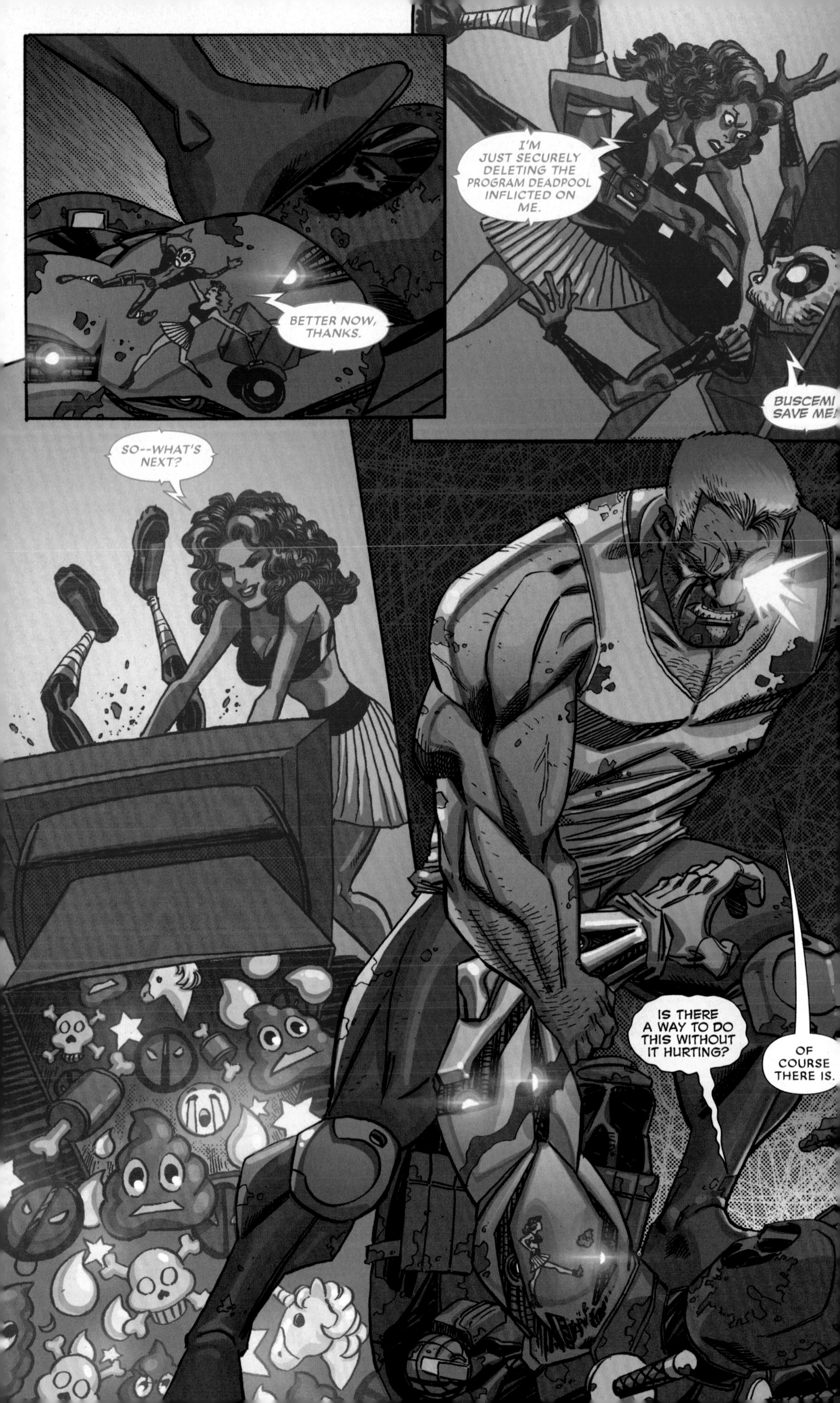
BETTER NOW, THANKS.
I'M JUST SECURELY DELETING THE PROGRAM DEADPOOL INFLICTED ON ME.
BUSCEMI SAVE ME!
SO--WHAT'S NEXT?
IS THERE A WAY TO DO THIS WITHOUT IT HURTING?
OF COURSE THERE IS.

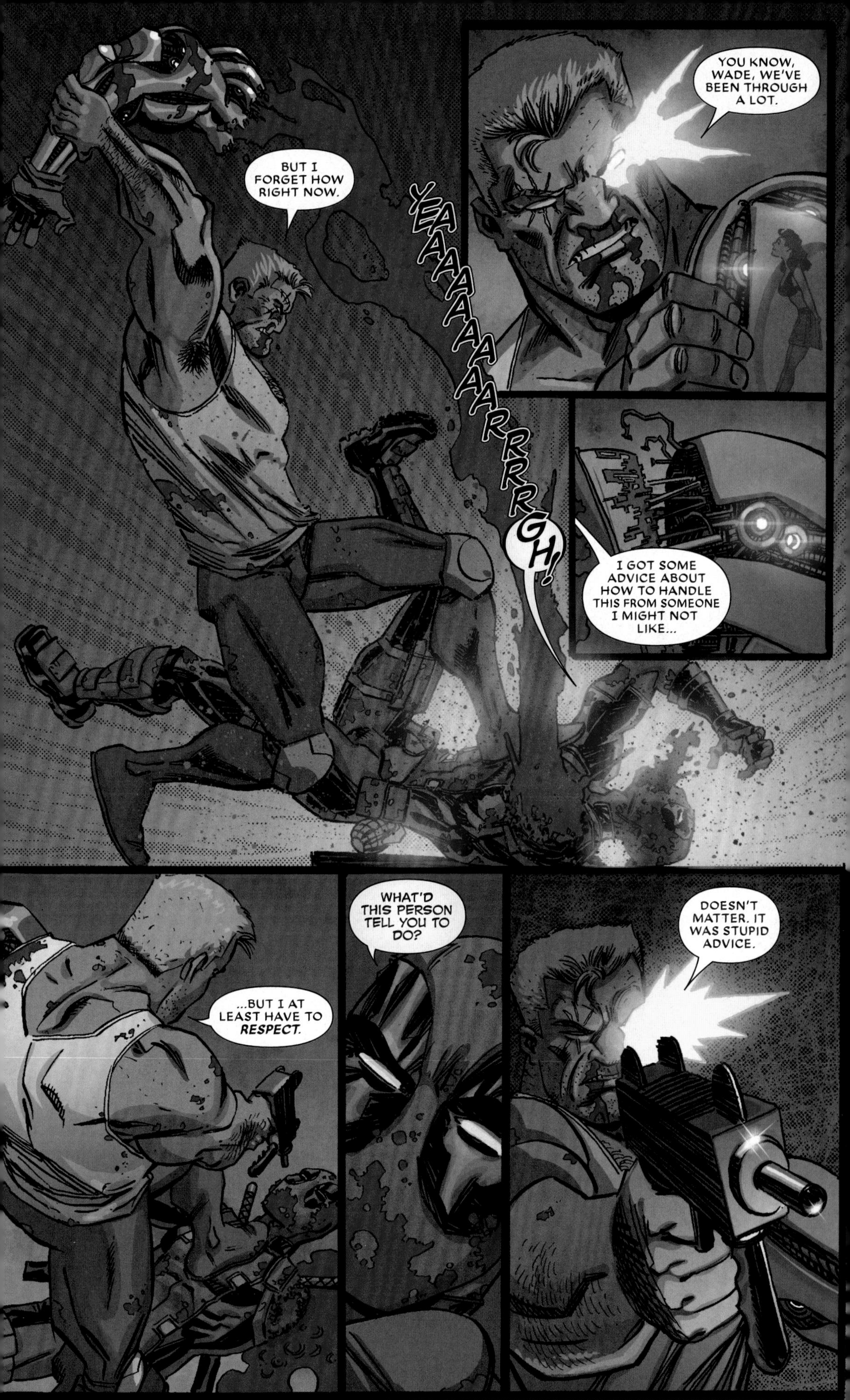
YOU KNOW, WADE, WE'VE BEEN THROUGH A LOT.
BUT I FORGET HOW RIGHT NOW.
YEAAAAAAAAARRRRGH!
I GOT SOME ADVICE ABOUT HOW TO HANDLE THIS FROM SOMEONE I MIGHT NOT LIKE...
...BUT I AT LEAST HAVE TO RESPECT.
WHAT'D THIS PERSON TELL YOU TO DO?
DOESN'T MATTER. IT WAS STUPID ADVICE.

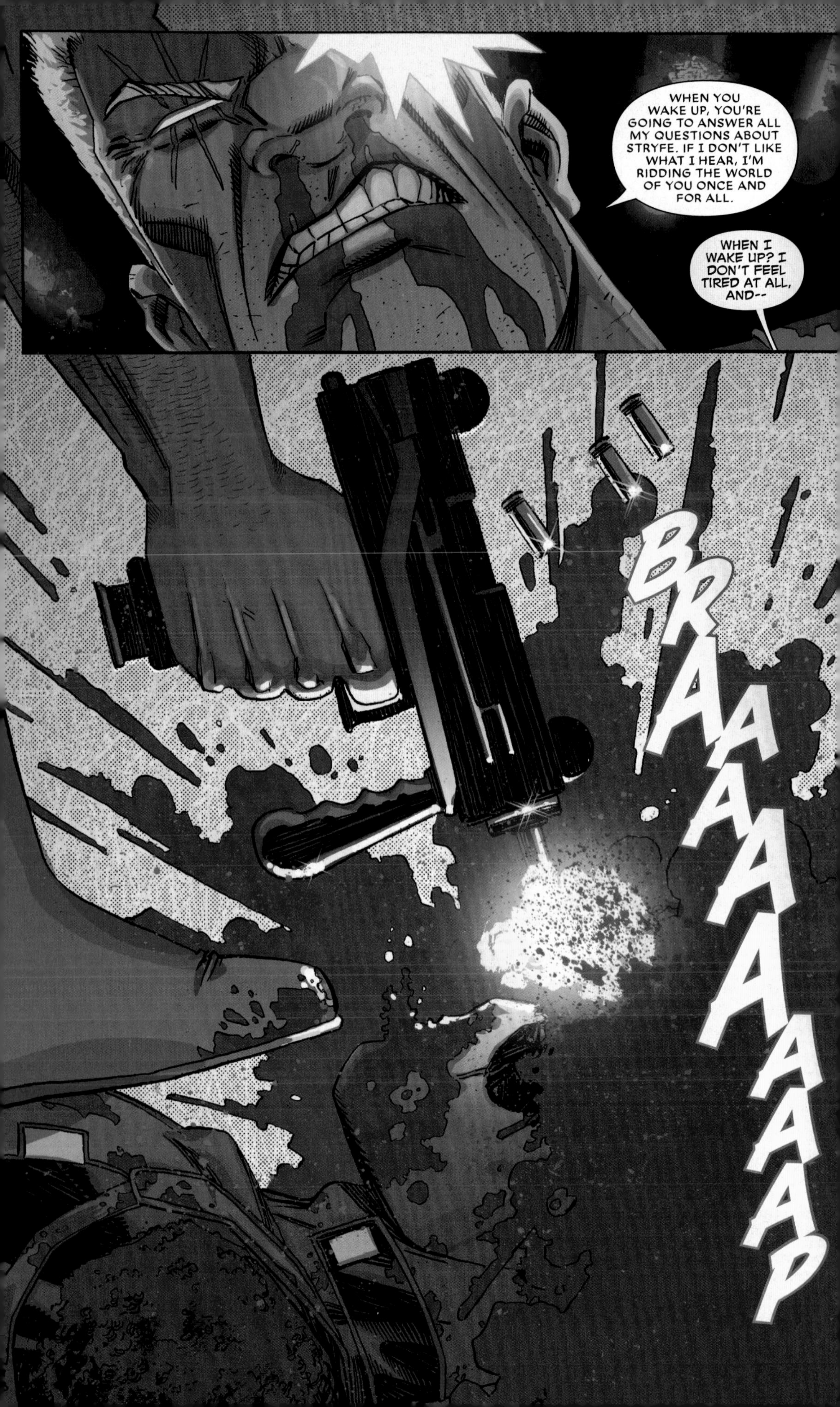
WHEN YOU WAKE UP, YOU'RE GOING TO ANSWER ALL MY QUESTIONS ABOUT STRYFE. IF I DON'T LIKE WHAT I HEAR, I'M RIDDING THE WORLD OF YOU ONCE AND FOR ALL.
WHEN I WAKE UP? I DON'T FEEL TIRED AT ALL, AND--
BRAAAAAAAAP

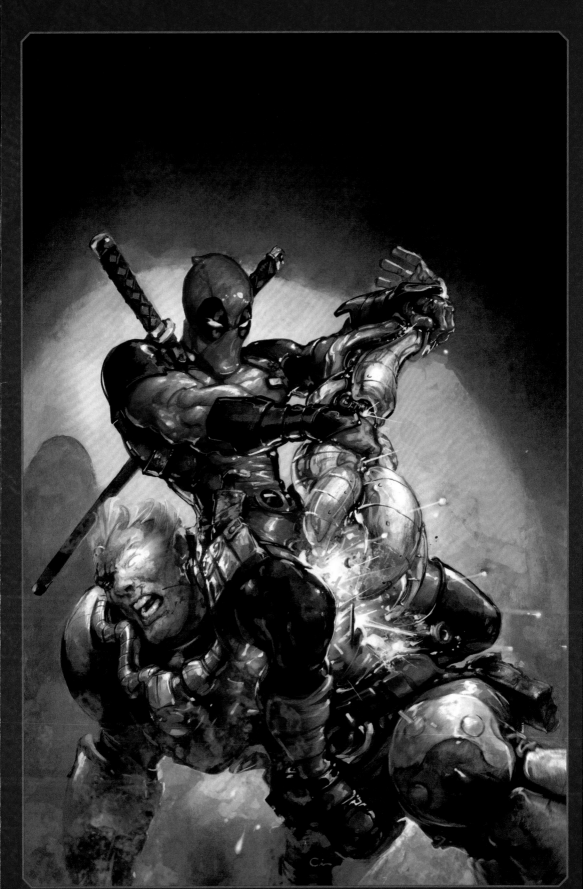

289 – Part Three: "It Was Good While It Lasted"

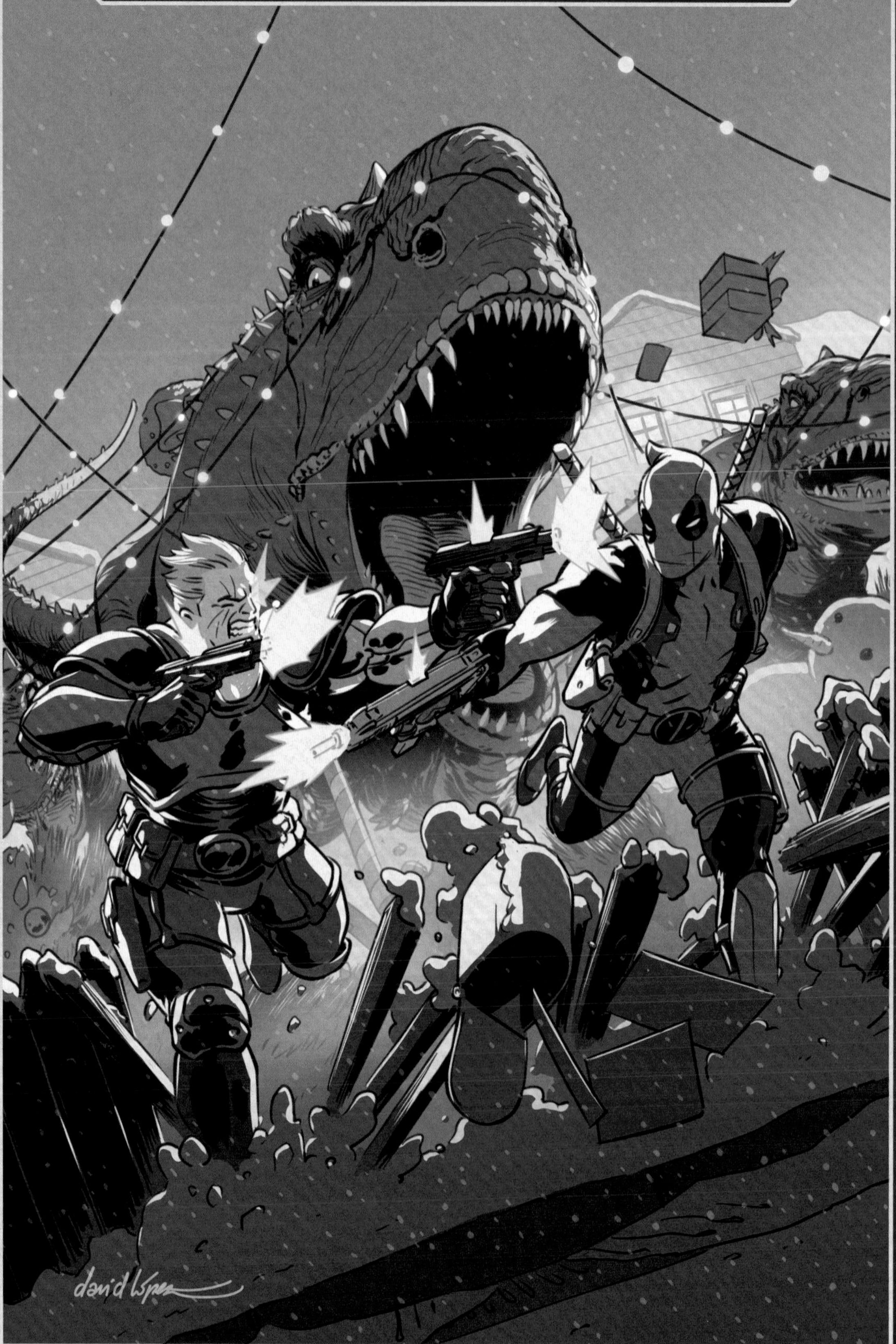

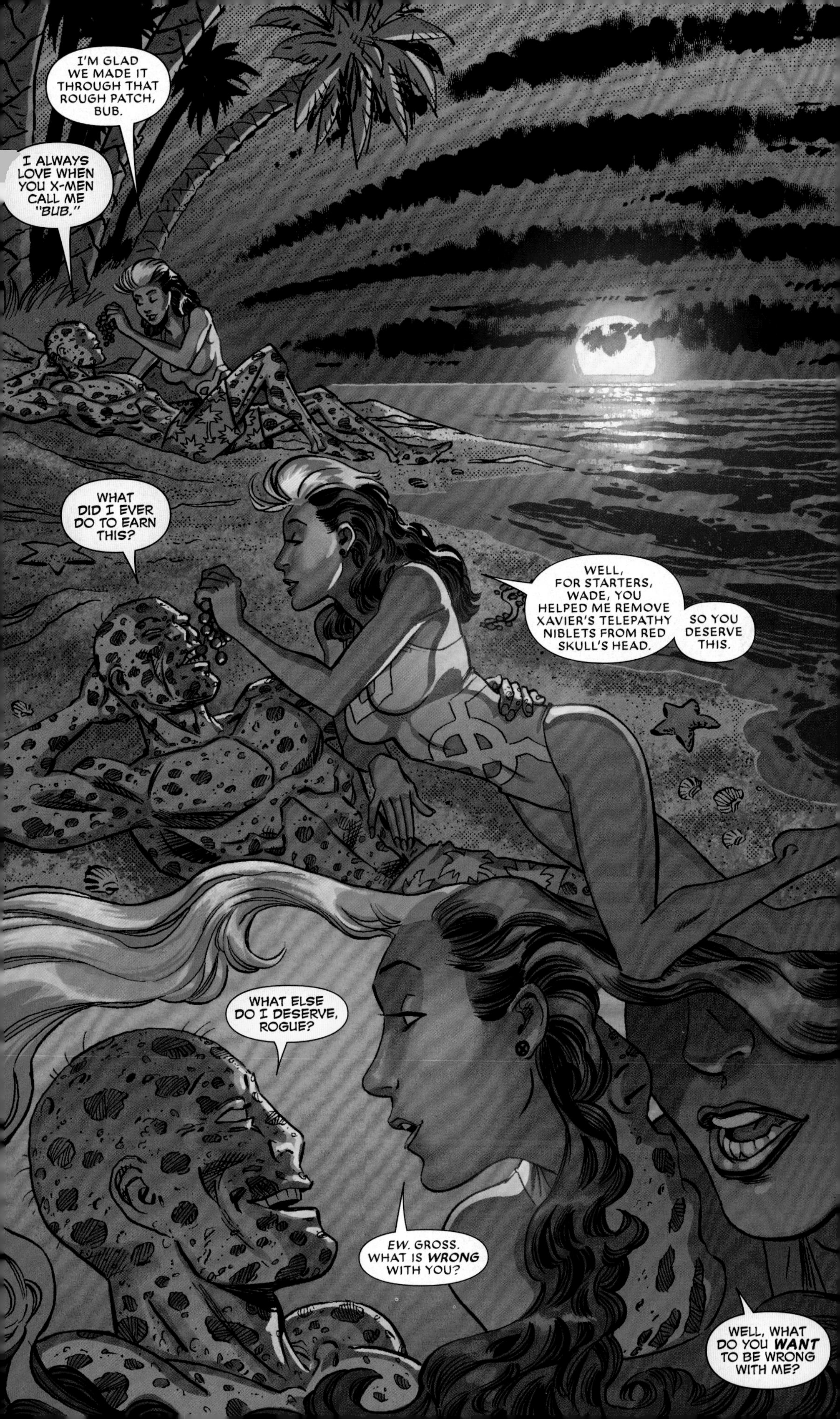
I'M GLAD WE MADE IT THROUGH THAT ROUGH PATCH, BUB.
I ALWAYS LOVE WHEN YOU X-MEN CALL ME "BUB."
WHAT DID I EVER DO TO EARN THIS?
WELL, FOR STARTERS, WADE, YOU HELPED ME REMOVE XAVIER'S TELEPATHY NIBLETS FROM RED SKULL'S HEAD.
SO YOU DESERVE THIS.
WHAT ELSE DO I DESERVE, ROGUE?
EW. GROSS. WHAT IS WRONG WITH YOU?
WELL, WHAT DO YOU WANT TO BE WRONG WITH ME?

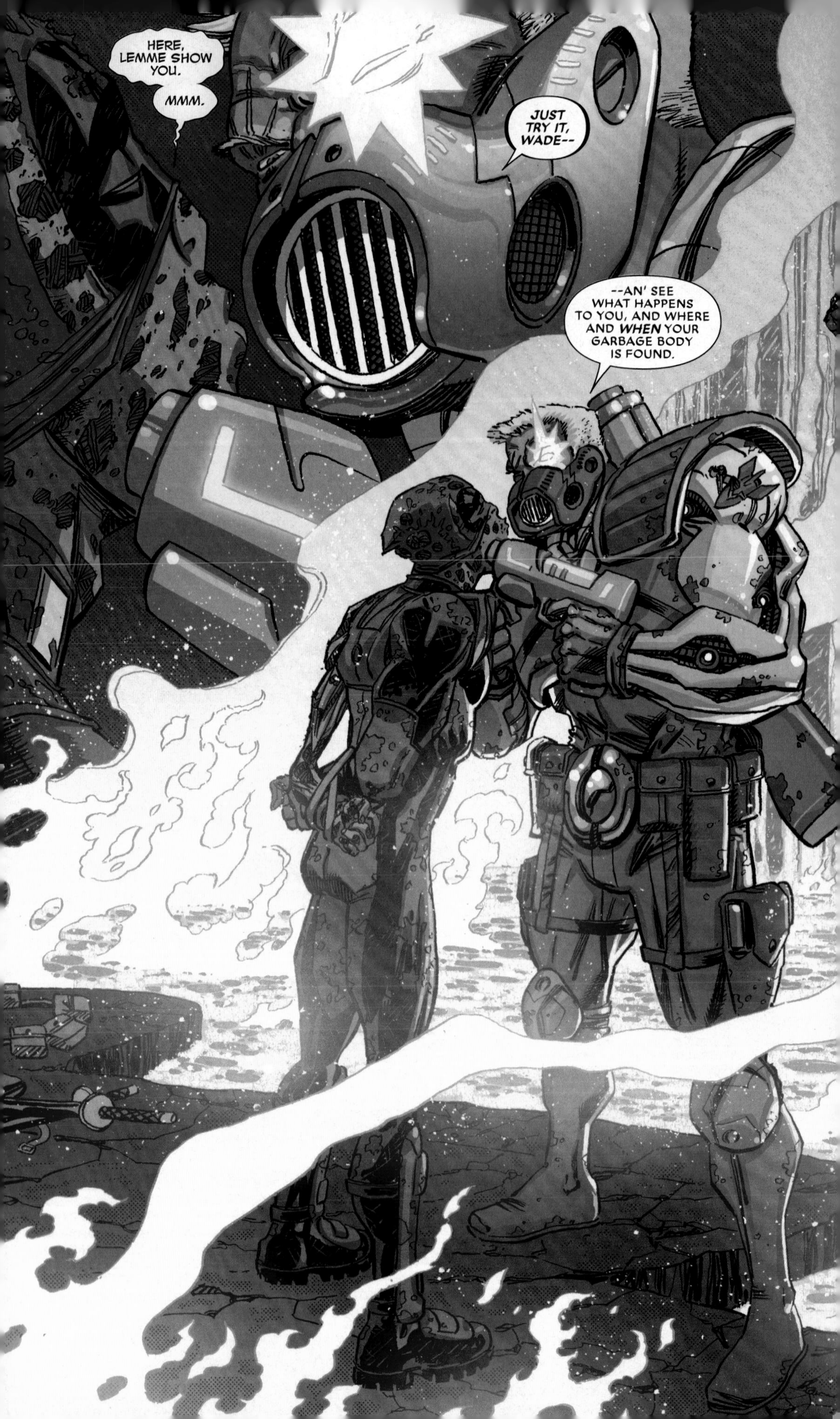
HERE, LEMME SHOW YOU.
MMM.
JUST TRY IT, WADE--
--AN' SEE WHAT HAPPENS TO YOU, AND WHERE AND WHEN YOUR GARBAGE BODY IS FOUND.

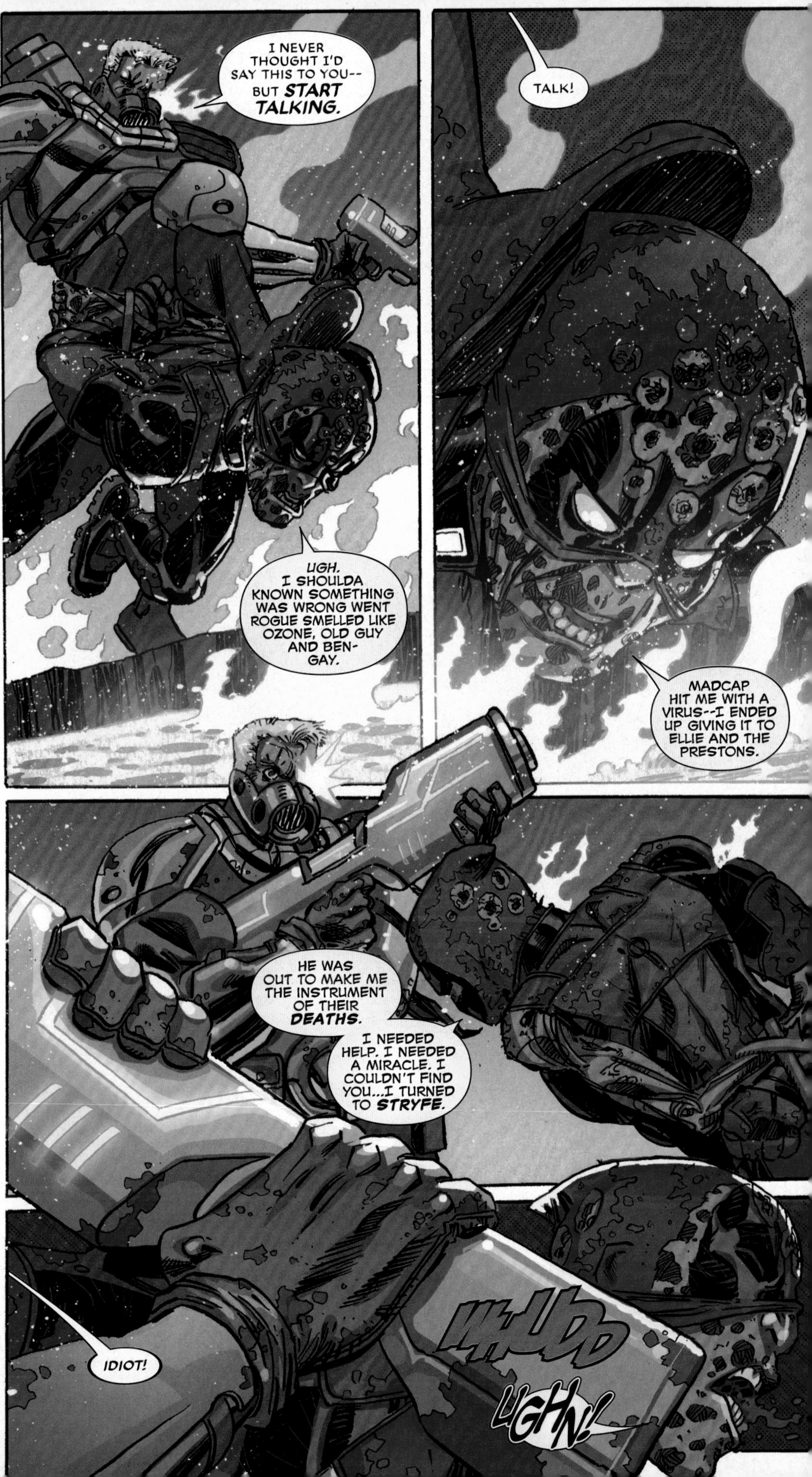
I NEVER THOUGHT I'D SAY THIS TO YOU-- BUT START TALKING.
UGH. I SHOULDA KNOWN SOMETHING WAS WRONG WENT ROGUE SMELLED LIKE OZONE, OLD GUY AND BEN-GAY.
TALK!
MADCAP HIT ME WITH A VIRUS--I ENDED UP GIVING IT TO ELLIE AND THE PRESTONS.
HE WAS OUT TO MAKE ME THE INSTRUMENT OF THEIR DEATHS.
I NEEDED HELP. I NEEDED A MIRACLE. I COULDN'T FIND YOU...I TURNED TO STRYFE.
IDIOT!
WHUDD
UGHN!

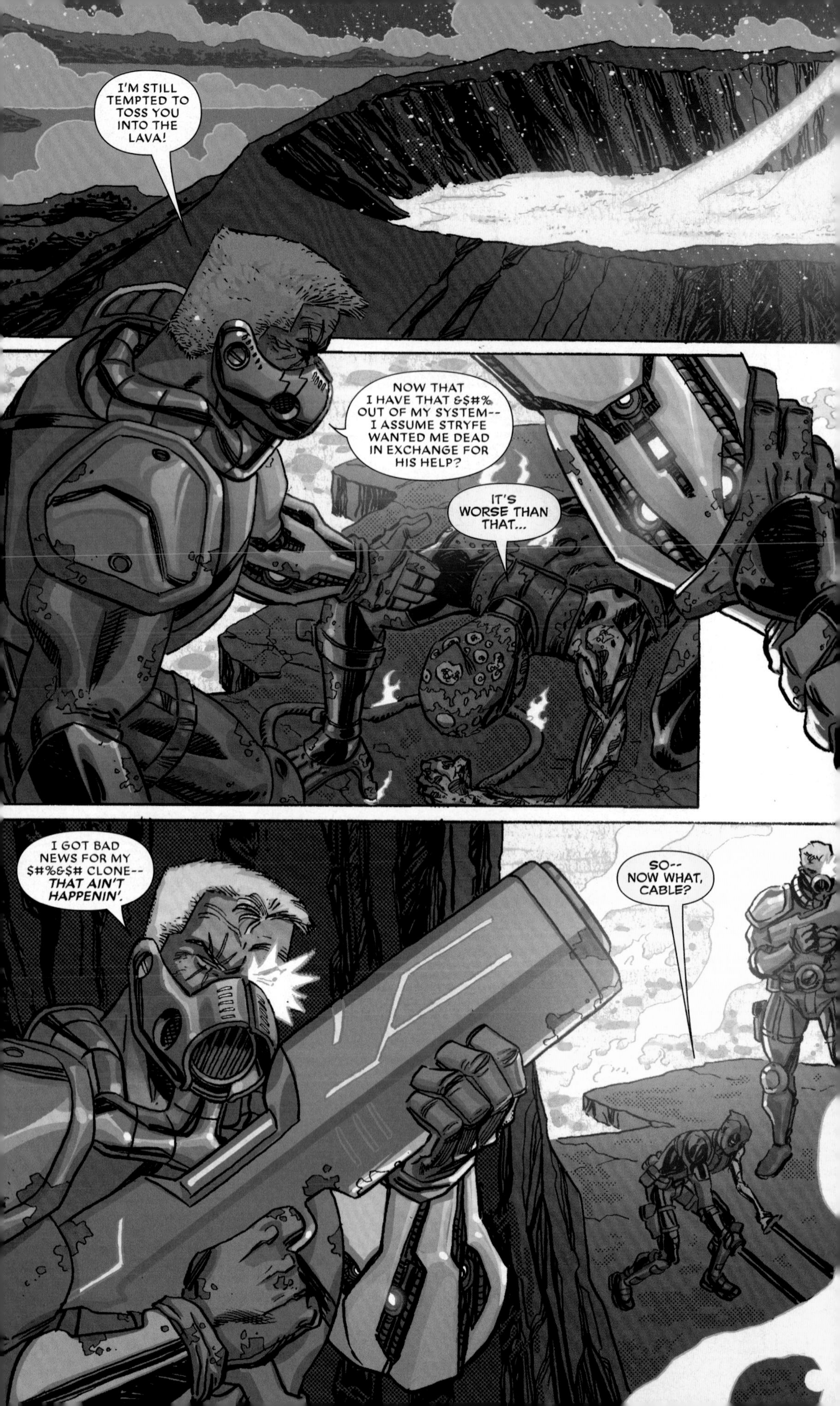
I'M STILL TEMPTED TO TOSS YOU INTO THE LAVA!
NOW THAT I HAVE THAT &$#% OUT OF MY SYSTEM-- I ASSUME STRYFE WANTED ME DEAD IN EXCHANGE FOR HIS HELP?
IT'S WORSE THAN THAT...
I GOT BAD NEWS FOR MY $#%&$# CLONE-- *THAT AIN'T HAPPENIN'.*
SO-- NOW WHAT, CABLE?

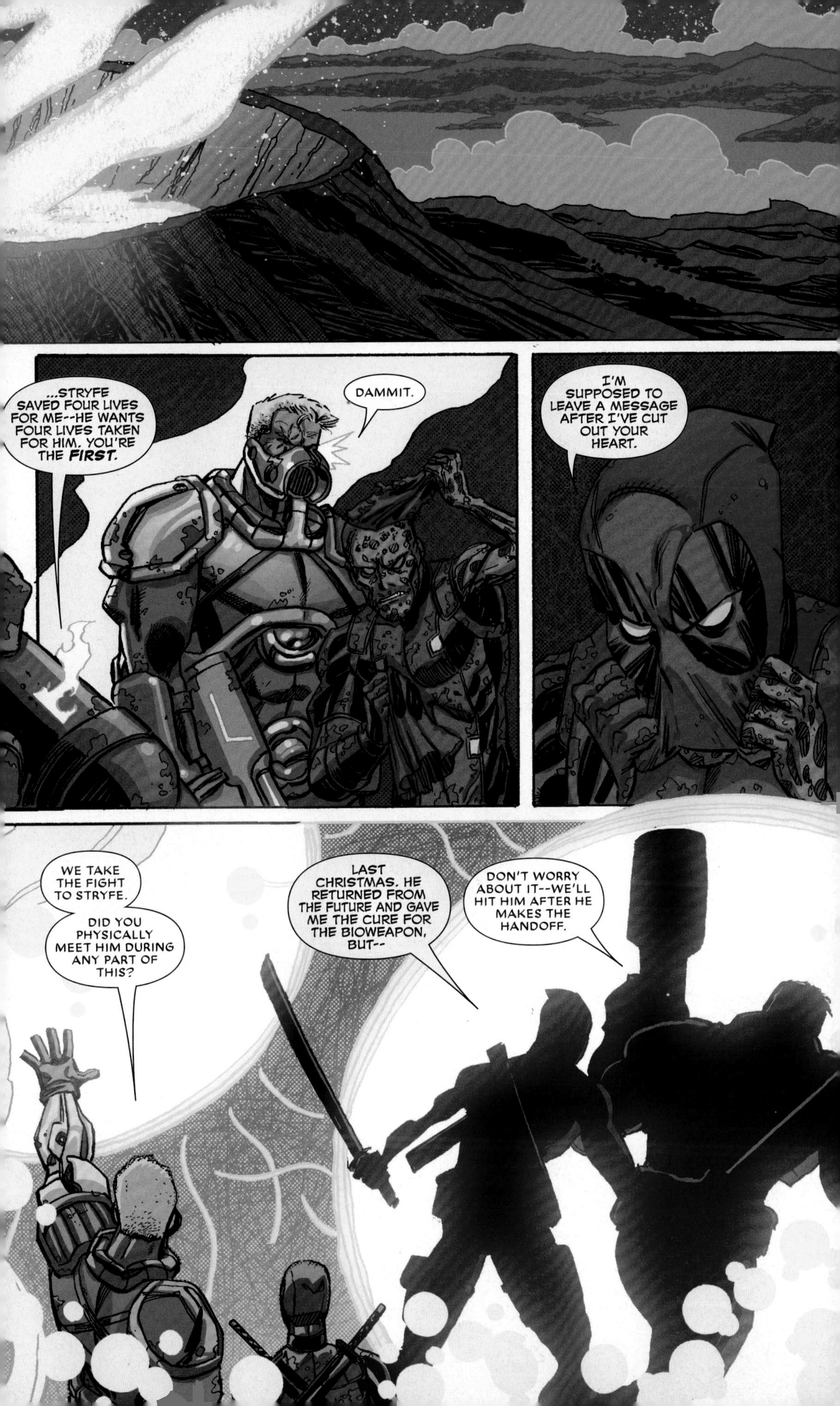
...STRYFE SAVED FOUR LIVES FOR ME--HE WANTS FOUR LIVES TAKEN FOR HIM. YOU'RE THE *FIRST.*
DAMMIT.
I'M SUPPOSED TO LEAVE A MESSAGE AFTER I'VE CUT OUT YOUR HEART.
WE TAKE THE FIGHT TO STRYFE.
DID YOU PHYSICALLY MEET HIM DURING ANY PART OF THIS?
LAST CHRISTMAS. HE RETURNED FROM THE FUTURE AND GAVE ME THE CURE FOR THE BIOWEAPON, BUT--
DON'T WORRY ABOUT IT--WE'LL HIT HIM AFTER HE MAKES THE HANDOFF.

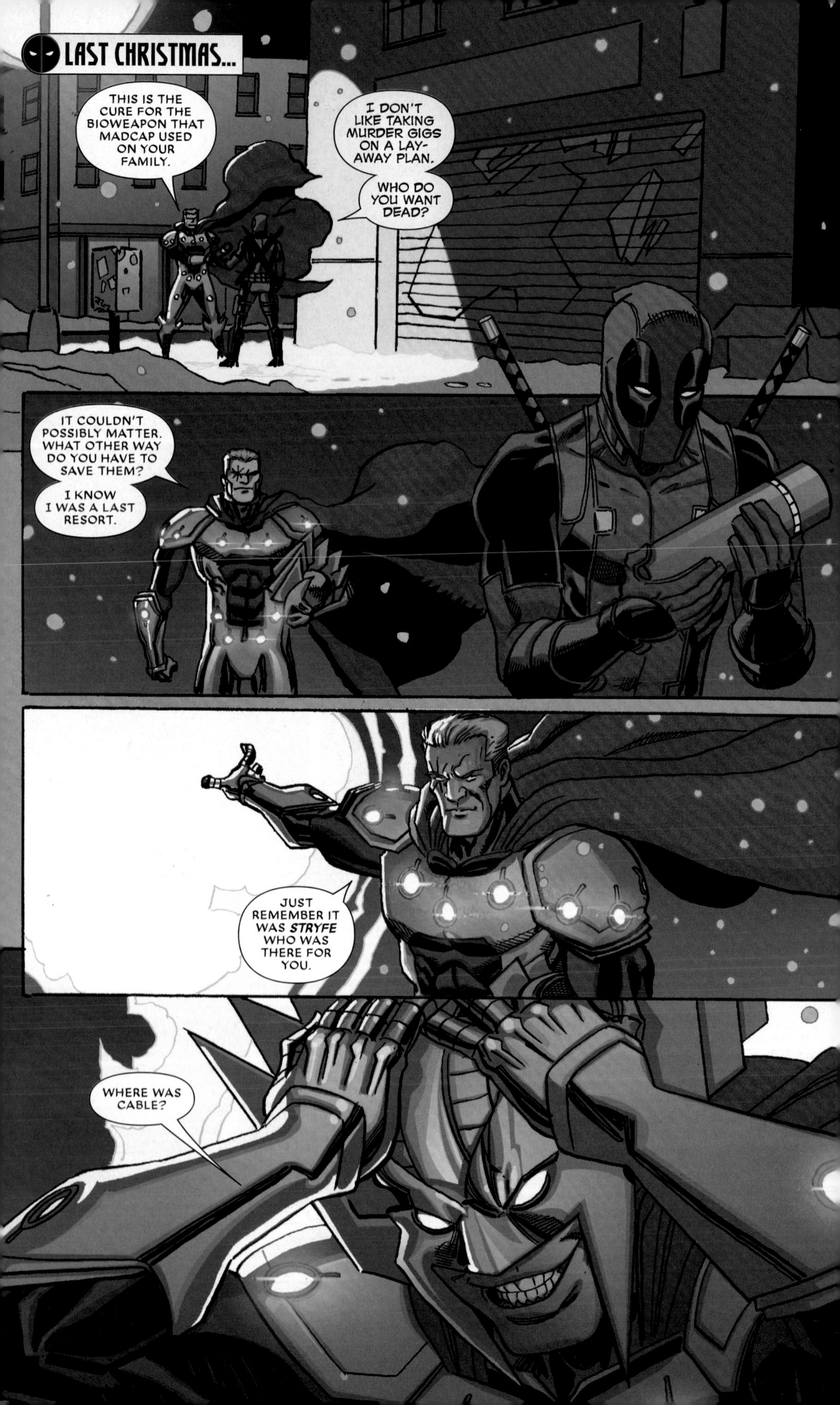
LAST CHRISTMAS...
THIS IS THE CURE FOR THE BIOWEAPON THAT MADCAP USED ON YOUR FAMILY.
I DON'T LIKE TAKING MURDER GIGS ON A LAY-AWAY PLAN.
WHO DO YOU WANT DEAD?
IT COULDN'T POSSIBLY MATTER. WHAT OTHER WAY DO YOU HAVE TO SAVE THEM?
I KNOW I WAS A LAST RESORT.
JUST REMEMBER IT WAS STRYFE WHO WAS THERE FOR YOU.
WHERE WAS CABLE?

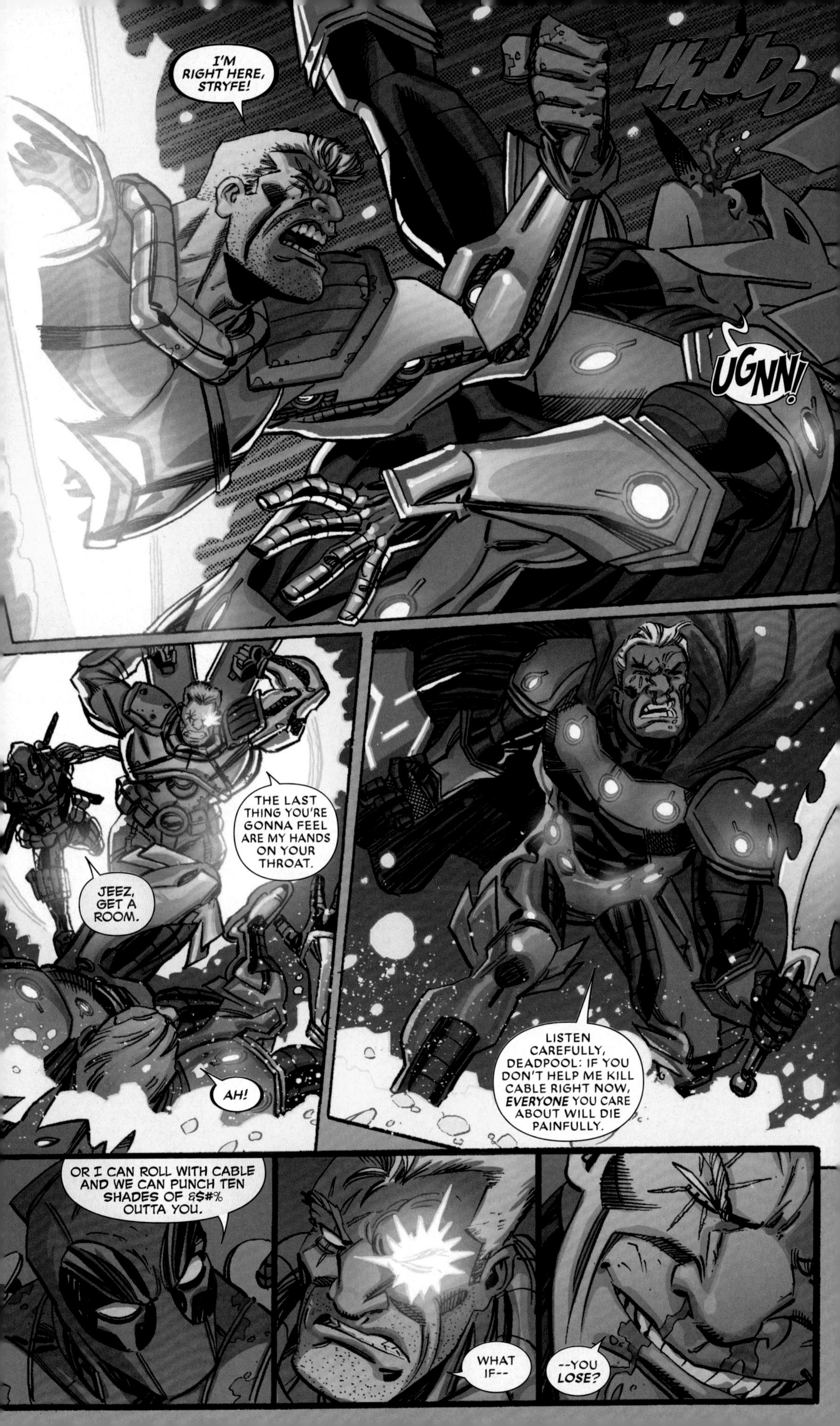
I'M RIGHT HERE, STRYFE!
WHUDD
UGNN!
THE LAST THING YOU'RE GONNA FEEL ARE MY HANDS ON YOUR THROAT.
JEEZ, GET A ROOM.
AH!
LISTEN CAREFULLY, DEADPOOL: IF YOU DON'T HELP ME KILL CABLE RIGHT NOW, EVERYONE YOU CARE ABOUT WILL DIE PAINFULLY.
OR I CAN ROLL WITH CABLE AND WE CAN PUNCH TEN SHADES OF &$#% OUTTA YOU.
WHAT IF--
--YOU LOSE?

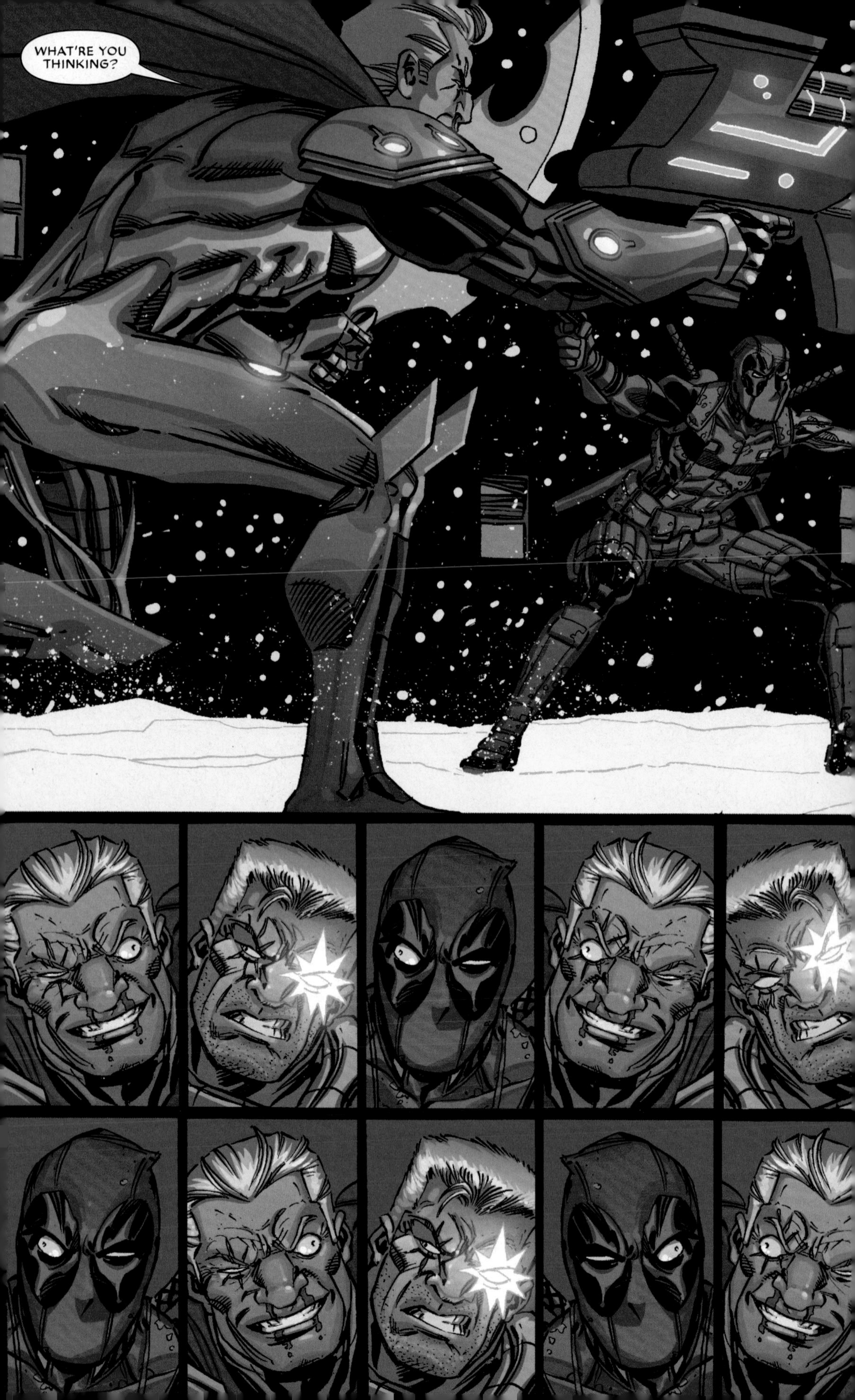
WHAT'RE YOU THINKING?

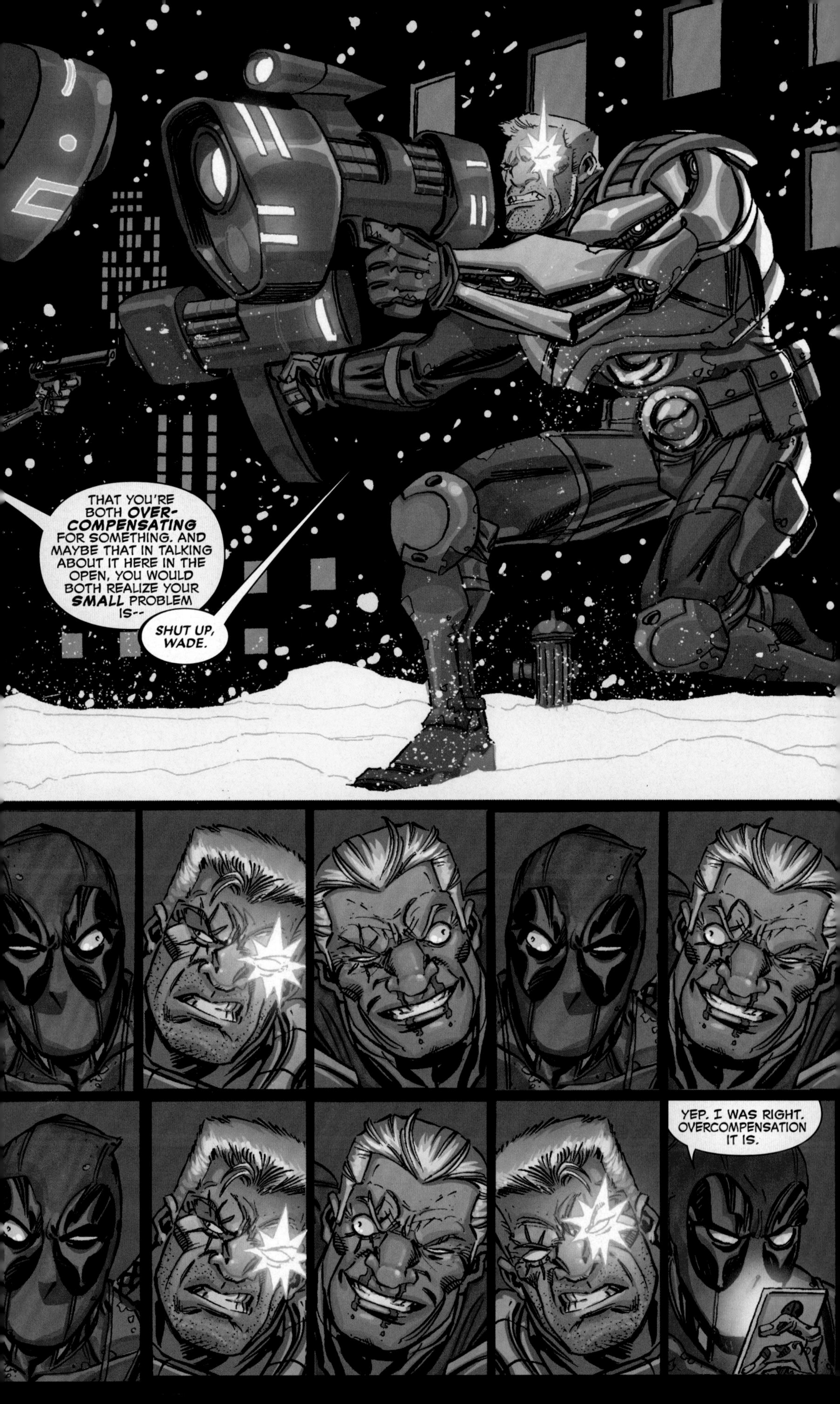
THAT YOU'RE BOTH **OVER-COMPENSATING** FOR SOMETHING. AND MAYBE THAT IN TALKING ABOUT IT HERE IN THE OPEN, YOU WOULD BOTH REALIZE YOUR **SMALL** PROBLEM IS--
SHUT UP, WADE.
YEP. I WAS RIGHT. OVERCOMPENSATION IT IS.

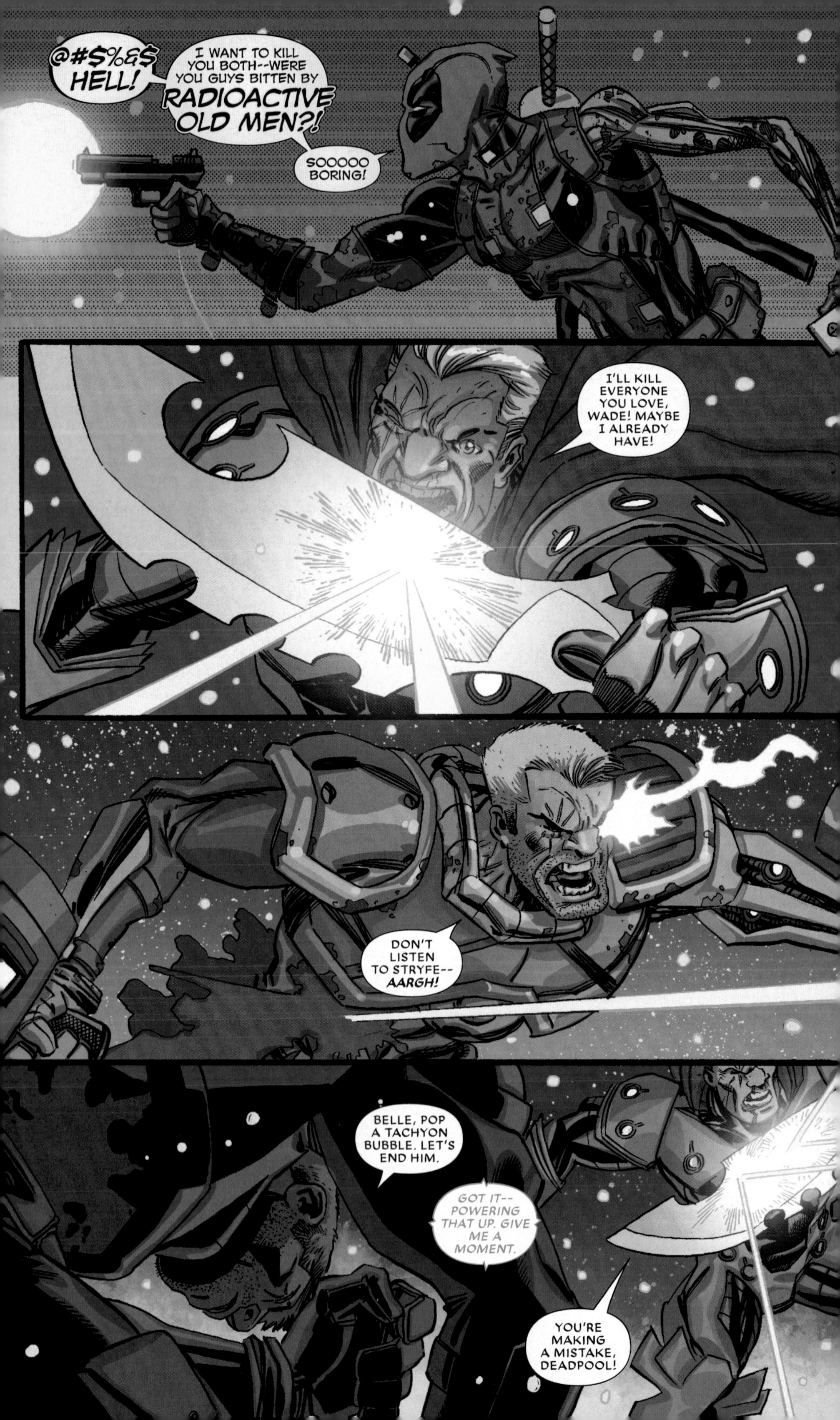
@#$%&$ HELL!
I WANT TO KILL YOU BOTH--WERE YOU GUYS BITTEN BY RADIOACTIVE OLD MEN?!
SOOOOO BORING!
I'LL KILL EVERYONE YOU LOVE, WADE! MAYBE I ALREADY HAVE!
DON'T LISTEN TO STRYFE-- AARGH!
BELLE, POP A TACHYON BUBBLE. LET'S END HIM.
GOT IT-- POWERING THAT UP. GIVE ME A MOMENT.
YOU'RE MAKING A MISTAKE, DEADPOOL!

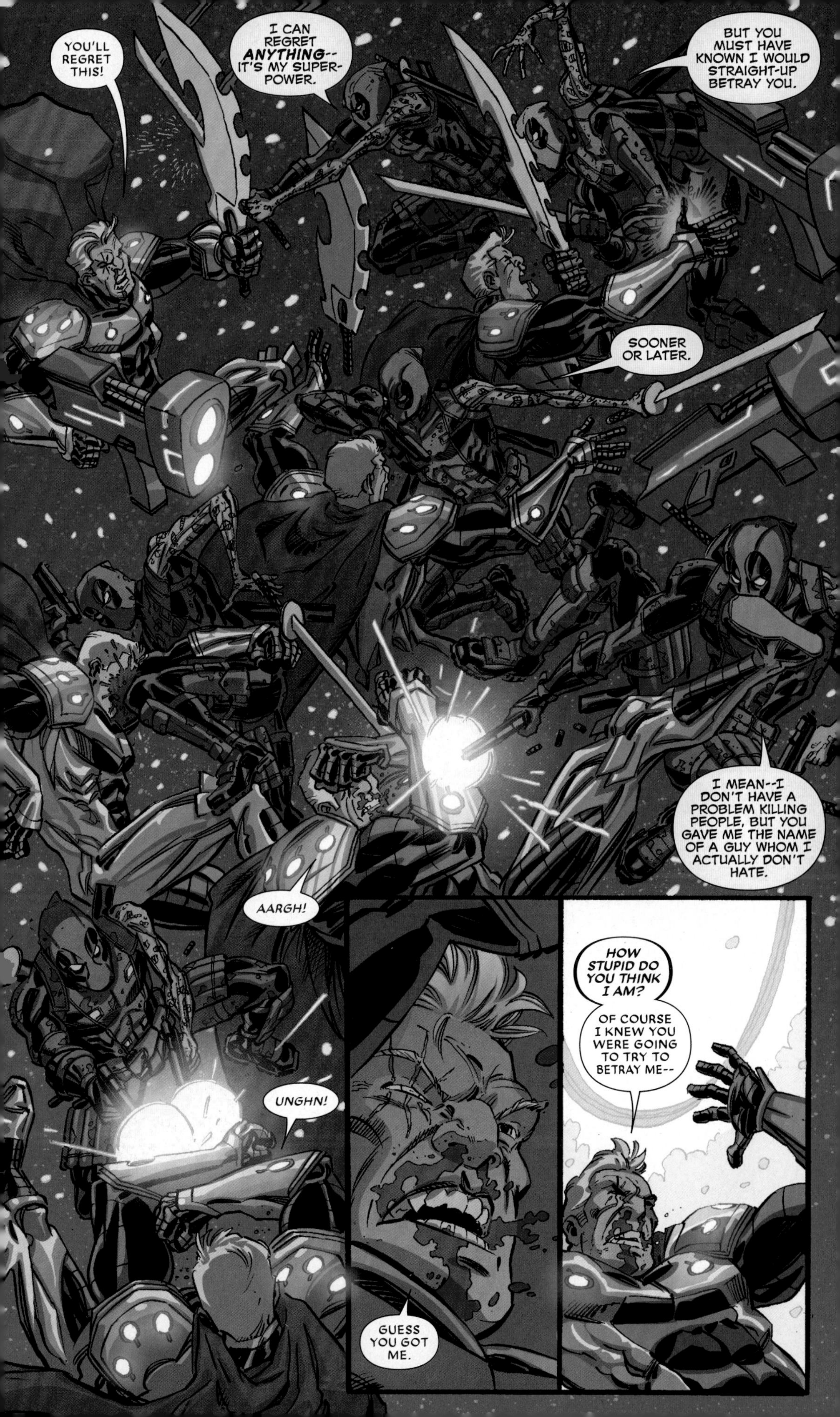

YOU'LL REGRET THIS!
I CAN REGRET ANYTHING-- IT'S MY SUPER-POWER.
BUT YOU MUST HAVE KNOWN I WOULD STRAIGHT-UP BETRAY YOU.
SOONER OR LATER.
I MEAN--I DON'T HAVE A PROBLEM KILLING PEOPLE, BUT YOU GAVE ME THE NAME OF A GUY WHOM I ACTUALLY DON'T HATE.
AARGH!
UNGHN!
GUESS YOU GOT ME.
HOW STUPID DO YOU THINK I AM?
OF COURSE I KNEW YOU WERE GOING TO TRY TO BETRAY ME--

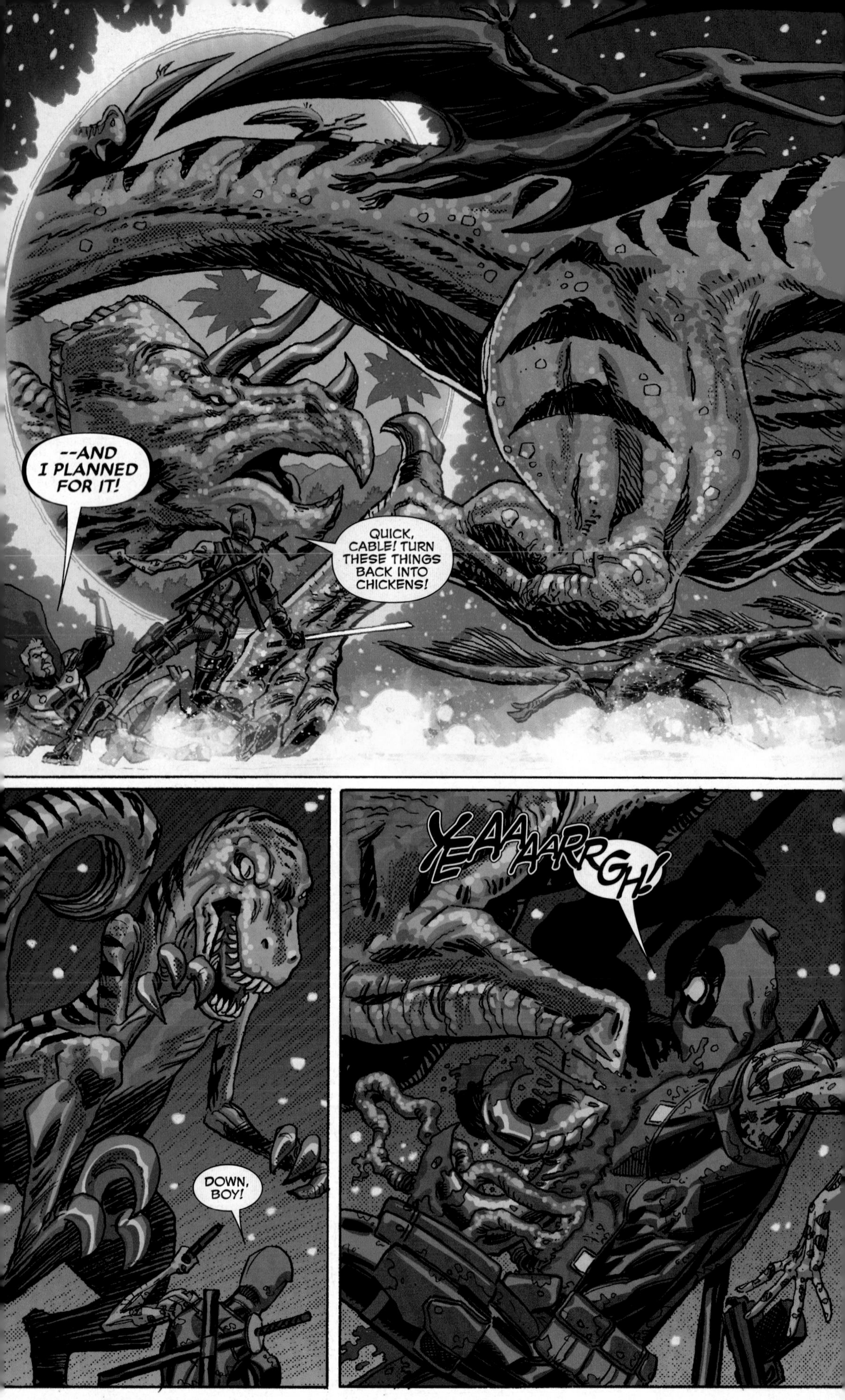
--AND I PLANNED FOR IT!
QUICK, CABLE! TURN THESE THINGS BACK INTO CHICKENS!
DOWN, BOY!
YEAAAAARRGH!

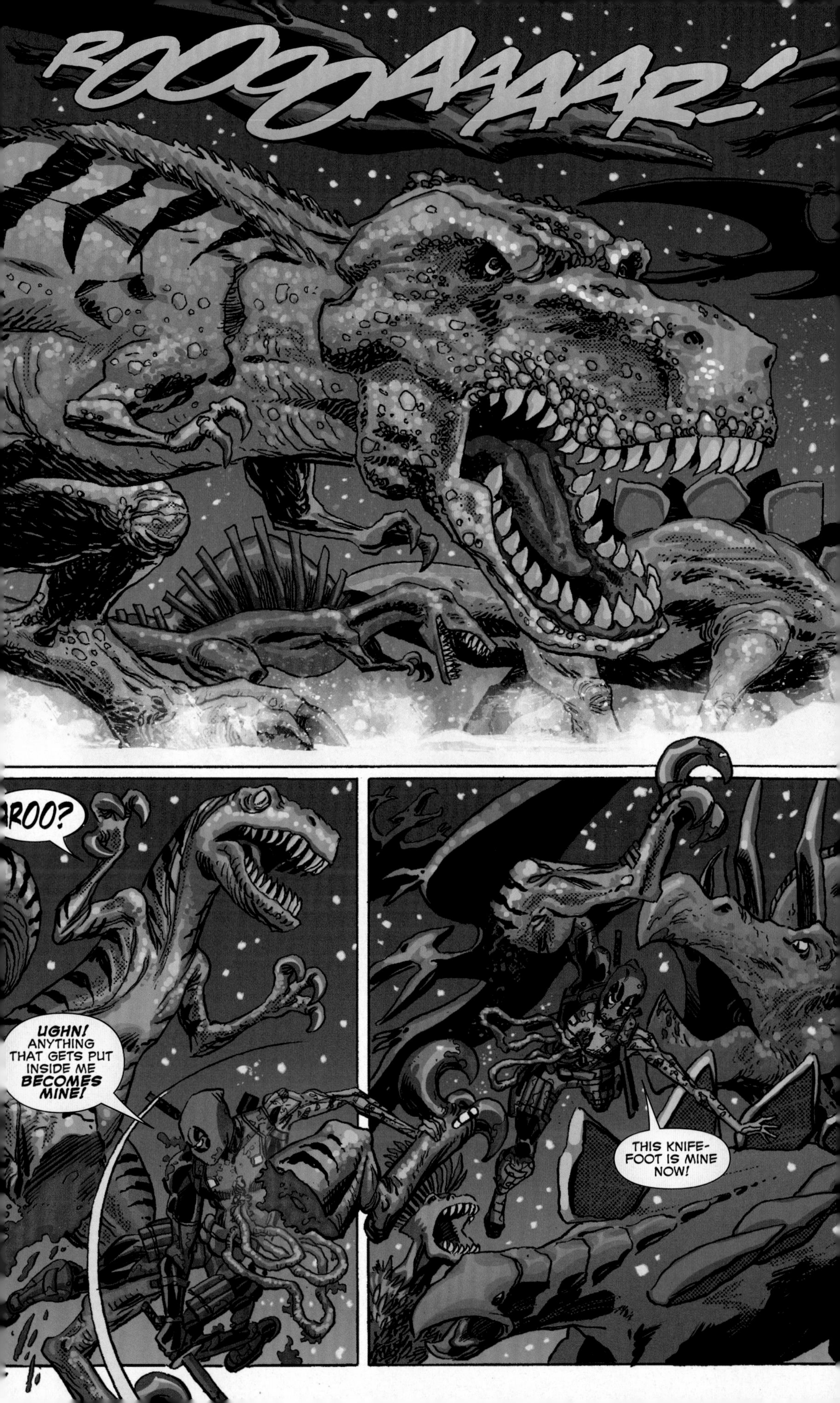

ROOOAAAAR!
ROO?
UGHN! ANYTHING THAT GETS PUT INSIDE ME BECOMES MINE!
THIS KNIFE-FOOT IS MINE NOW!

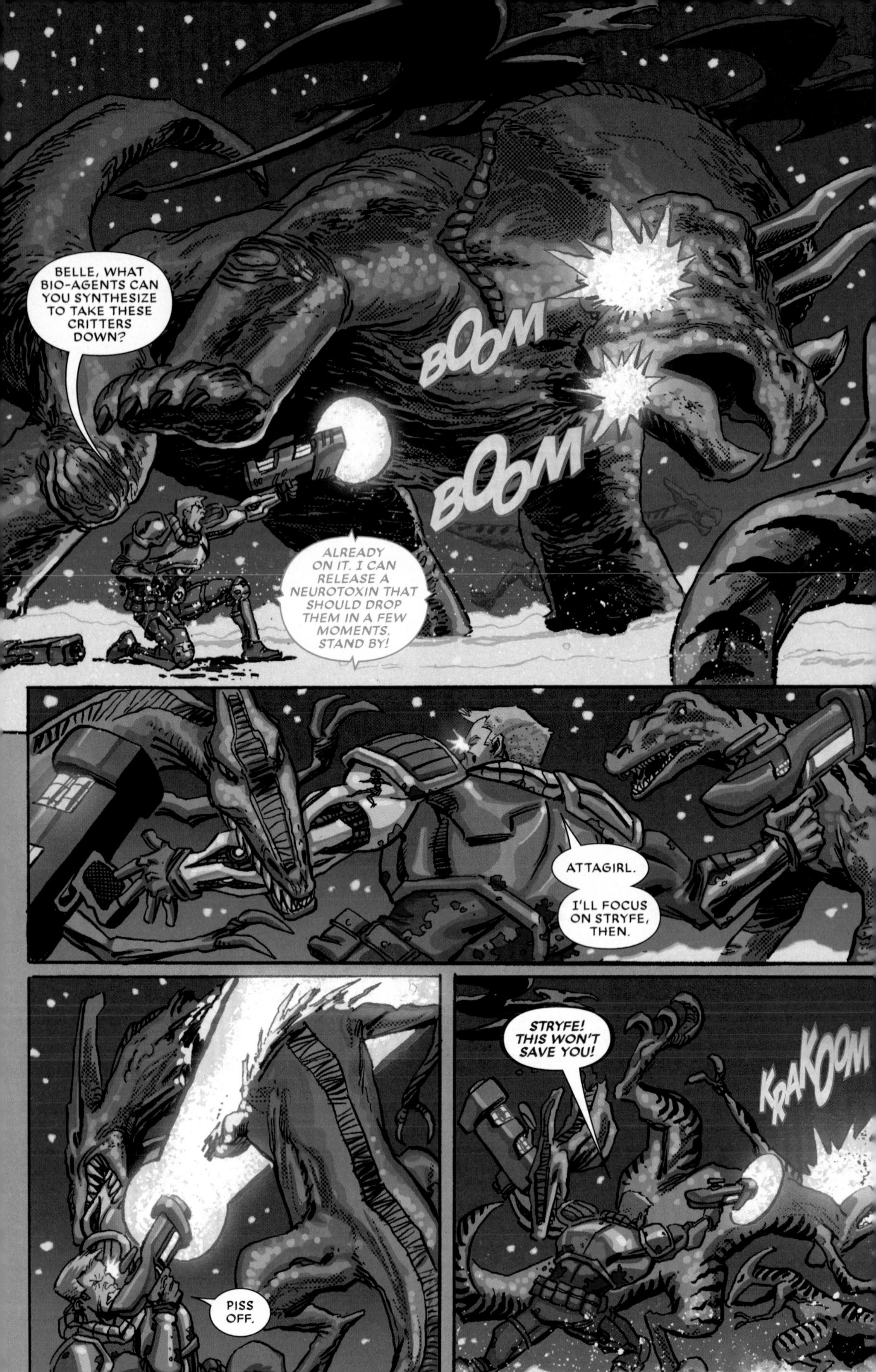
BELLE, WHAT BIO-AGENTS CAN YOU SYNTHESIZE TO TAKE THESE CRITTERS DOWN?
BOOM
BOOM
ALREADY ON IT. I CAN RELEASE A NEUROTOXIN THAT SHOULD DROP THEM IN A FEW MOMENTS. STAND BY!
ATTAGIRL.
I'LL FOCUS ON STRYFE, THEN.
PISS OFF.
STRYFE! THIS WON'T SAVE YOU!
KRAKOOM

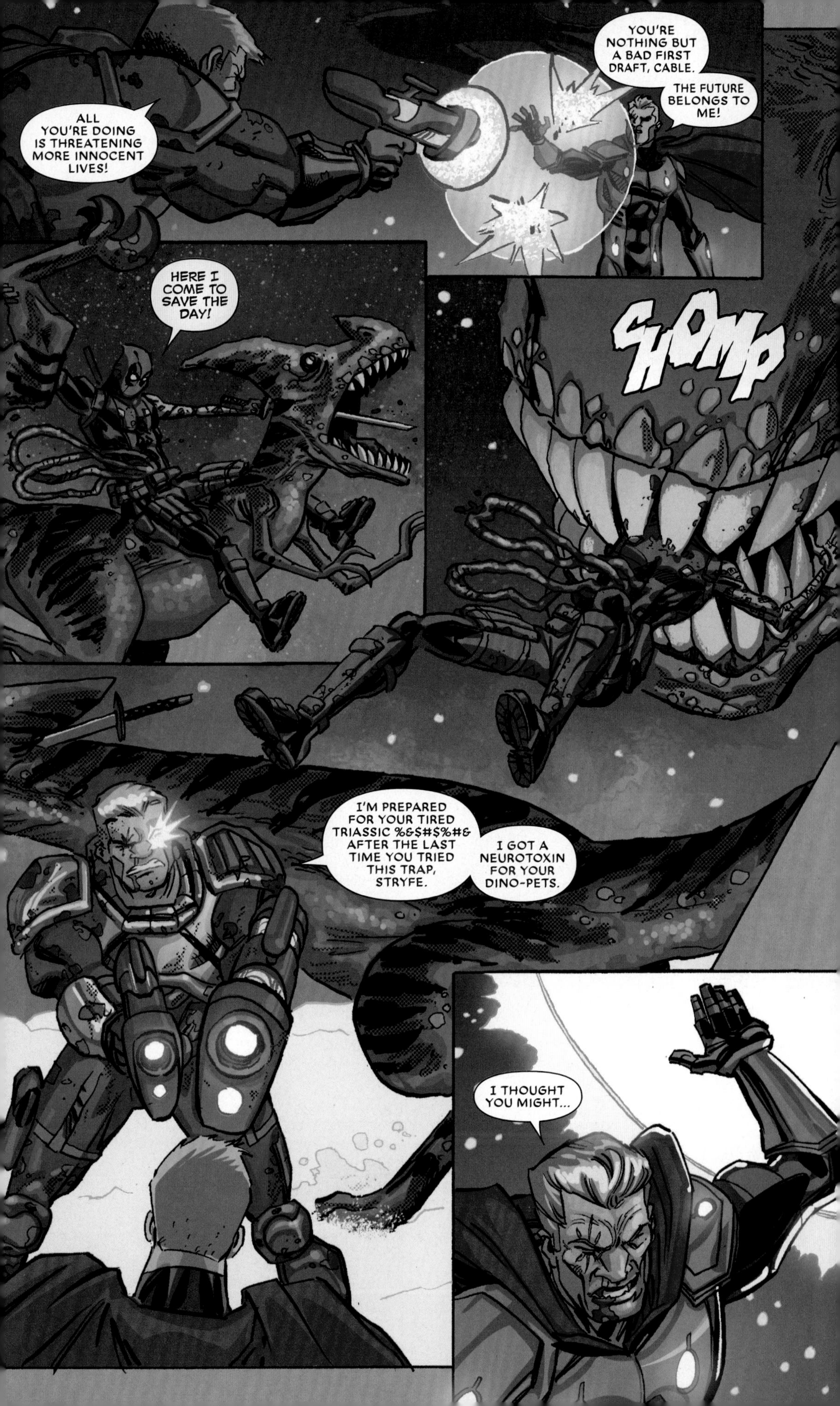

ALL YOU'RE DOING IS THREATENING MORE INNOCENT LIVES!
YOU'RE NOTHING BUT A BAD FIRST DRAFT, CABLE.
THE FUTURE BELONGS TO ME!
HERE I COME TO SAVE THE DAY!
CHOMP
I'M PREPARED FOR YOUR TIRED TRIASSIC %&$#$%#& AFTER THE LAST TIME YOU TRIED THIS TRAP, STRYFE.
I GOT A NEUROTOXIN FOR YOUR DINO-PETS.
I THOUGHT YOU MIGHT...

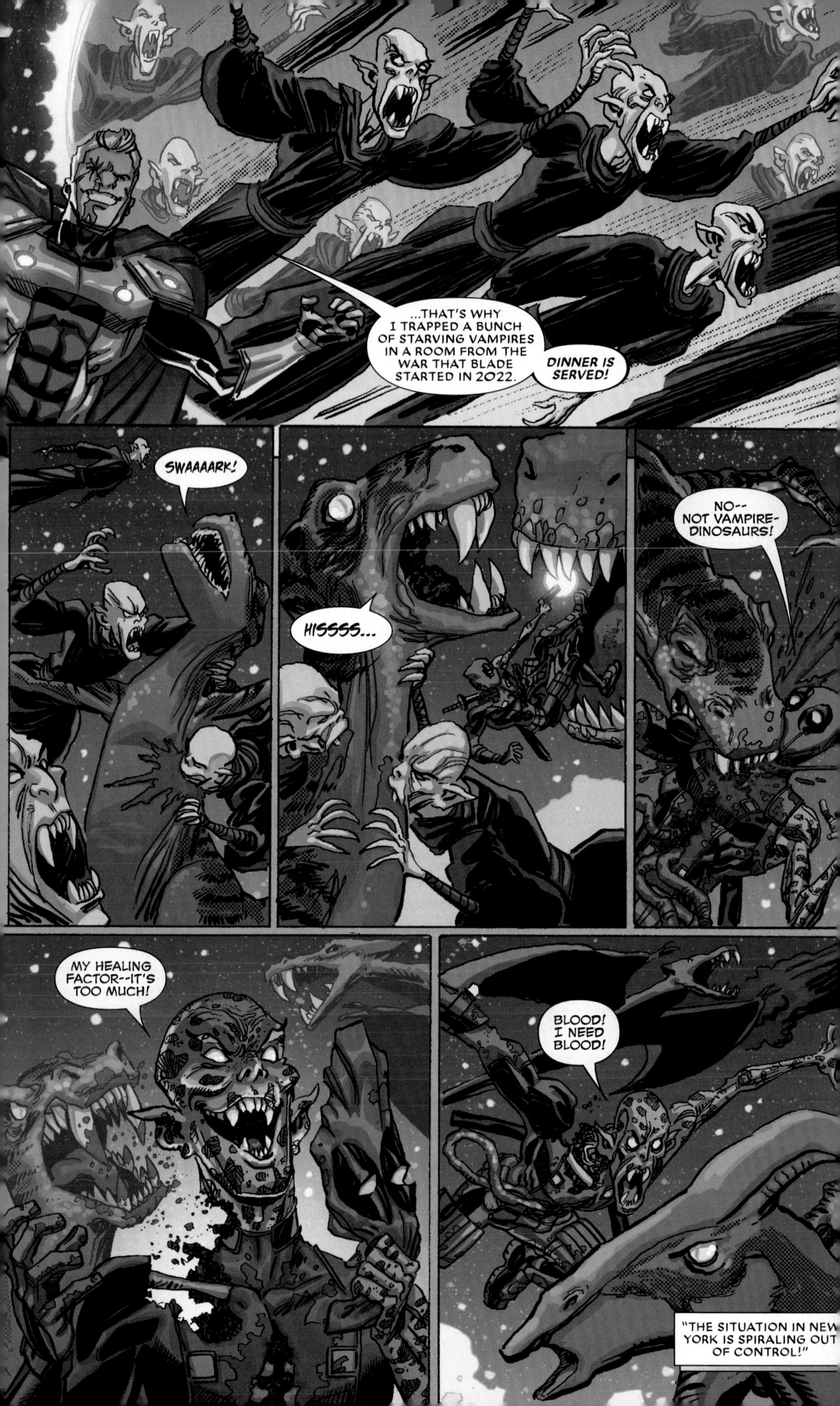
...THAT'S WHY I TRAPPED A BUNCH OF STARVING VAMPIRES IN A ROOM FROM THE WAR THAT BLADE STARTED IN 2022.
DINNER IS SERVED!
SWAAAARK!
HISSSS...
NO-- NOT VAMPIRE-DINOSAURS!
MY HEALING FACTOR--IT'S TOO MUCH!
BLOOD! I NEED BLOOD!
"THE SITUATION IN NEW YORK IS SPIRALING OUT OF CONTROL!"

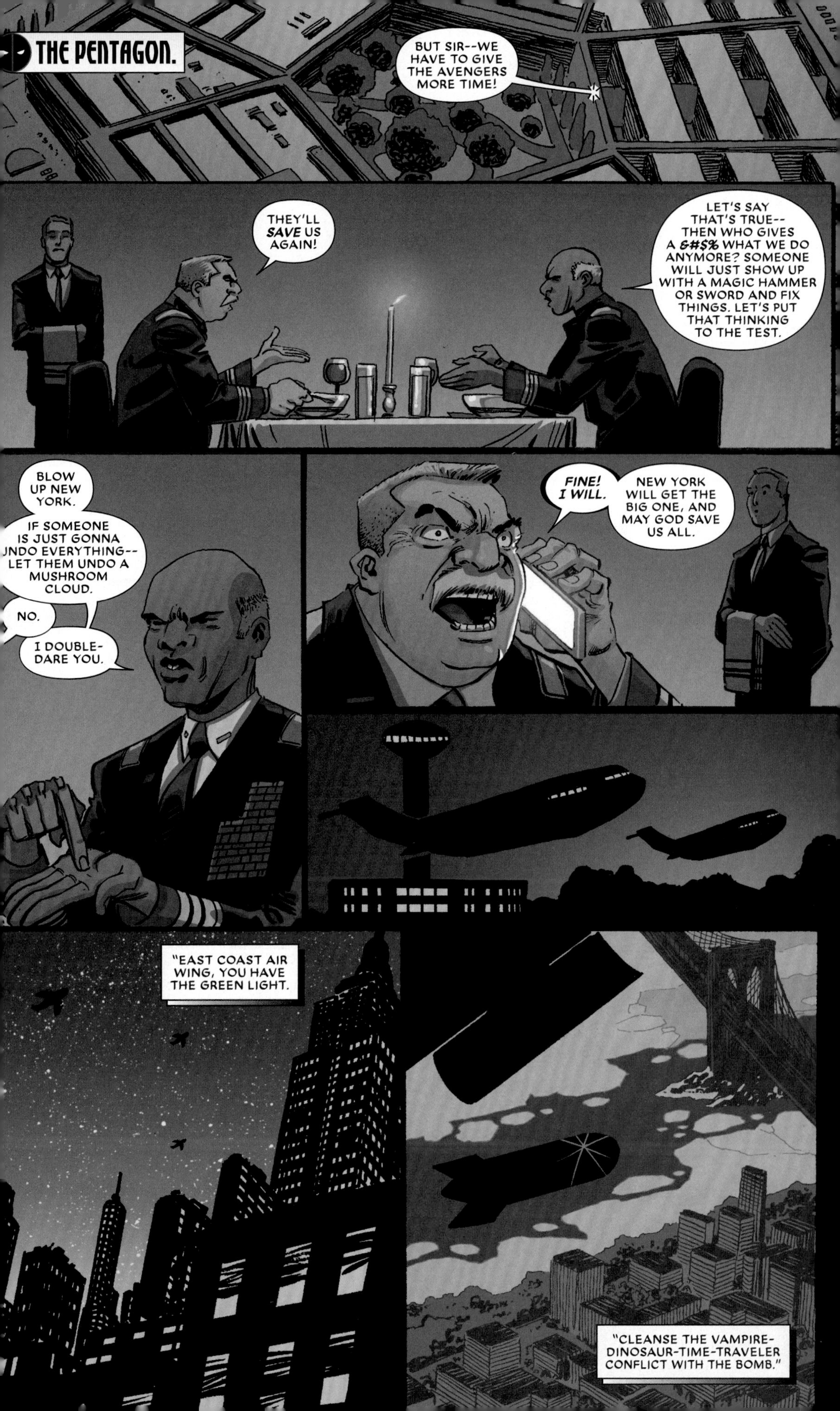
THE PENTAGON.
BUT SIR--WE HAVE TO GIVE THE AVENGERS MORE TIME!
THEY'LL *SAVE* US AGAIN!
LET'S SAY THAT'S TRUE-- THEN WHO GIVES A &#$% WHAT WE DO ANYMORE? SOMEONE WILL JUST SHOW UP WITH A MAGIC HAMMER OR SWORD AND FIX THINGS. LET'S PUT THAT THINKING TO THE TEST.
BLOW UP NEW YORK.
IF SOMEONE IS JUST GONNA UNDO EVERYTHING-- LET THEM UNDO A MUSHROOM CLOUD.
NO.
I DOUBLE-DARE YOU.
FINE! I WILL.
NEW YORK WILL GET THE BIG ONE, AND MAY GOD SAVE US ALL.
"EAST COAST AIR WING, YOU HAVE THE GREEN LIGHT.
"CLEANSE THE VAMPIRE-DINOSAUR-TIME-TRAVELER CONFLICT WITH THE BOMB."

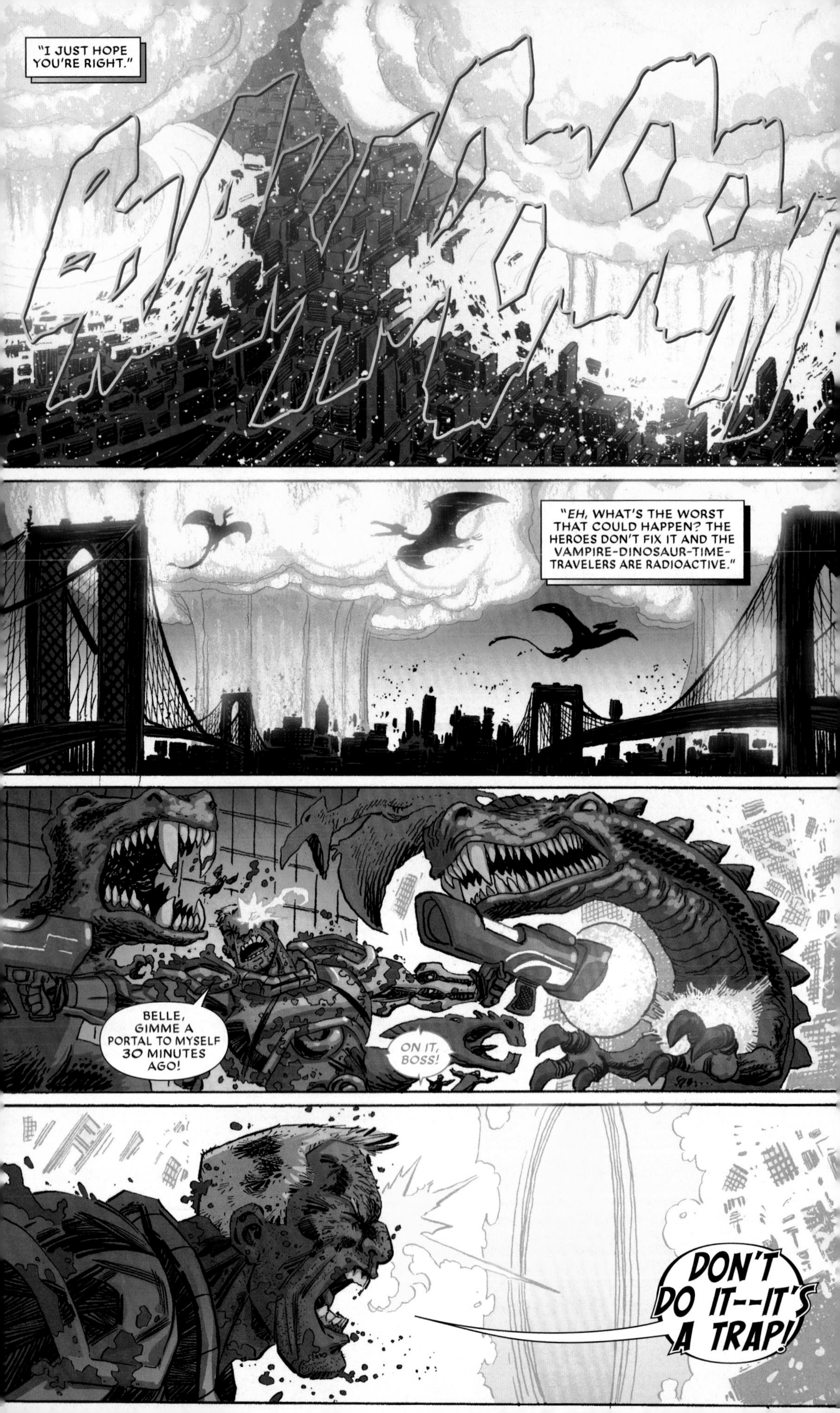
"I JUST HOPE YOU'RE RIGHT."
"EH, WHAT'S THE WORST THAT COULD HAPPEN? THE HEROES DON'T FIX IT AND THE VAMPIRE-DINOSAUR-TIME-TRAVELERS ARE RADIOACTIVE."
BELLE, GIMME A PORTAL TO MYSELF 30 MINUTES AGO!
ON IT, BOSS!
DON'T DO IT--IT'S A TRAP!

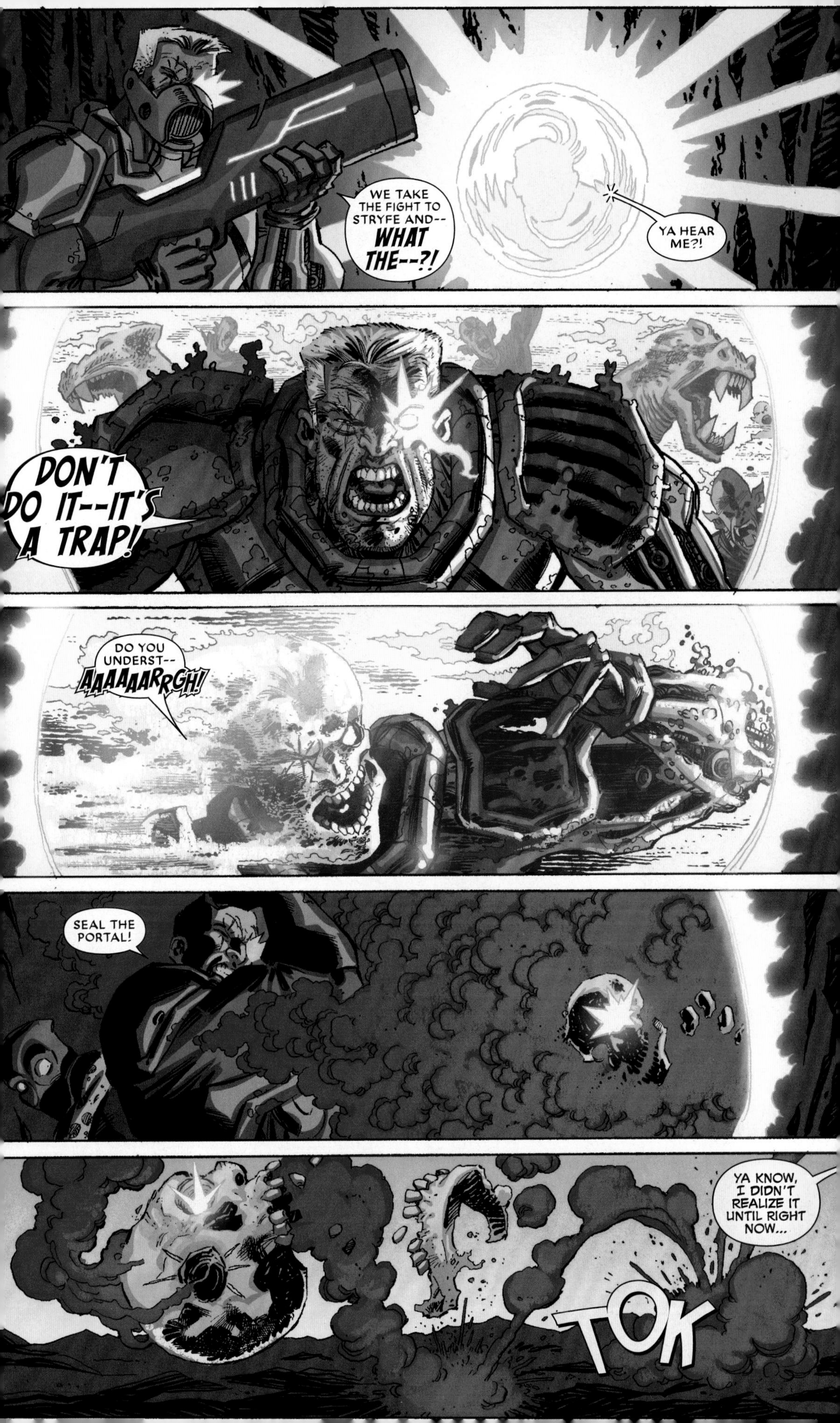

WE TAKE THE FIGHT TO STRYFE AND-- WHAT THE--?!
YA HEAR ME?!
DON'T DO IT--IT'S A TRAP!
DO YOU UNDERST-- AAAAAARRGH!
SEAL THE PORTAL!
YA KNOW, I DIDN'T REALIZE IT UNTIL RIGHT NOW...
TOK

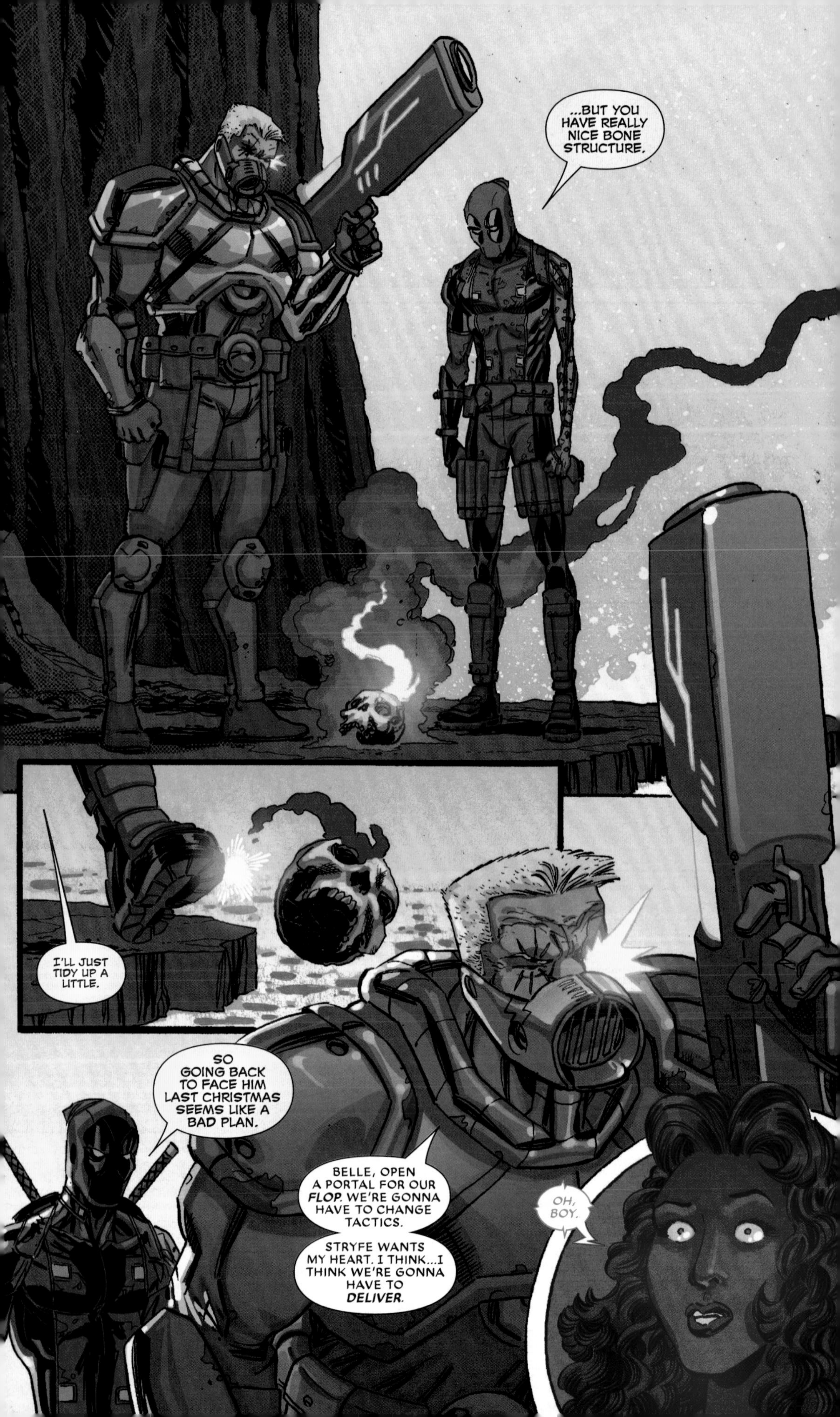
...BUT YOU HAVE REALLY NICE BONE STRUCTURE.
I'LL JUST TIDY UP A LITTLE.
SO GOING BACK TO FACE HIM LAST CHRISTMAS SEEMS LIKE A BAD PLAN.
BELLE, OPEN A PORTAL FOR OUR FLOP. WE'RE GONNA HAVE TO CHANGE TACTICS.
STRYFE WANTS MY HEART. I THINK...I THINK WE'RE GONNA HAVE TO DELIVER.
OH, BOY.

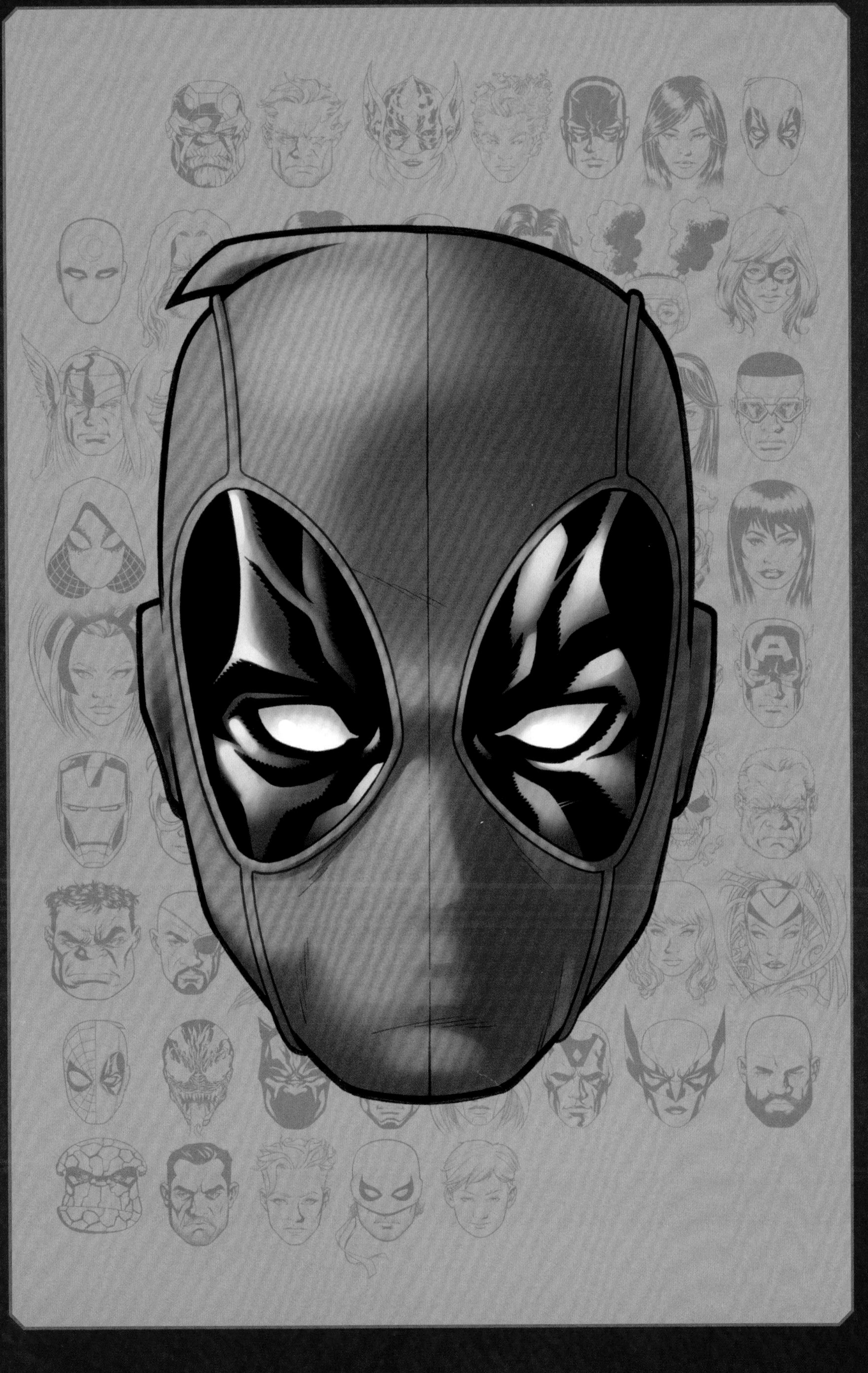

#287 LEGACY HEADSHOT VARIANT BY **MIKE McKONE**

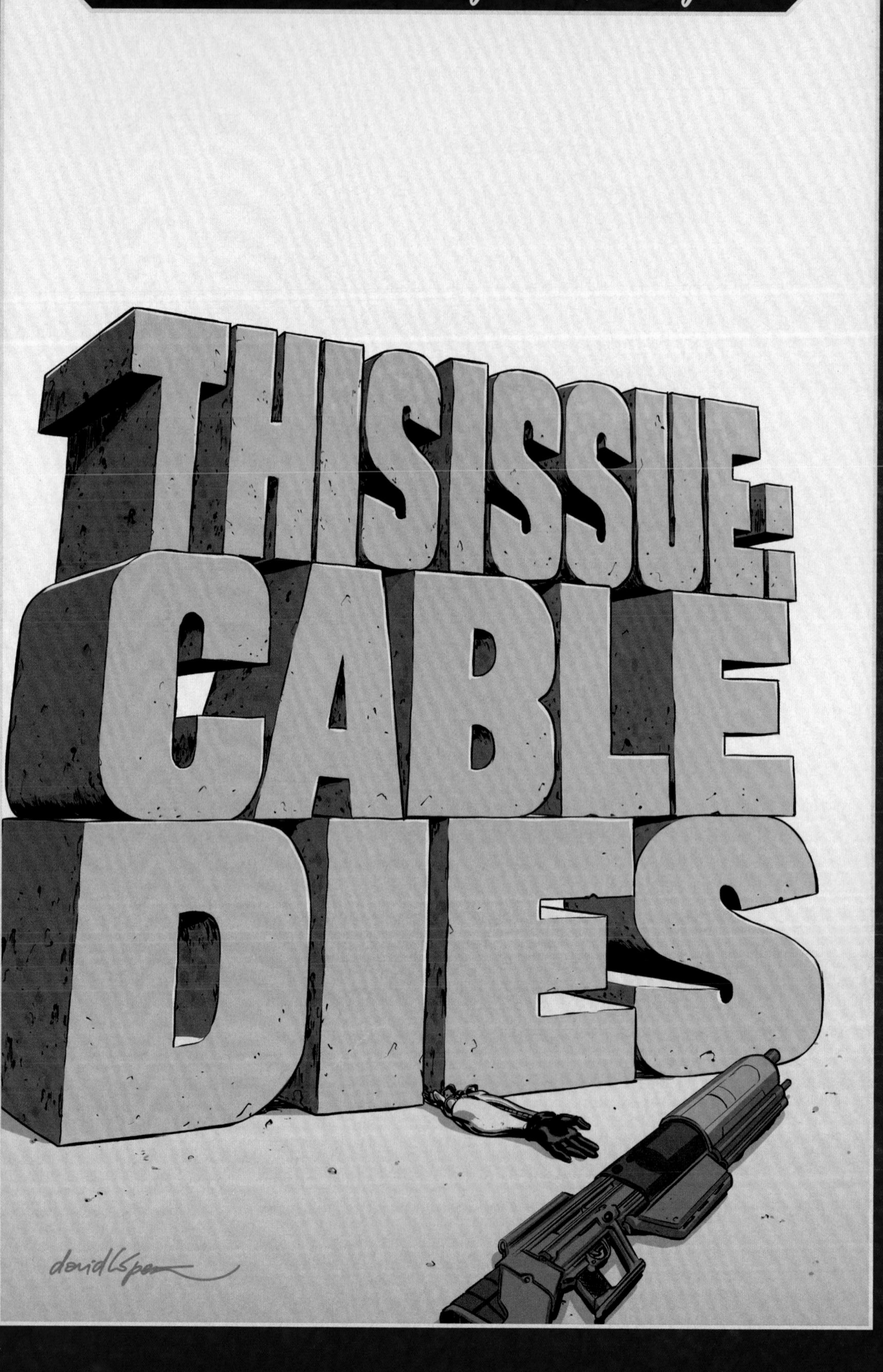
THIS ISSUE:
CABLE
DIES
davidLspa

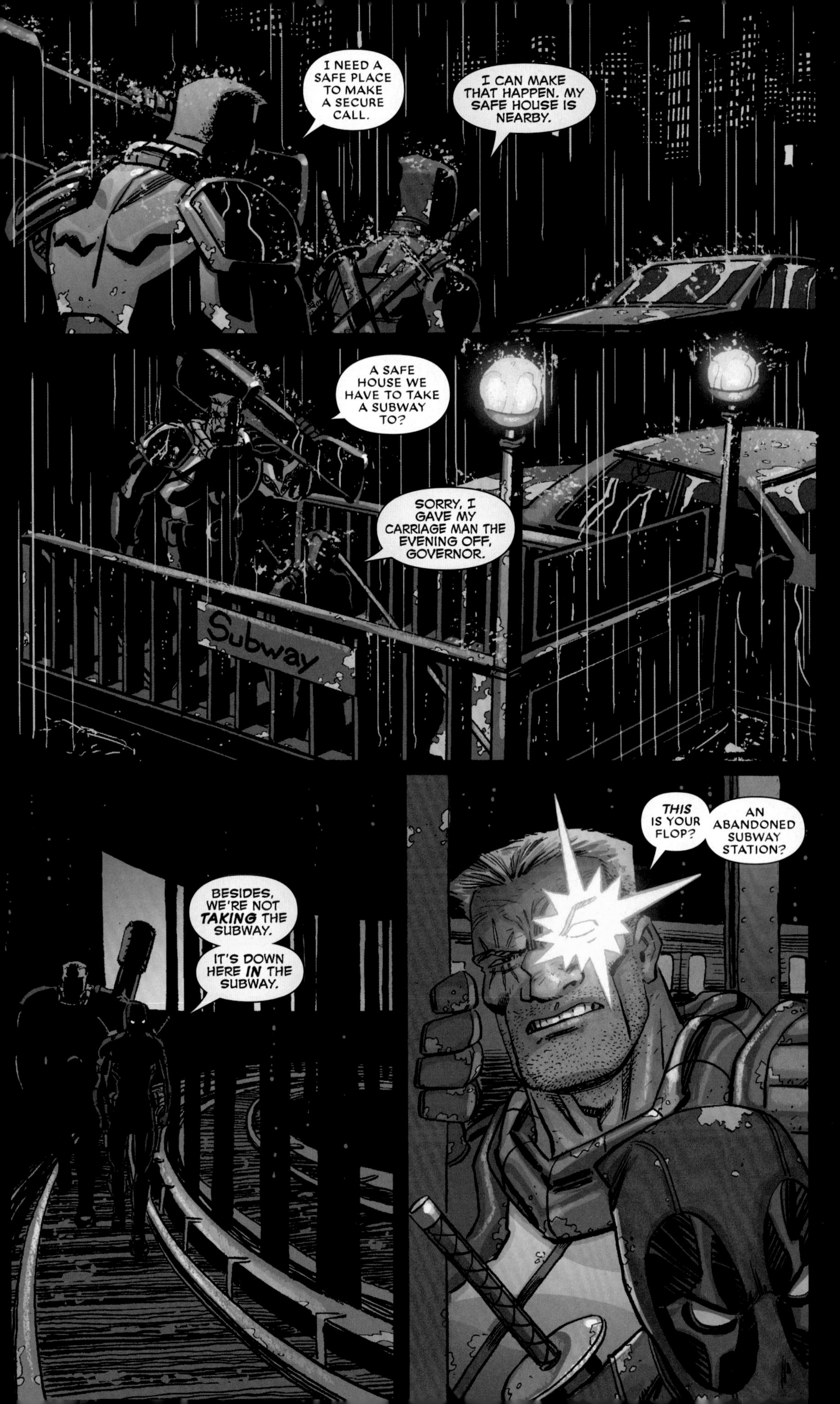
I NEED A SAFE PLACE TO MAKE A SECURE CALL.
I CAN MAKE THAT HAPPEN. MY SAFE HOUSE IS NEARBY.
A SAFE HOUSE WE HAVE TO TAKE A SUBWAY TO?
SORRY, I GAVE MY CARRIAGE MAN THE EVENING OFF, GOVERNOR.
Subway
BESIDES, WE'RE NOT *TAKING* THE SUBWAY.
IT'S DOWN HERE *IN* THE SUBWAY.
THIS IS YOUR FLOP?
AN ABANDONED SUBWAY STATION?

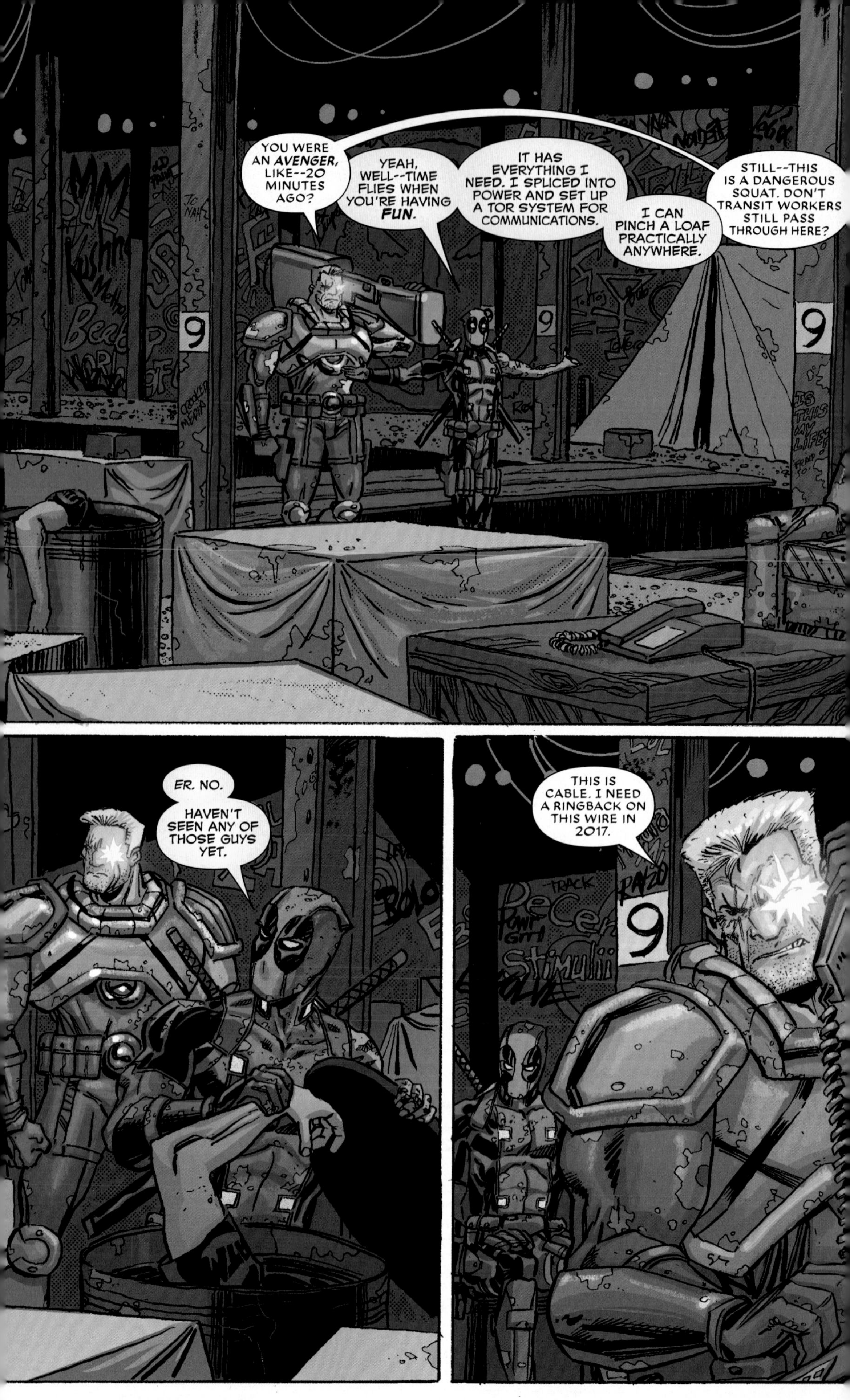
YOU WERE AN *AVENGER*, LIKE--20 MINUTES AGO?
YEAH, WELL--TIME FLIES WHEN YOU'RE HAVING ***FUN***.
IT HAS EVERYTHING I NEED. I SPLICED INTO POWER AND SET UP A TOR SYSTEM FOR COMMUNICATIONS.
I CAN PINCH A LOAF PRACTICALLY ANYWHERE.
STILL--THIS IS A DANGEROUS SQUAT. DON'T TRANSIT WORKERS STILL PASS THROUGH HERE?
IS THIS MY LIFE?
ER. NO.
HAVEN'T SEEN ANY OF THOSE GUYS YET.
THIS IS CABLE. I NEED A RINGBACK ON THIS WIRE IN 2017.

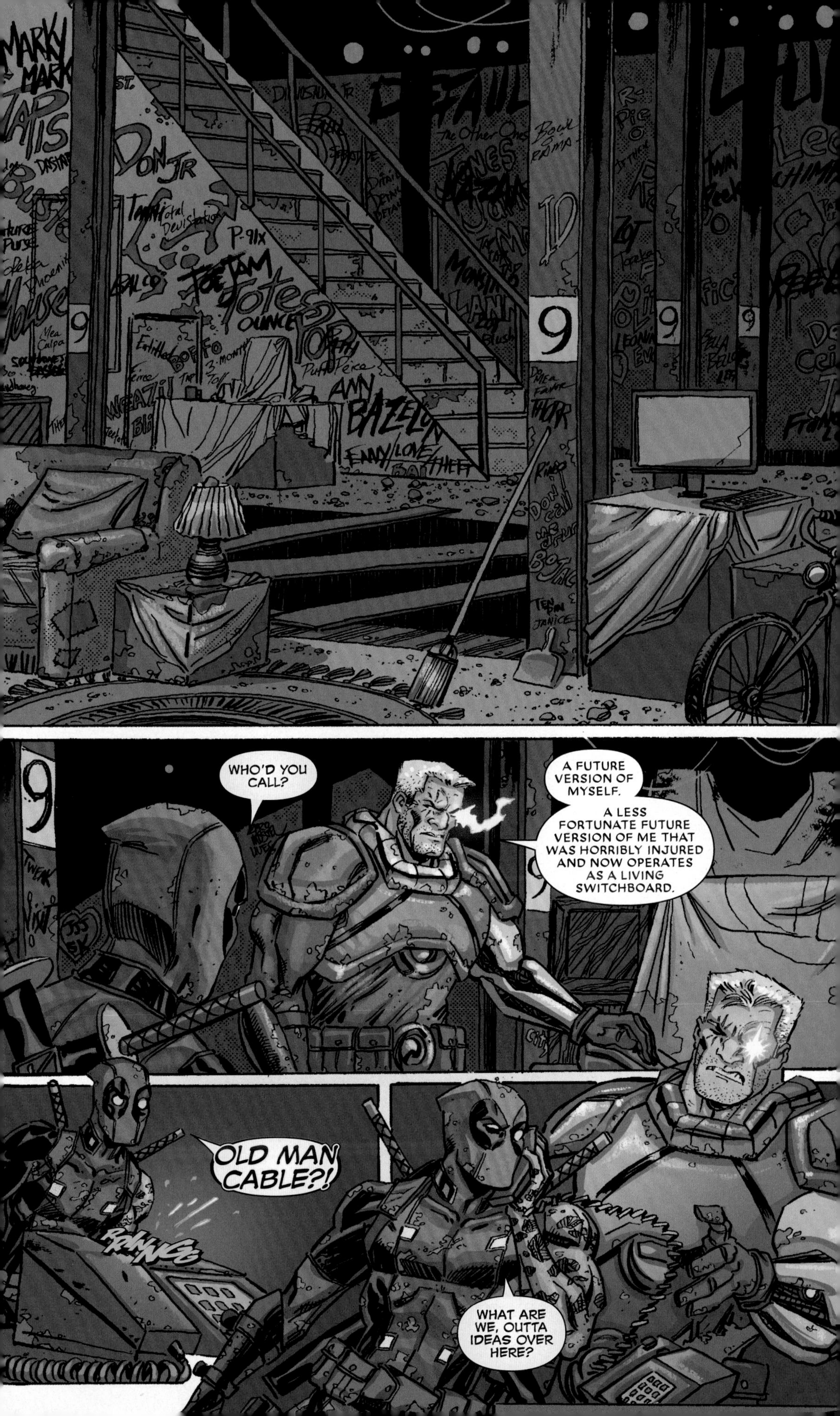
WHO'D YOU CALL?
A FUTURE VERSION OF MYSELF.
A LESS FORTUNATE FUTURE VERSION OF ME THAT WAS HORRIBLY INJURED AND NOW OPERATES AS A LIVING SWITCHBOARD.
OLD MAN CABLE?!
WHAT ARE WE, OUTTA IDEAS OVER HERE?

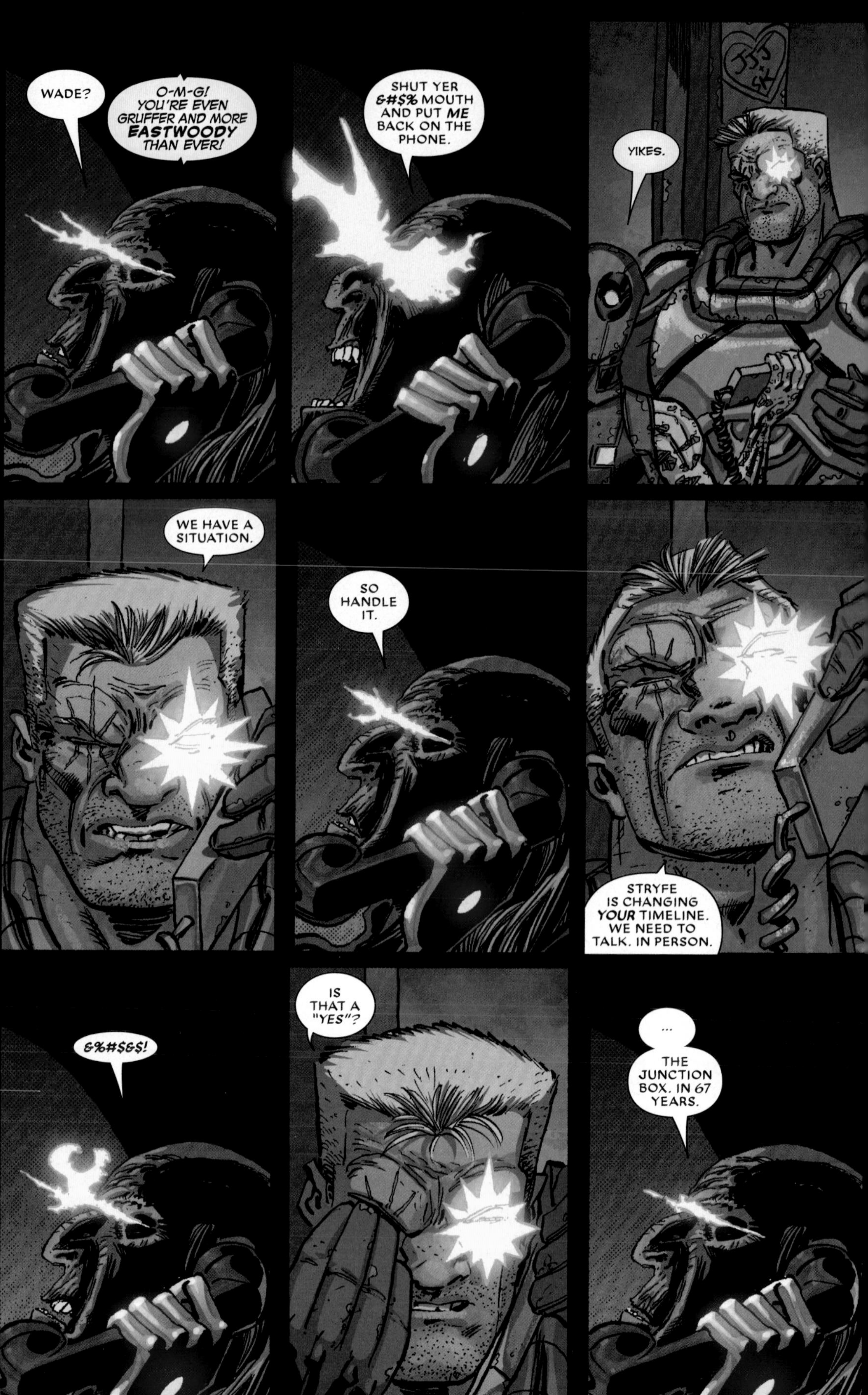
WADE?
O-M-G! YOU'RE EVEN GRUFFER AND MORE EASTWOODY THAN EVER!
SHUT YER &#$% MOUTH AND PUT ME BACK ON THE PHONE.
YIKES.
WE HAVE A SITUATION.
SO HANDLE IT.
STRYFE IS CHANGING YOUR TIMELINE. WE NEED TO TALK. IN PERSON.
&%#$&$!
IS THAT A "YES"?
...
THE JUNCTION BOX. IN 67 YEARS.

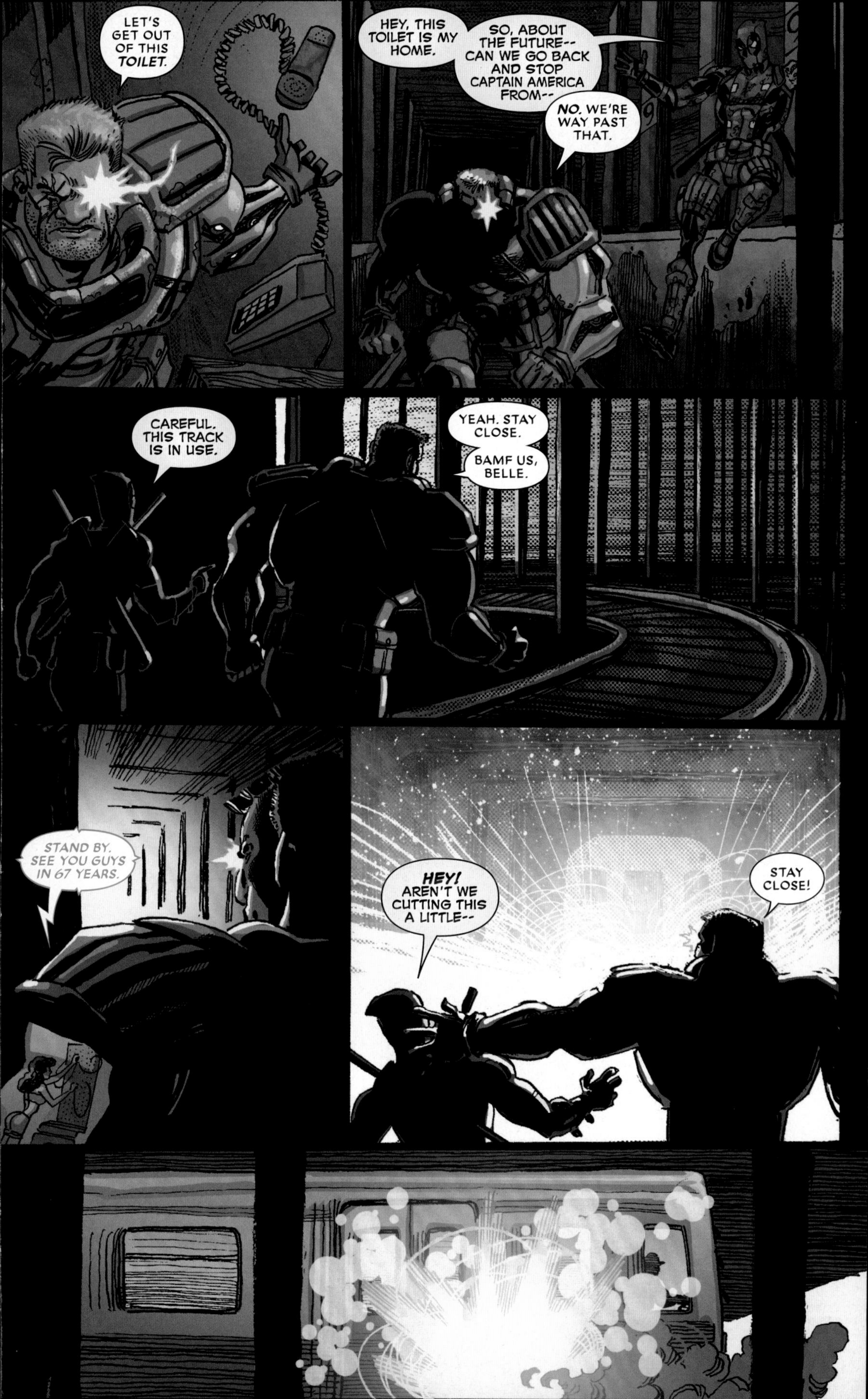
LET'S GET OUT OF THIS *TOILET*.
HEY, THIS TOILET IS MY HOME.
SO, ABOUT THE FUTURE-- CAN WE GO BACK AND STOP CAPTAIN AMERICA FROM--
NO. WE'RE WAY PAST THAT.
CAREFUL. THIS TRACK IS IN USE.
YEAH. STAY CLOSE.
BAMF US, BELLE.
STAND BY. SEE YOU GUYS IN 67 YEARS.
HEY! AREN'T WE CUTTING THIS A LITTLE--
STAY CLOSE!

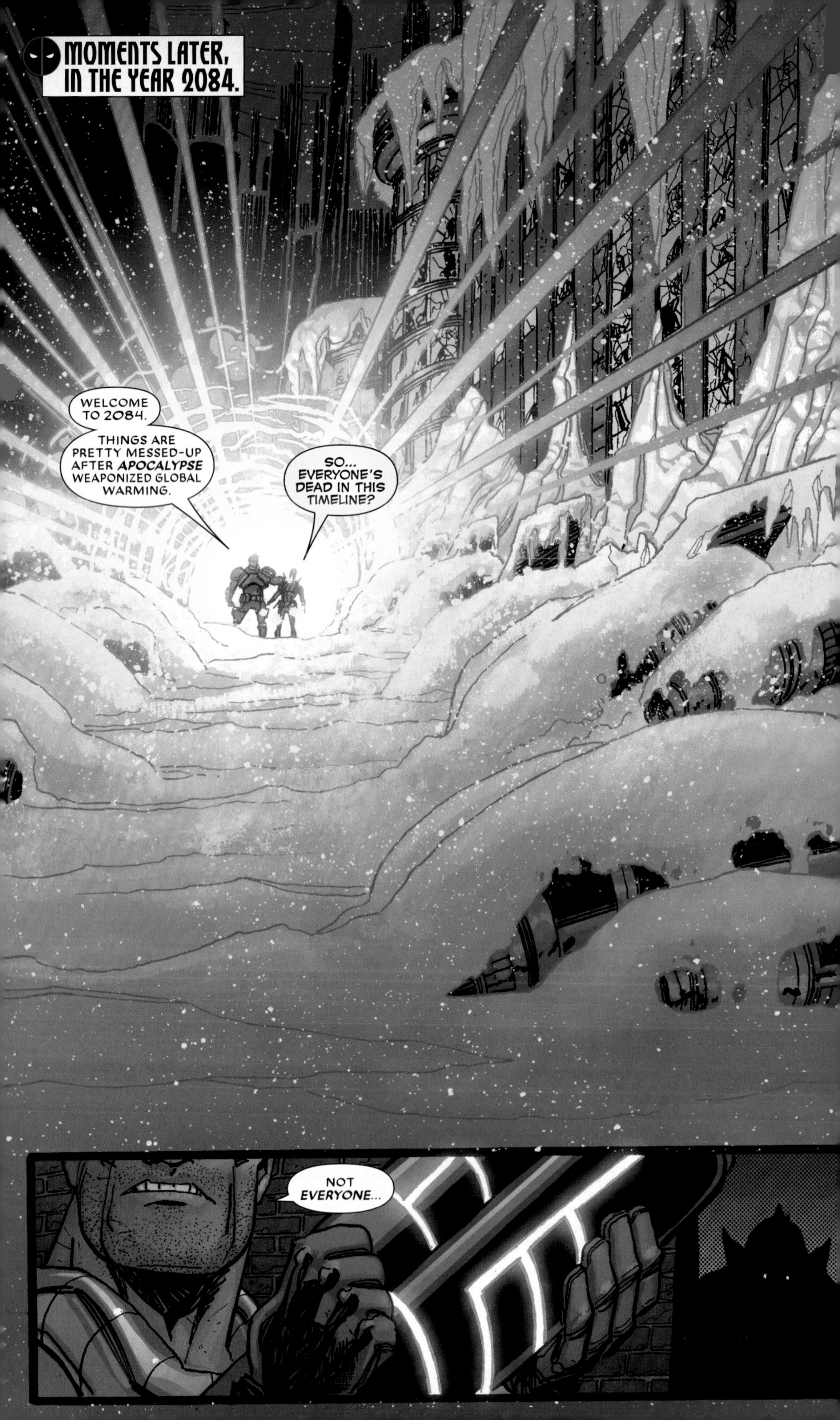
MOMENTS LATER, IN THE YEAR 2084.
WELCOME TO 2084.
THINGS ARE PRETTY MESSED-UP AFTER APOCALYPSE WEAPONIZED GLOBAL WARMING.
SO... EVERYONE'S DEAD IN THIS TIMELINE?
NOT EVERYONE...

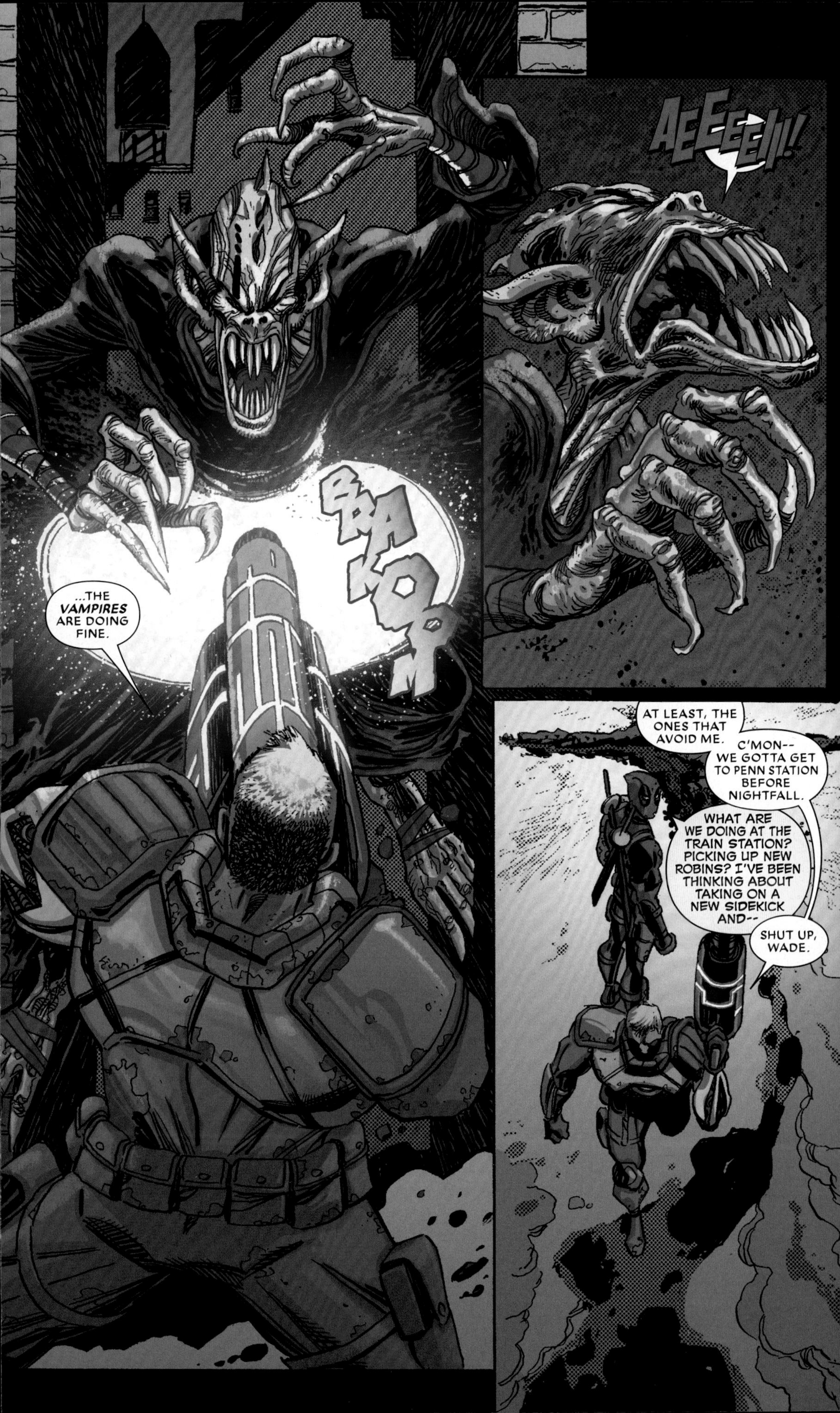
AEEEEIII!
BRAKOOM
...THE VAMPIRES ARE DOING FINE.
AT LEAST, THE ONES THAT AVOID ME.
C'MON-- WE GOTTA GET TO PENN STATION BEFORE NIGHTFALL.
WHAT ARE WE DOING AT THE TRAIN STATION? PICKING UP NEW ROBINS? I'VE BEEN THINKING ABOUT TAKING ON A NEW SIDEKICK AND--
SHUT UP, WADE.

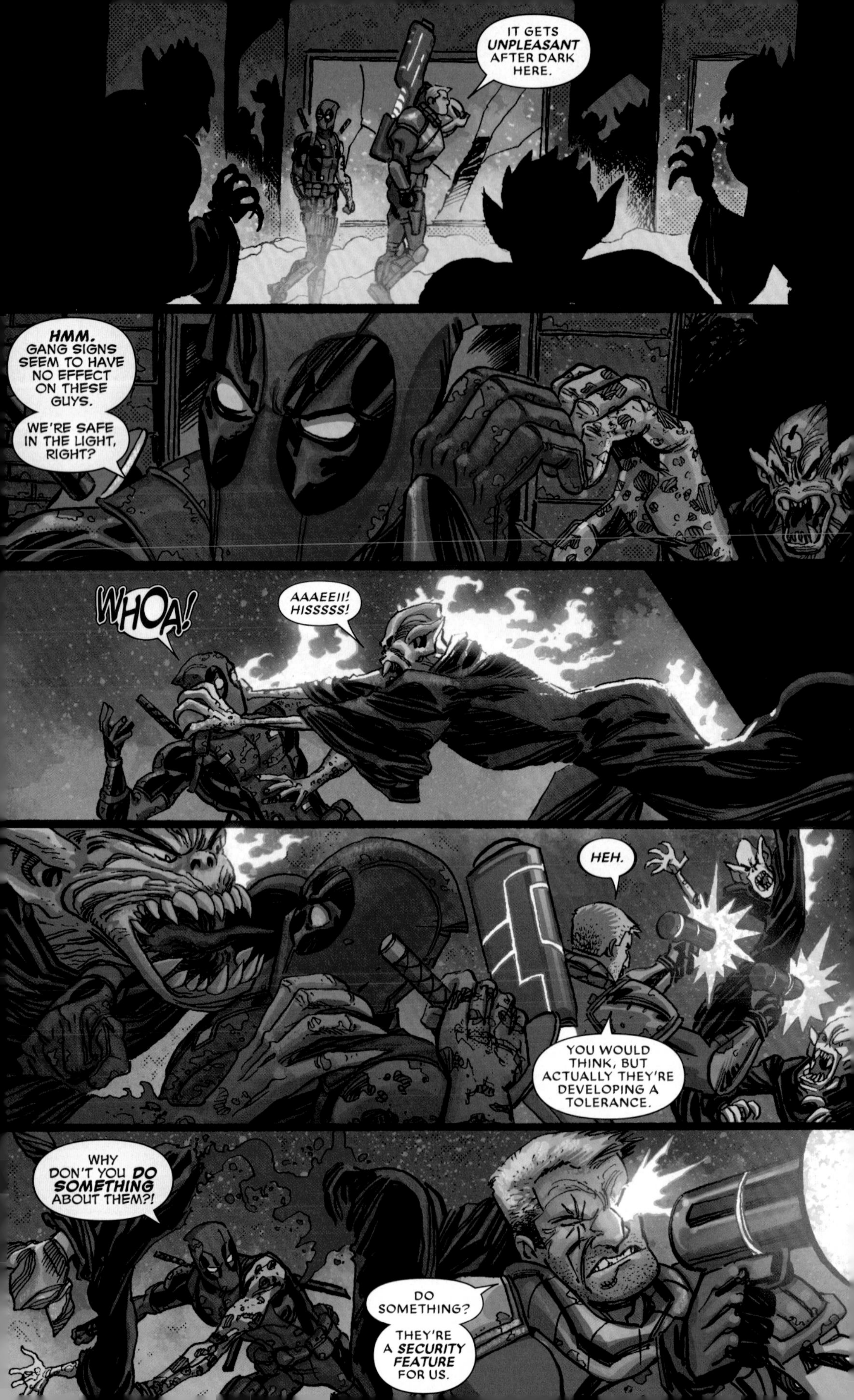
IT GETS UNPLEASANT AFTER DARK HERE.
HMM. GANG SIGNS SEEM TO HAVE NO EFFECT ON THESE GUYS.
WE'RE SAFE IN THE LIGHT, RIGHT?
WHOA!
AAAEEII! HISSSSS!
HEH.
YOU WOULD THINK, BUT ACTUALLY THEY'RE DEVELOPING A TOLERANCE.
WHY DON'T YOU DO SOMETHING ABOUT THEM?!
DO SOMETHING?
THEY'RE A SECURITY FEATURE FOR US.

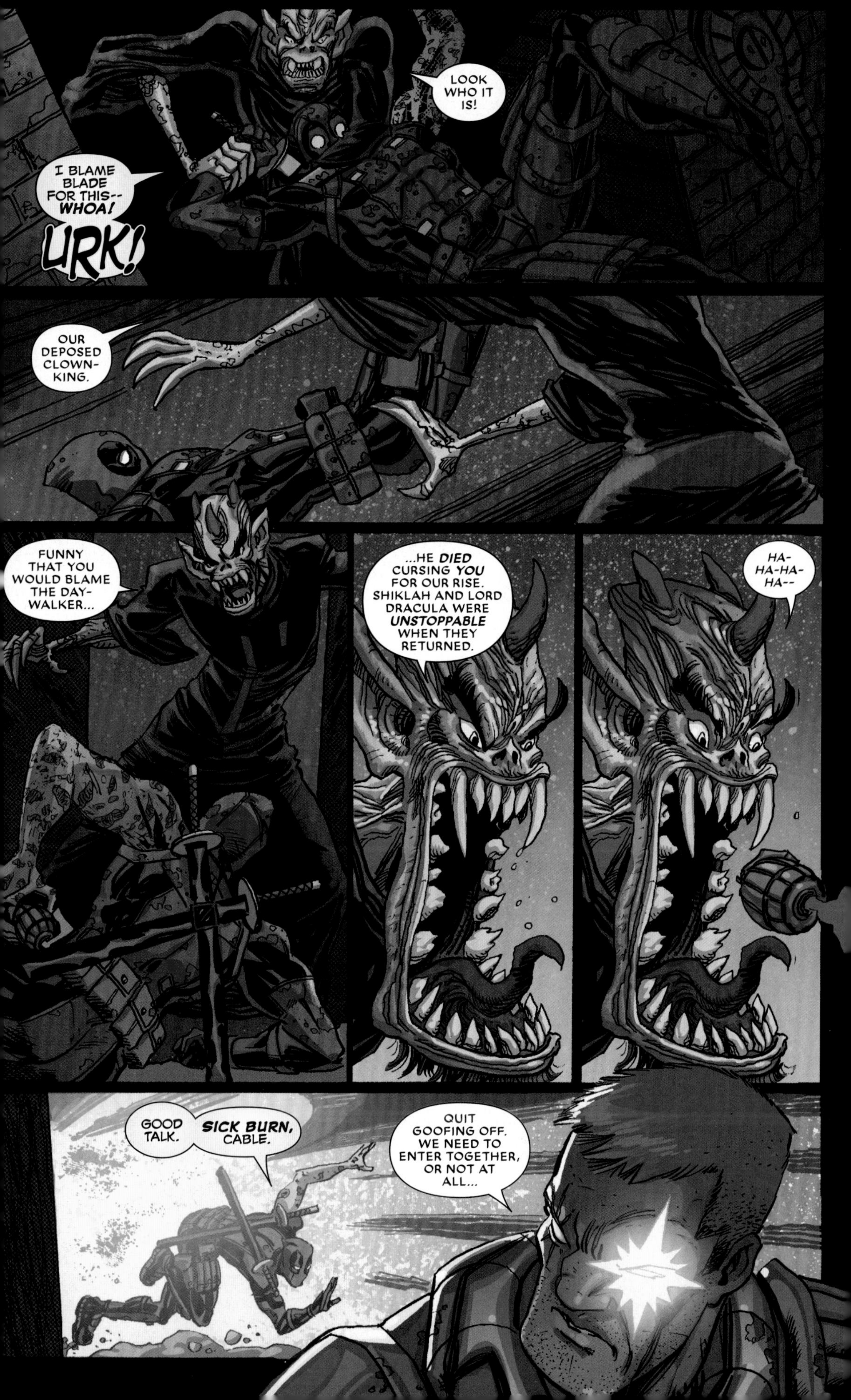
LOOK WHO IT IS!
I BLAME BLADE FOR THIS-- WHOA!
URK!
OUR DEPOSED CLOWN-KING.
FUNNY THAT YOU WOULD BLAME THE DAY-WALKER...
...HE DIED CURSING YOU FOR OUR RISE. SHIKLAH AND LORD DRACULA WERE UNSTOPPABLE WHEN THEY RETURNED.
HA-HA-HA-HA--
GOOD TALK.
SICK BURN, CABLE.
QUIT GOOFING OFF. WE NEED TO ENTER TOGETHER, OR NOT AT ALL...

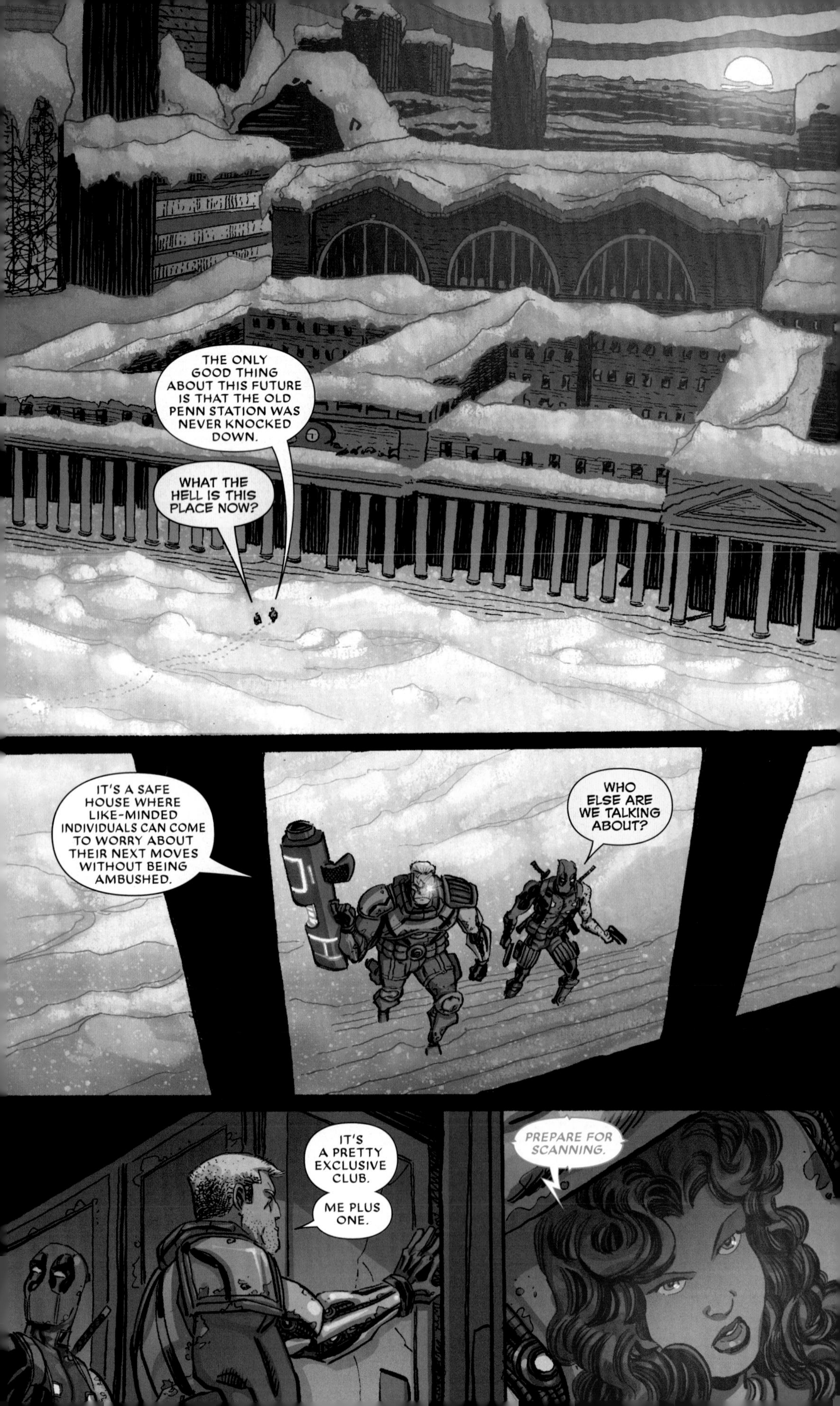

THE ONLY GOOD THING ABOUT THIS FUTURE IS THAT THE OLD PENN STATION WAS NEVER KNOCKED DOWN.
WHAT THE HELL IS THIS PLACE NOW?
IT'S A SAFE HOUSE WHERE LIKE-MINDED INDIVIDUALS CAN COME TO WORRY ABOUT THEIR NEXT MOVES WITHOUT BEING AMBUSHED.
WHO ELSE ARE WE TALKING ABOUT?
IT'S A PRETTY EXCLUSIVE CLUB.
ME PLUS ONE.
PREPARE FOR SCANNING.

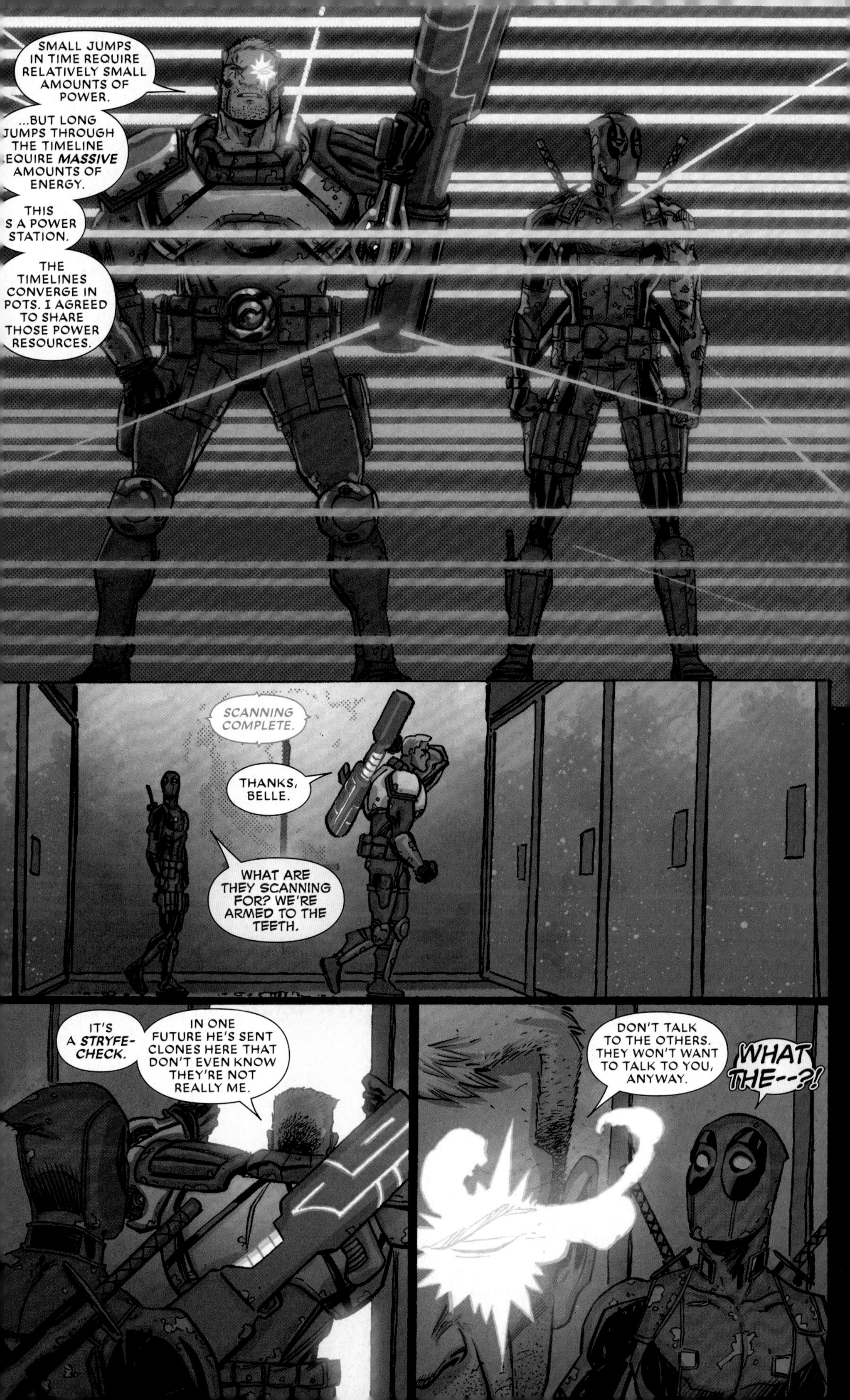
SMALL JUMPS IN TIME REQUIRE RELATIVELY SMALL AMOUNTS OF POWER.
...BUT LONG JUMPS THROUGH THE TIMELINE EQUIRE *MASSIVE* AMOUNTS OF ENERGY.
THIS S A POWER STATION.
THE TIMELINES CONVERGE IN POTS. I AGREED TO SHARE THOSE POWER RESOURCES.
SCANNING COMPLETE.
THANKS, BELLE.
WHAT ARE THEY SCANNING FOR? WE'RE ARMED TO THE TEETH.
IT'S A *STRYFE-CHECK.*
IN ONE FUTURE HE'S SENT CLONES HERE THAT DON'T EVEN KNOW THEY'RE NOT REALLY ME.
DON'T TALK TO THE OTHERS. THEY WON'T WANT TO TALK TO YOU, ANYWAY.
WHAT THE--?!

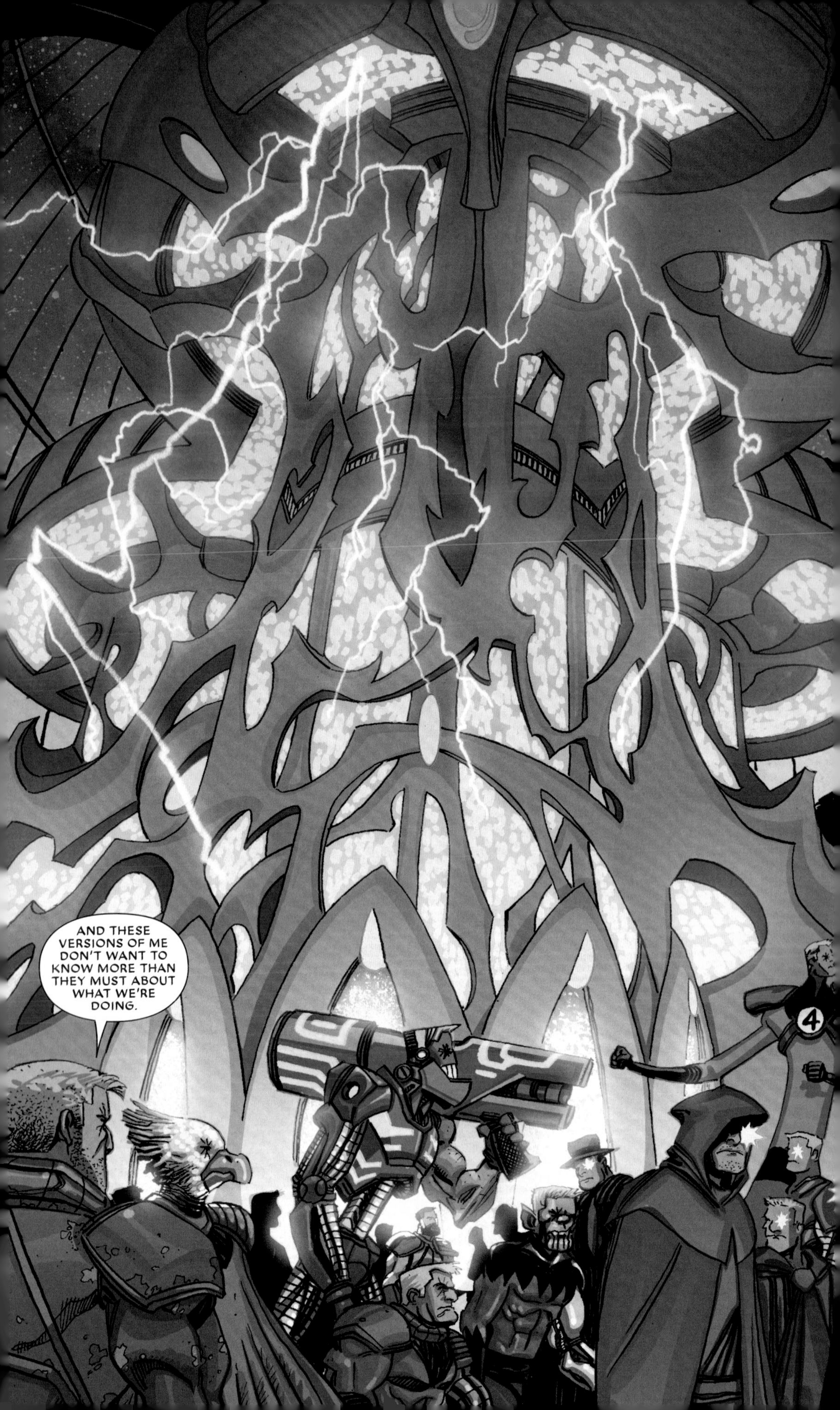
AND THESE VERSIONS OF ME DON'T WANT TO KNOW MORE THAN THEY MUST ABOUT WHAT WE'RE DOING.
4

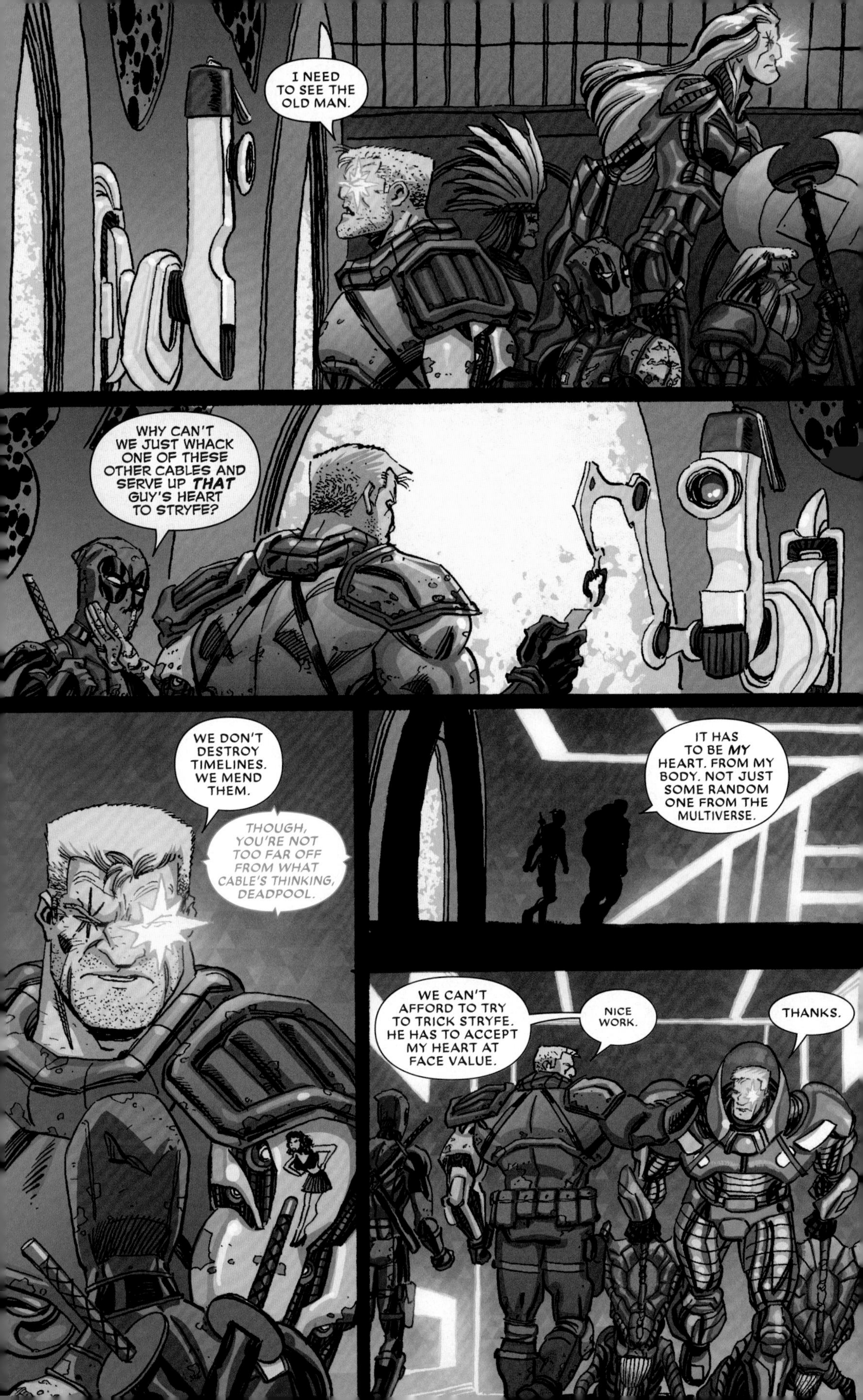
I NEED TO SEE THE OLD MAN.
WHY CAN'T WE JUST WHACK ONE OF THESE OTHER CABLES AND SERVE UP **THAT** GUY'S HEART TO STRYFE?
WE DON'T DESTROY TIMELINES. WE MEND THEM.
THOUGH, YOU'RE NOT TOO FAR OFF FROM WHAT CABLE'S THINKING, DEADPOOL.
IT HAS TO BE ***MY*** HEART. FROM MY BODY. NOT JUST SOME RANDOM ONE FROM THE MULTIVERSE.
WE CAN'T AFFORD TO TRY TO TRICK STRYFE. HE HAS TO ACCEPT MY HEART AT FACE VALUE.
NICE WORK.
THANKS.

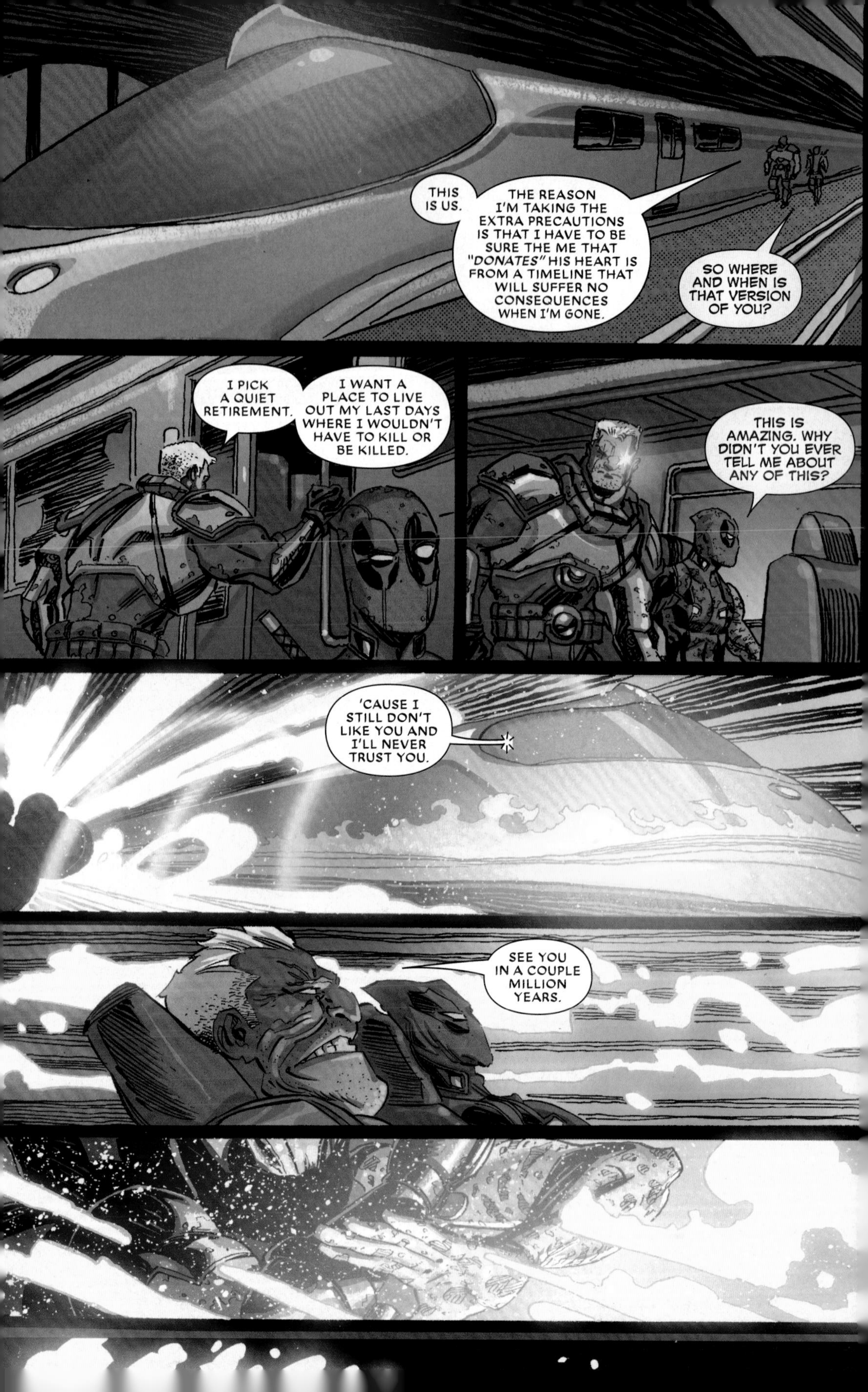
THIS IS US.
THE REASON I'M TAKING THE EXTRA PRECAUTIONS IS THAT I HAVE TO BE SURE THE ME THAT "DONATES" HIS HEART IS FROM A TIMELINE THAT WILL SUFFER NO CONSEQUENCES WHEN I'M GONE.
SO WHERE AND WHEN IS THAT VERSION OF YOU?
I PICK A QUIET RETIREMENT.
I WANT A PLACE TO LIVE OUT MY LAST DAYS WHERE I WOULDN'T HAVE TO KILL OR BE KILLED.
THIS IS AMAZING. WHY DIDN'T YOU EVER TELL ME ABOUT ANY OF THIS?
'CAUSE I STILL DON'T LIKE YOU AND I'LL NEVER TRUST YOU.
SEE YOU IN A COUPLE MILLION YEARS.

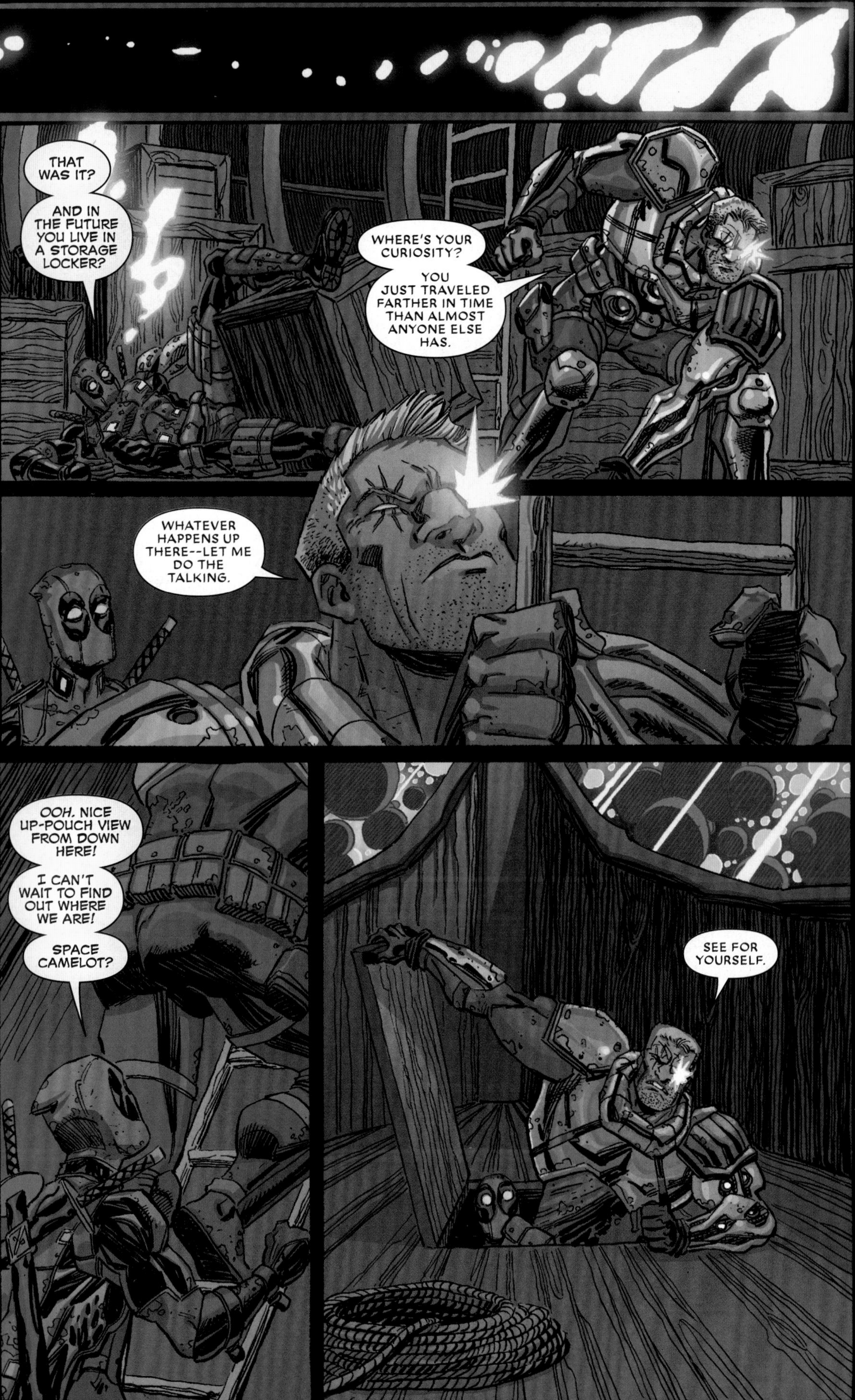
THAT WAS IT?
AND IN THE FUTURE YOU LIVE IN A STORAGE LOCKER?
WHERE'S YOUR CURIOSITY?
YOU JUST TRAVELED FARTHER IN TIME THAN ALMOST ANYONE ELSE HAS.
WHATEVER HAPPENS UP THERE--LET ME DO THE TALKING.
OOH. NICE UP-POUCH VIEW FROM DOWN HERE!
I CAN'T WAIT TO FIND OUT WHERE WE ARE!
SPACE CAMELOT?
SEE FOR YOURSELF.

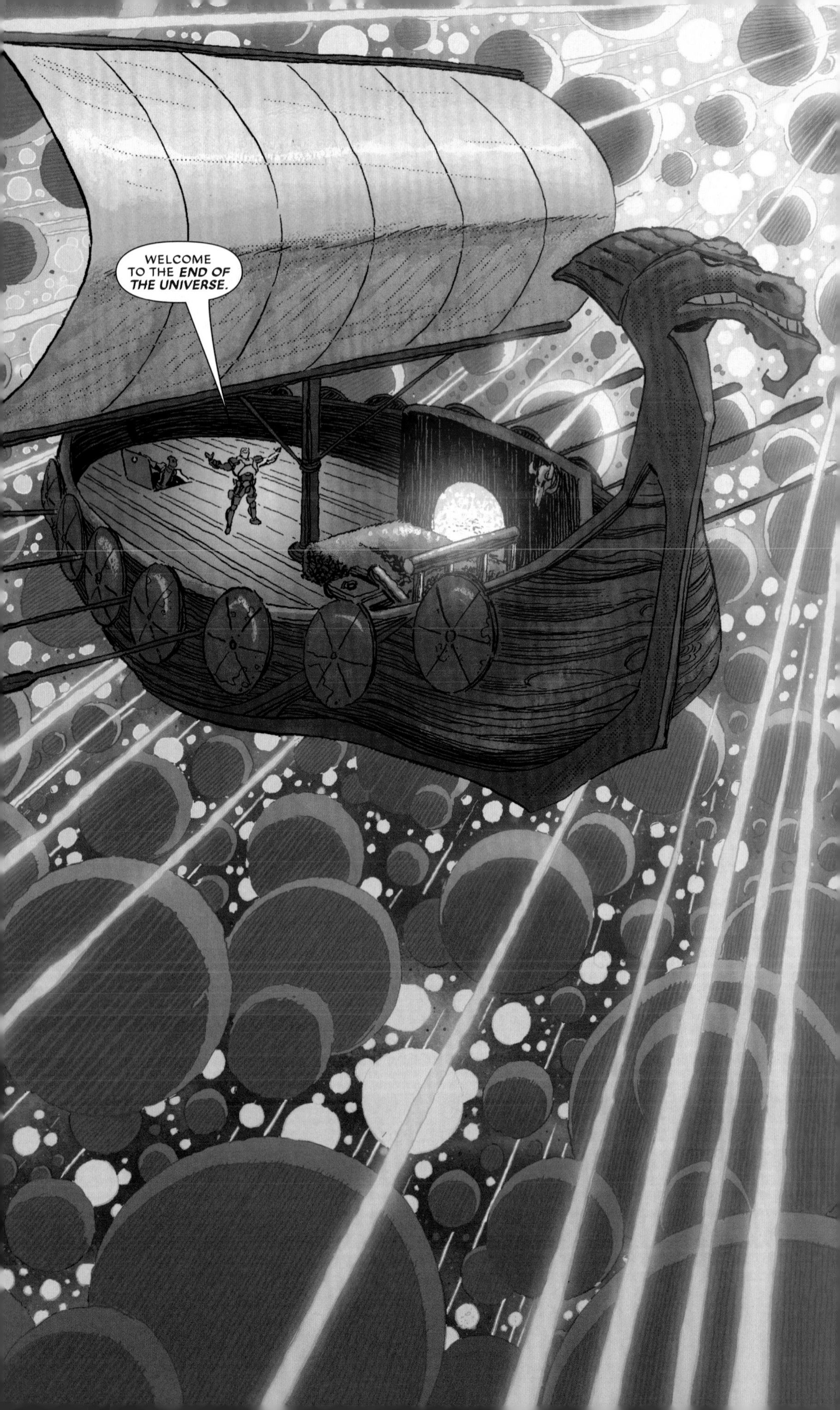
WELCOME TO THE *END OF THE UNIVERSE.*

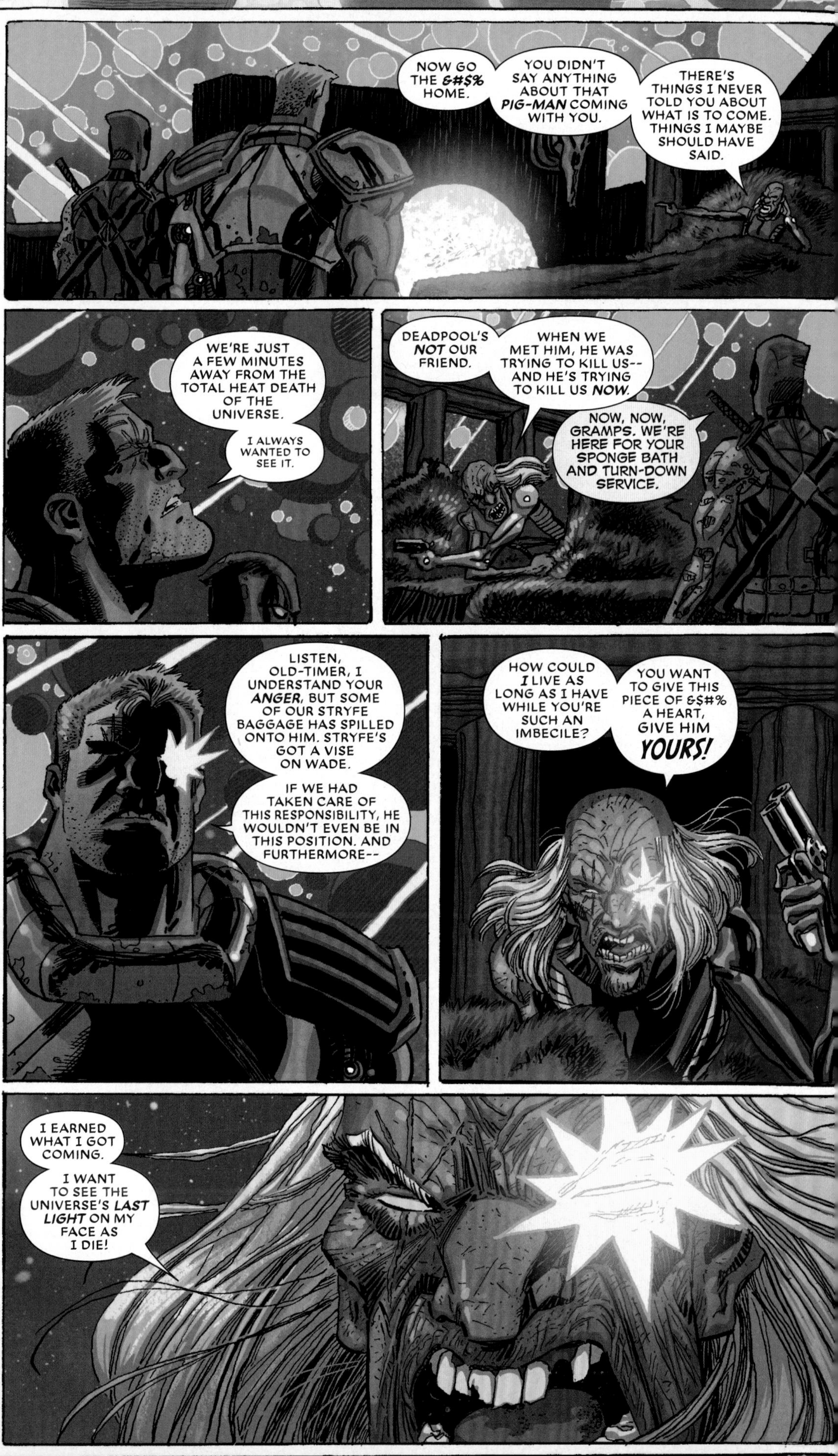
NOW GO THE &#$% HOME.
YOU DIDN'T SAY ANYTHING ABOUT THAT PIG-MAN COMING WITH YOU.
THERE'S THINGS I NEVER TOLD YOU ABOUT WHAT IS TO COME. THINGS I MAYBE SHOULD HAVE SAID.
WE'RE JUST A FEW MINUTES AWAY FROM THE TOTAL HEAT DEATH OF THE UNIVERSE.
I ALWAYS WANTED TO SEE IT.
DEADPOOL'S NOT OUR FRIEND.
WHEN WE MET HIM, HE WAS TRYING TO KILL US-- AND HE'S TRYING TO KILL US NOW.
NOW, NOW, GRAMPS. WE'RE HERE FOR YOUR SPONGE BATH AND TURN-DOWN SERVICE.
LISTEN, OLD-TIMER, I UNDERSTAND YOUR ANGER, BUT SOME OF OUR STRYFE BAGGAGE HAS SPILLED ONTO HIM. STRYFE'S GOT A VISE ON WADE.
IF WE HAD TAKEN CARE OF THIS RESPONSIBILITY, HE WOULDN'T EVEN BE IN THIS POSITION. AND FURTHERMORE--
HOW COULD I LIVE AS LONG AS I HAVE WHILE YOU'RE SUCH AN IMBECILE?
YOU WANT TO GIVE THIS PIECE OF &$#% A HEART, GIVE HIM YOURS!
I EARNED WHAT I GOT COMING.
I WANT TO SEE THE UNIVERSE'S LAST LIGHT ON MY FACE AS I DIE!

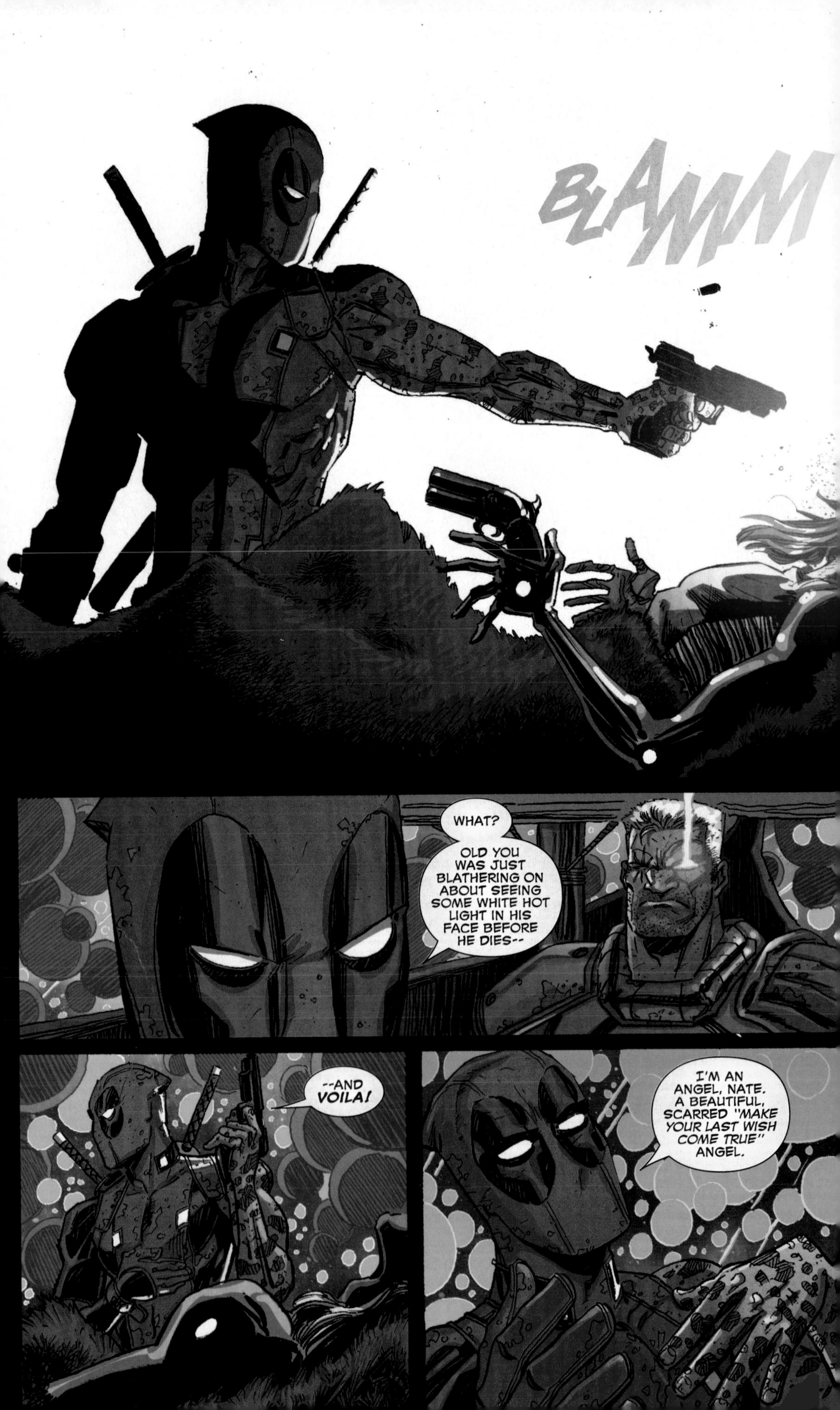
BLAMM
WHAT?
OLD YOU WAS JUST BLATHERING ON ABOUT SEEING SOME WHITE HOT LIGHT IN HIS FACE BEFORE HE DIES--
--AND VOILA!
I'M AN ANGEL, NATE. A BEAUTIFUL, SCARRED "MAKE YOUR LAST WISH COME TRUE" ANGEL.

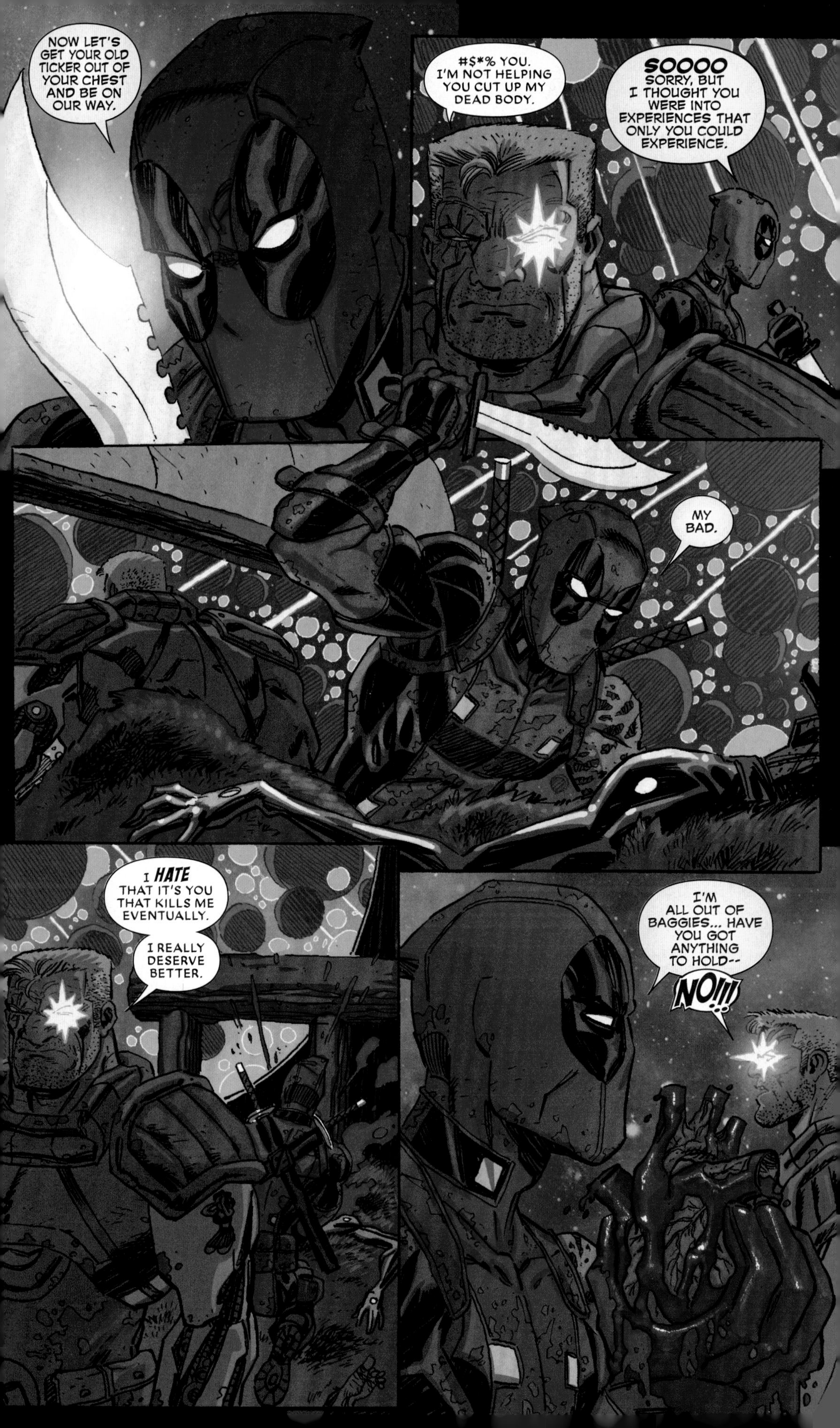
NOW LET'S GET YOUR OLD TICKER OUT OF YOUR CHEST AND BE ON OUR WAY.
#$*% YOU. I'M NOT HELPING YOU CUT UP MY DEAD BODY.
SOOOO SORRY, BUT I THOUGHT YOU WERE INTO EXPERIENCES THAT ONLY YOU COULD EXPERIENCE.
MY BAD.
I HATE THAT IT'S YOU THAT KILLS ME EVENTUALLY.
I REALLY DESERVE BETTER.
I'M ALL OUT OF BAGGIES... HAVE YOU GOT ANYTHING TO HOLD--
NO!!!

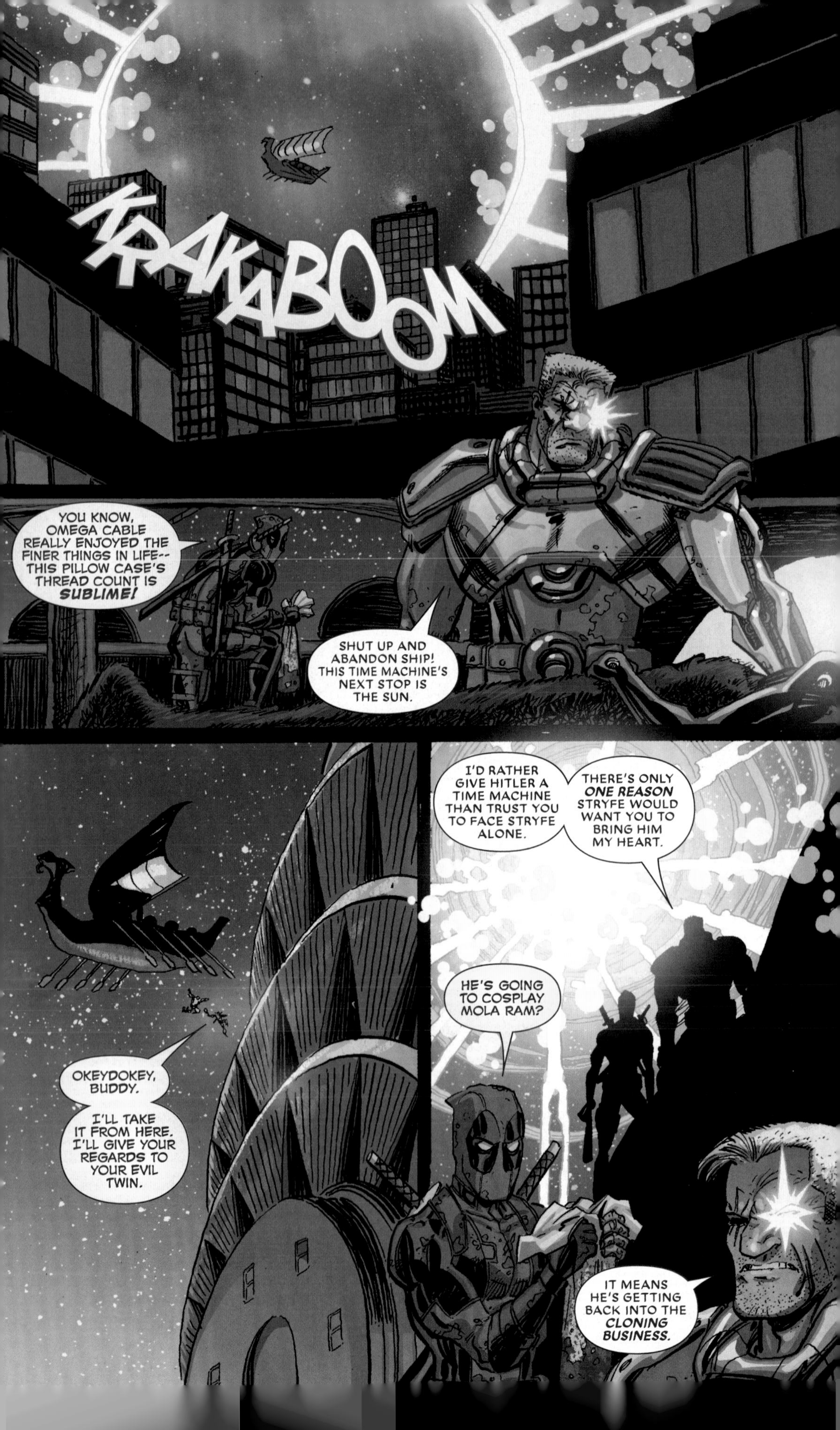
KRAKABOOM
YOU KNOW, OMEGA CABLE REALLY ENJOYED THE FINER THINGS IN LIFE-- THIS PILLOW CASE'S THREAD COUNT IS SUBLIME!
SHUT UP AND ABANDON SHIP! THIS TIME MACHINE'S NEXT STOP IS THE SUN.
OKEYDOKEY, BUDDY.
I'LL TAKE IT FROM HERE. I'LL GIVE YOUR REGARDS TO YOUR EVIL TWIN.
I'D RATHER GIVE HITLER A TIME MACHINE THAN TRUST YOU TO FACE STRYFE ALONE.
THERE'S ONLY ONE REASON STRYFE WOULD WANT YOU TO BRING HIM MY HEART.
HE'S GOING TO COSPLAY MOLA RAM?
IT MEANS HE'S GETTING BACK INTO THE CLONING BUSINESS.

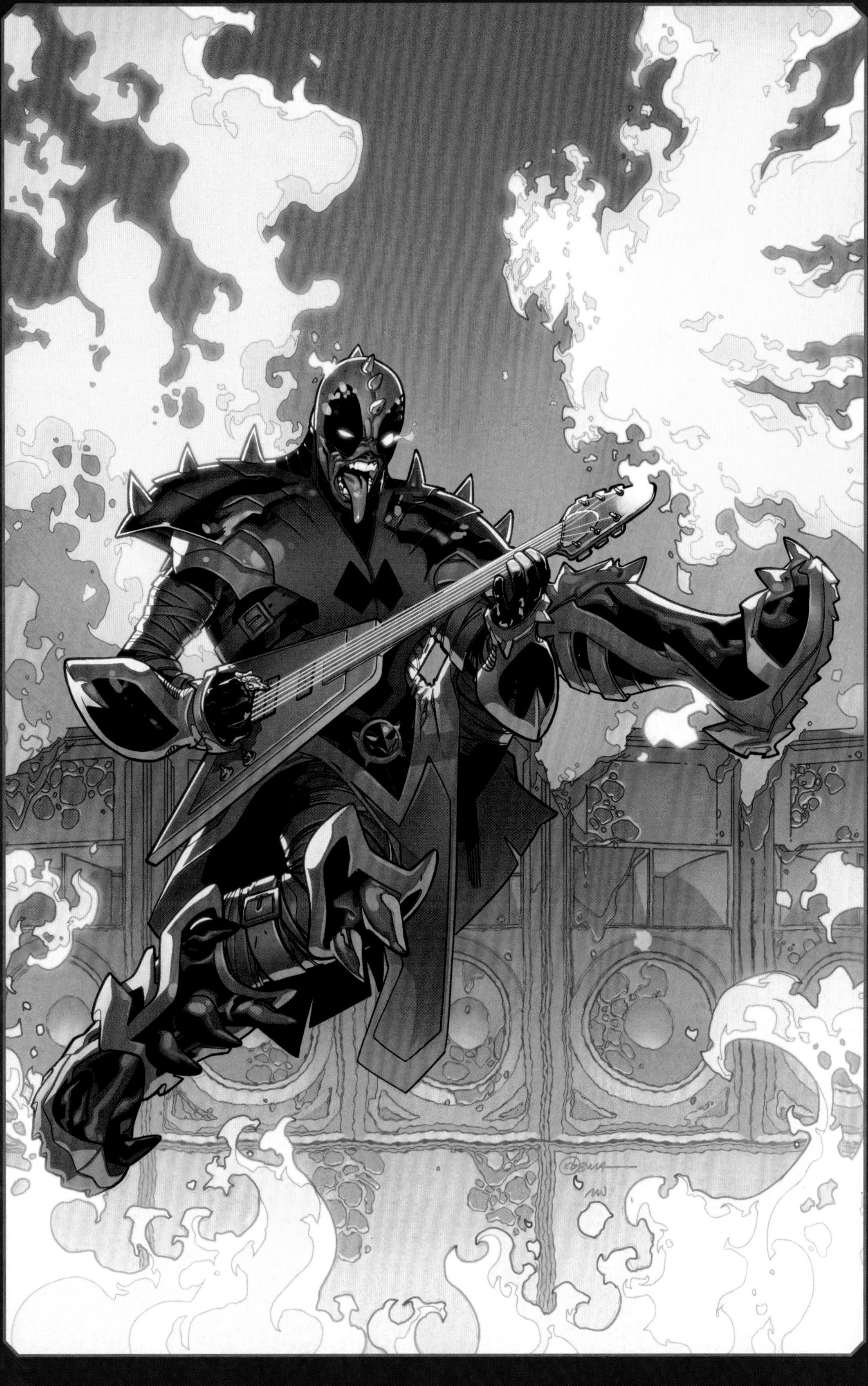

#290 PHOENIX VARIANT BY R.B. SILVA & NOLAN WOODARD

291 – Part Five: "Great Scott"

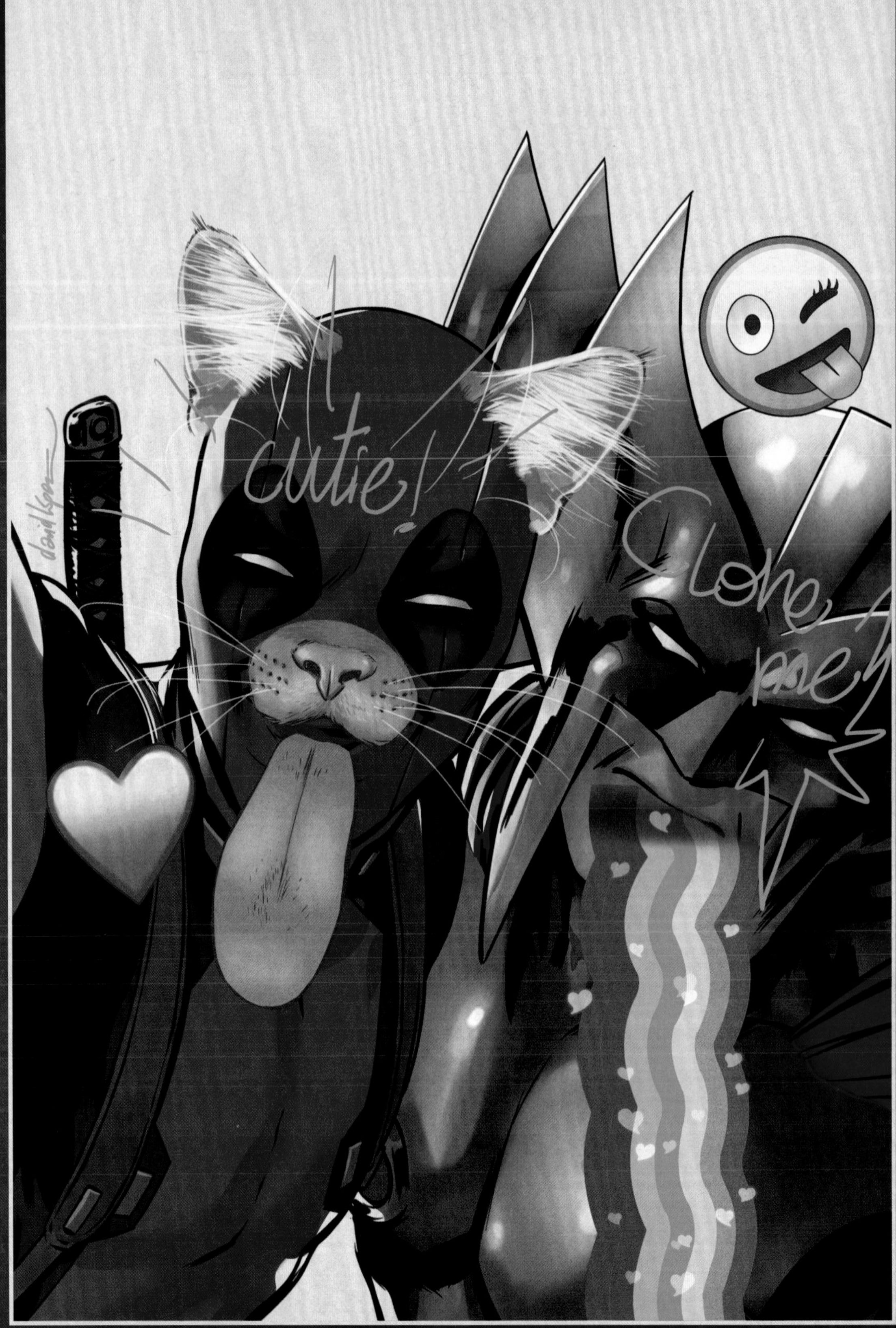
cutie!
Clone me!

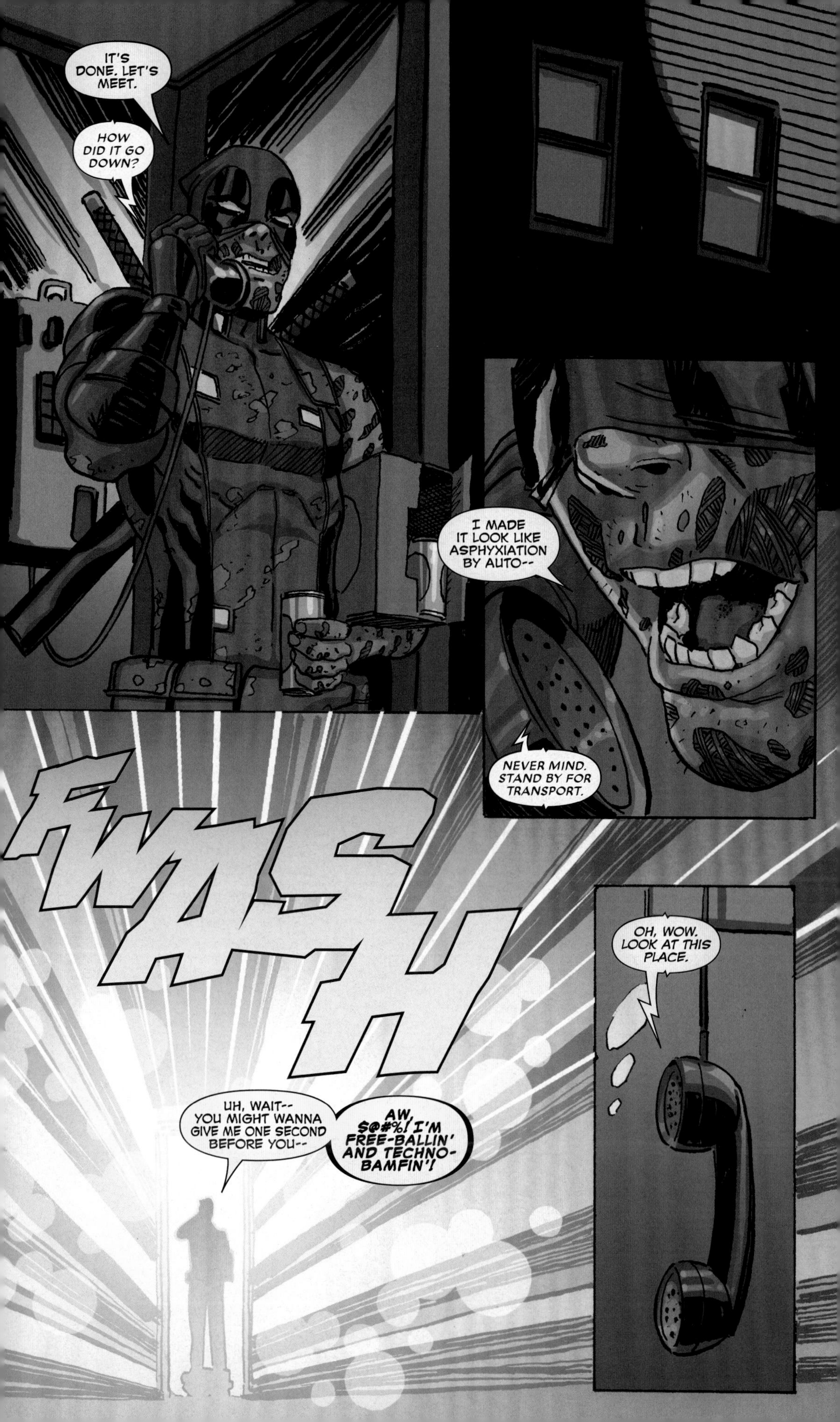
IT'S DONE. LET'S MEET.
HOW DID IT GO DOWN?
I MADE IT LOOK LIKE ASPHYXIATION BY AUTO--
NEVER MIND. STAND BY FOR TRANSPORT.
FWASH
UH, WAIT-- YOU MIGHT WANNA GIVE ME ONE SECOND BEFORE YOU--
AW, $@#%! I'M FREE-BALLIN' AND TECHNO-BAMFIN'!
OH, WOW. LOOK AT THIS PLACE.

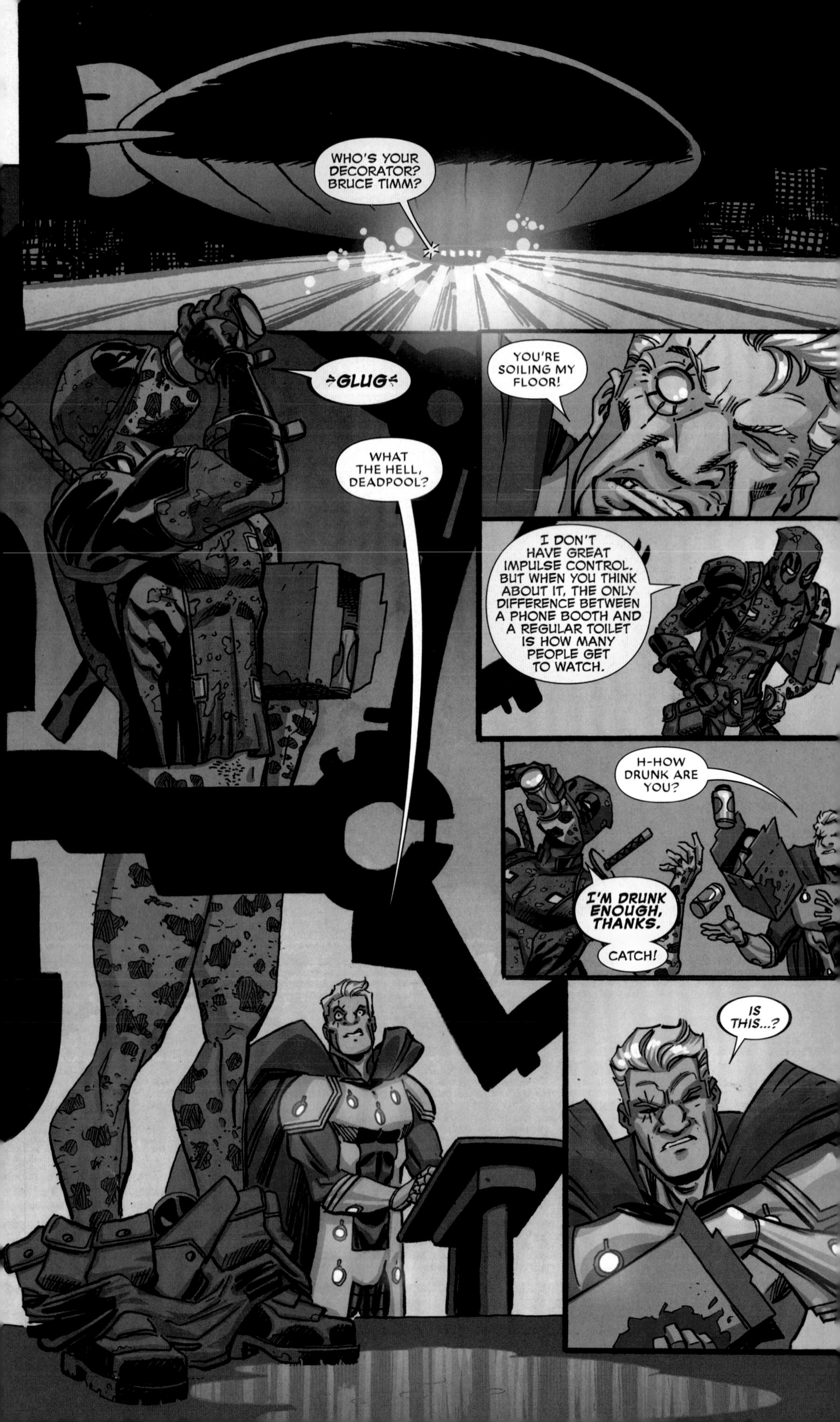
WHO'S YOUR DECORATOR? BRUCE TIMM?
GLUG
WHAT THE HELL, DEADPOOL?
YOU'RE SOILING MY FLOOR!
I DON'T HAVE GREAT IMPULSE CONTROL. BUT WHEN YOU THINK ABOUT IT, THE ONLY DIFFERENCE BETWEEN A PHONE BOOTH AND A REGULAR TOILET IS HOW MANY PEOPLE GET TO WATCH.
H-HOW DRUNK ARE YOU?
I'M DRUNK ENOUGH, THANKS.
CATCH!
IS THIS...?

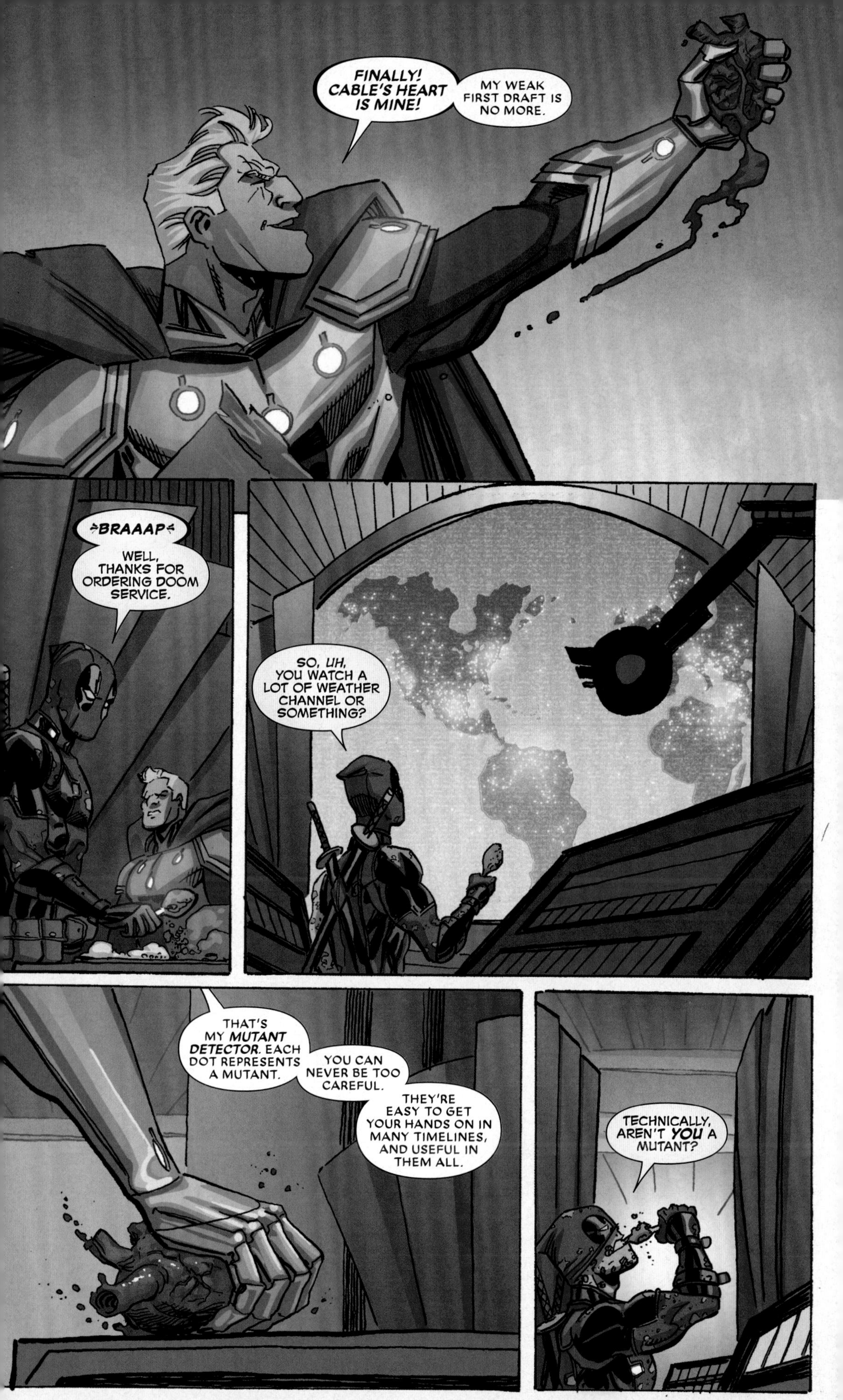

FINALLY! CABLE'S HEART IS MINE!
MY WEAK FIRST DRAFT IS NO MORE.
BRAAAP
WELL, THANKS FOR ORDERING DOOM SERVICE.
SO, UH, YOU WATCH A LOT OF WEATHER CHANNEL OR SOMETHING?
THAT'S MY MUTANT DETECTOR. EACH DOT REPRESENTS A MUTANT.
YOU CAN NEVER BE TOO CAREFUL.
THEY'RE EASY TO GET YOUR HANDS ON IN MANY TIMELINES, AND USEFUL IN THEM ALL.
TECHNICALLY, AREN'T YOU A MUTANT?

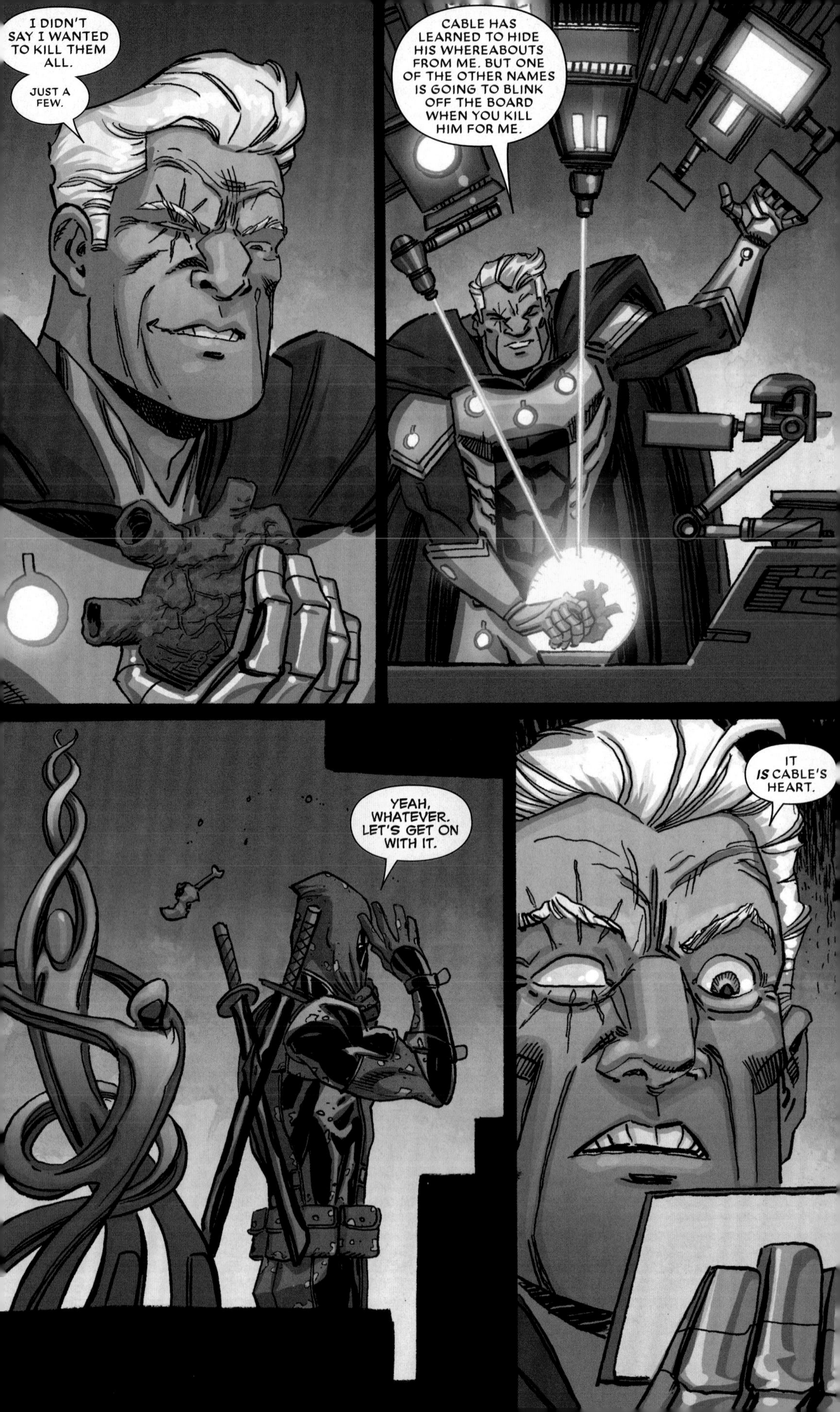
I DIDN'T SAY I WANTED TO KILL THEM ALL.
JUST A FEW.
CABLE HAS LEARNED TO HIDE HIS WHEREABOUTS FROM ME. BUT ONE OF THE OTHER NAMES IS GOING TO BLINK OFF THE BOARD WHEN YOU KILL HIM FOR ME.
YEAH, WHATEVER. LET'S GET ON WITH IT.
IT *IS* CABLE'S HEART.

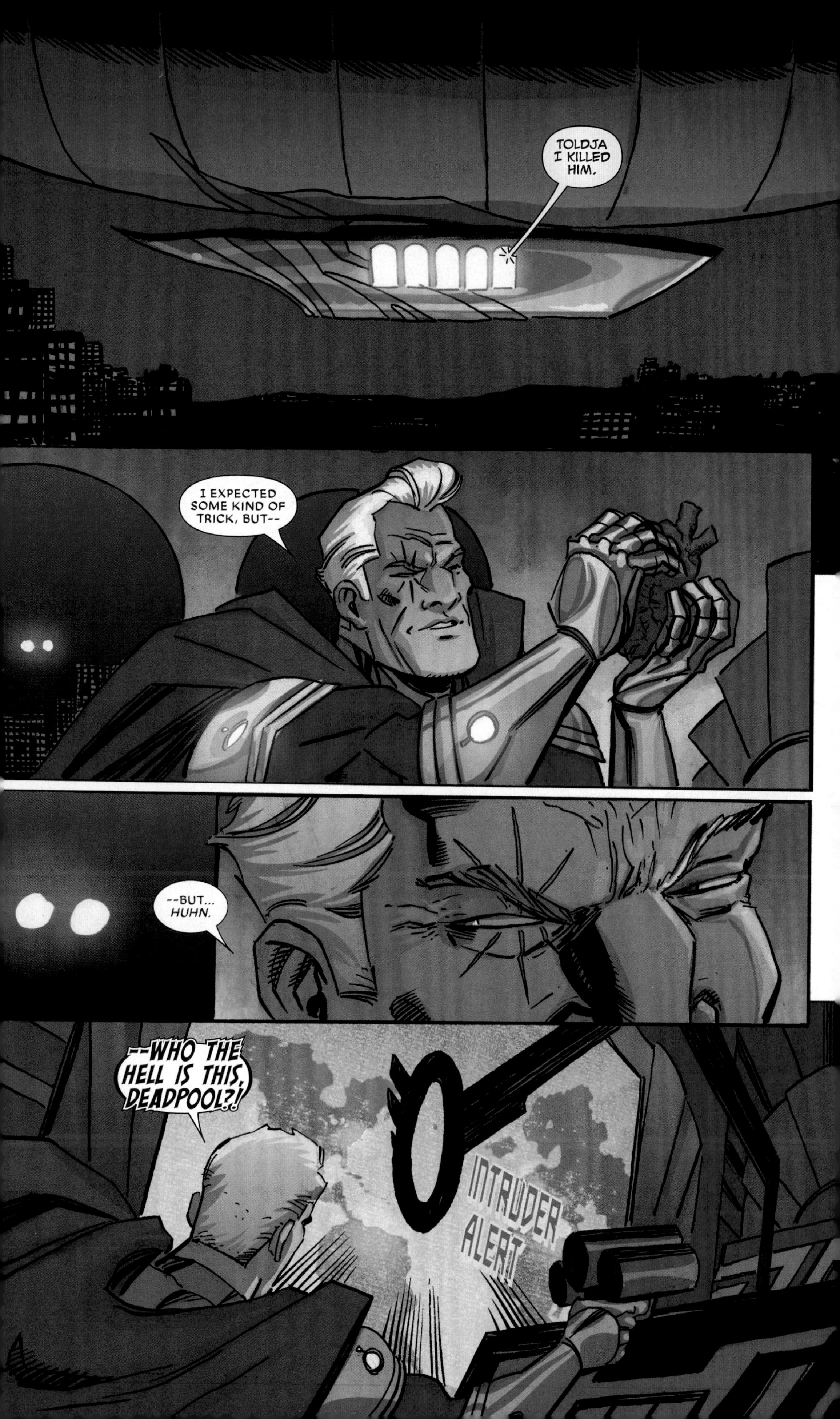
TOLDJA I KILLED HIM.
I EXPECTED SOME KIND OF TRICK, BUT--
--BUT... HUHN.
--WHO THE HELL IS THIS, DEADPOOL?!
INTRUDER ALERT!

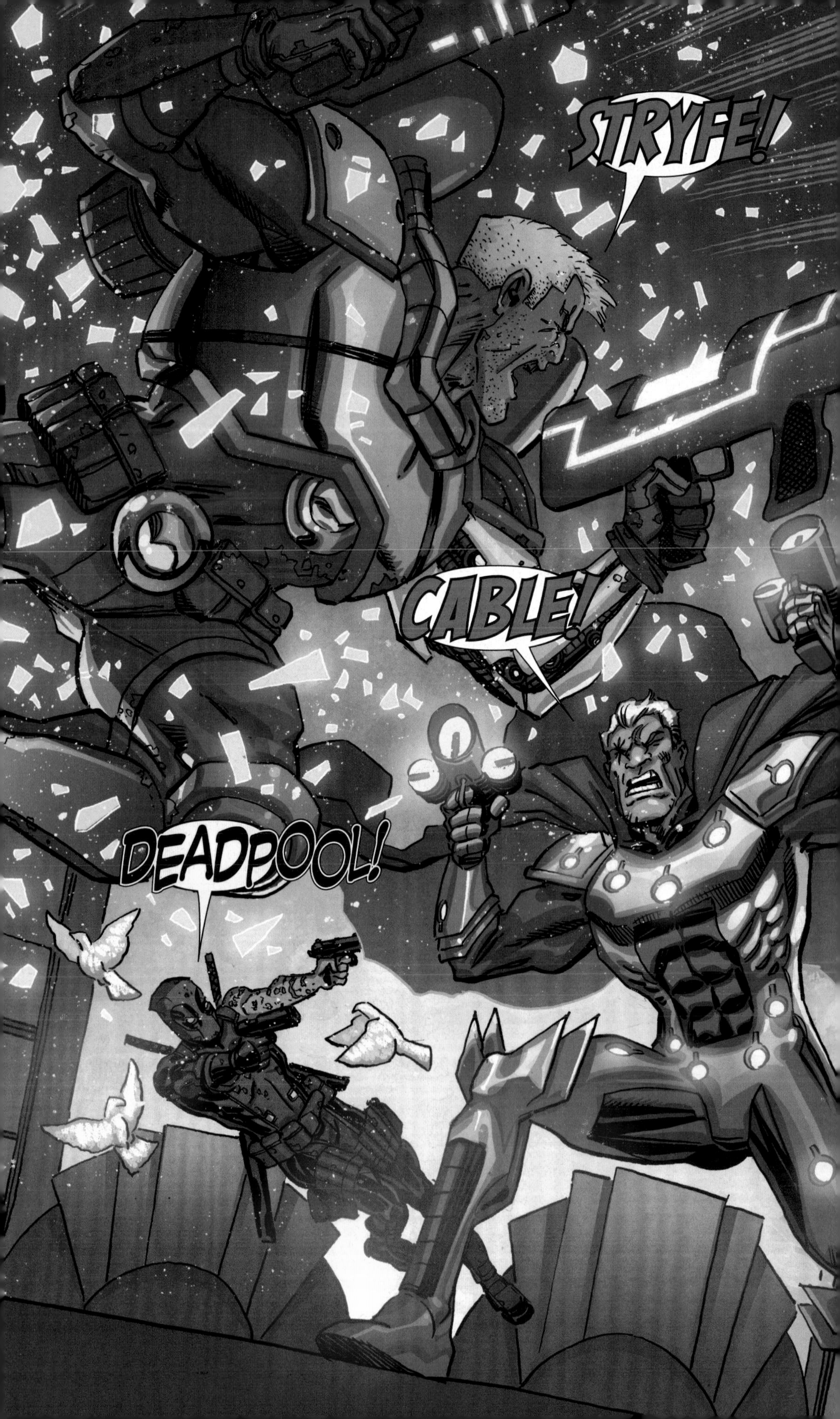
STRYFE!
CABLE!
DEADPOOL!

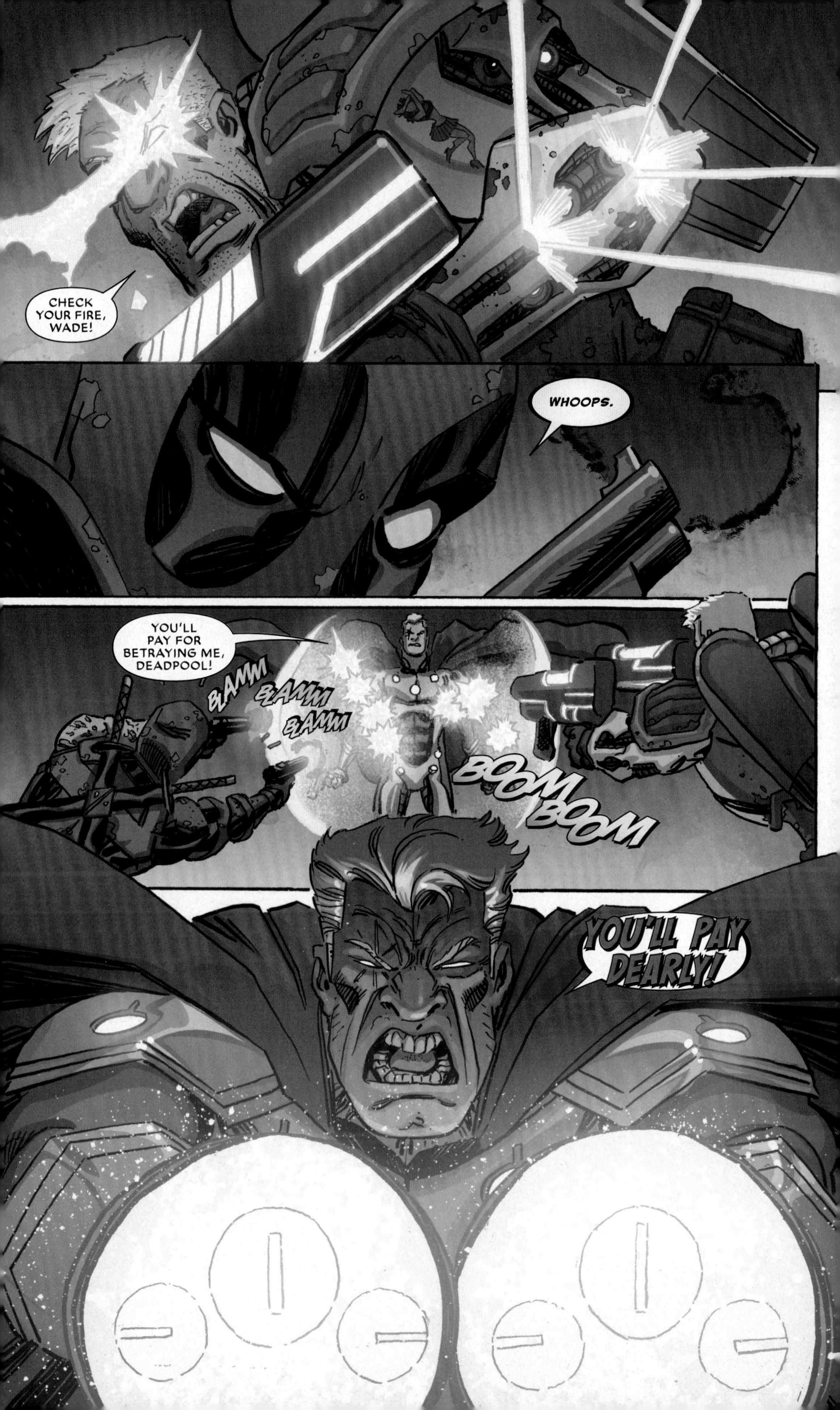
CHECK YOUR FIRE, WADE!
WHOOPS.
YOU'LL PAY FOR BETRAYING ME, DEADPOOL!
BLAMM
BLAMM
BLAMM
BOOM BOOM
YOU'LL PAY DEARLY!

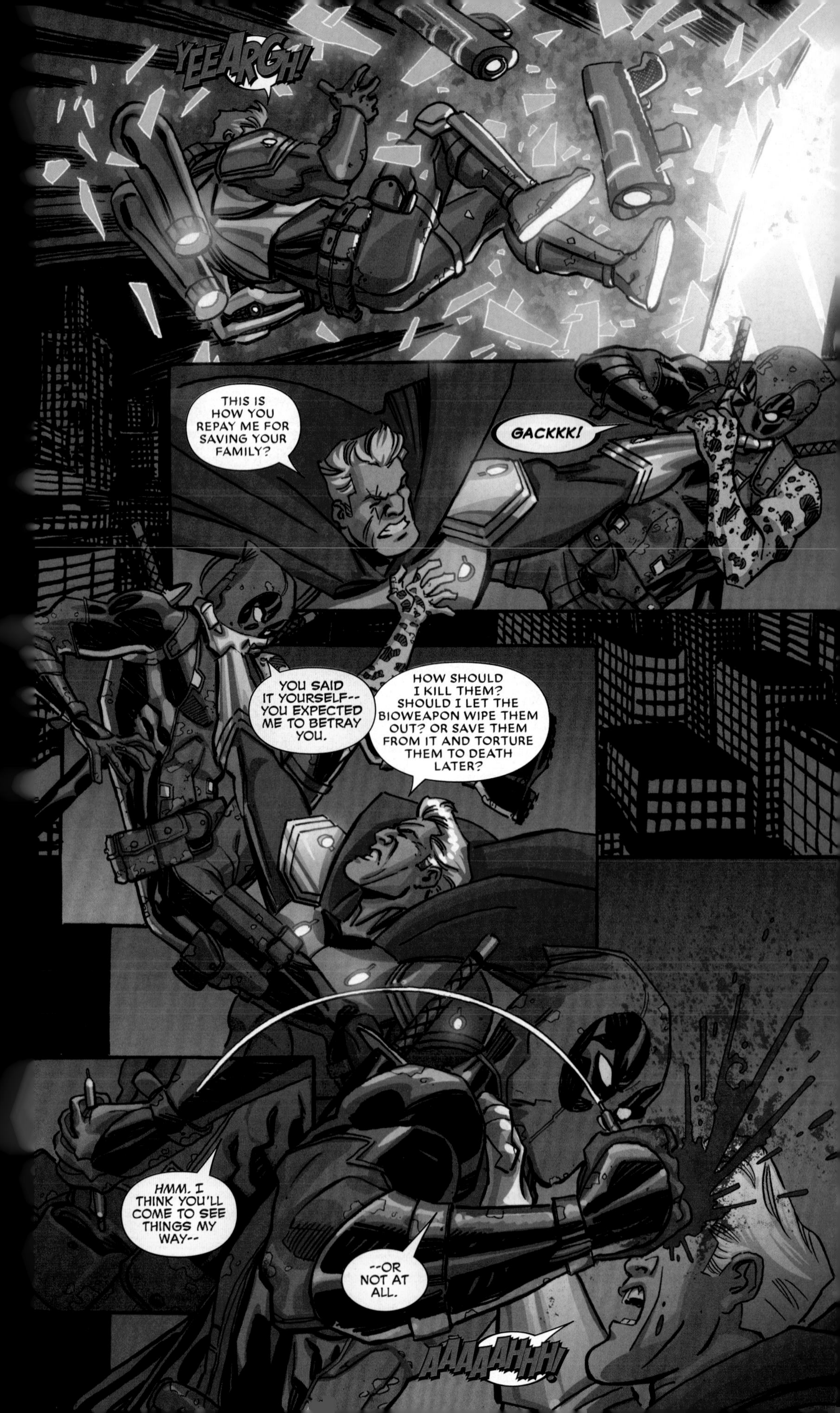

YEEARGH!
THIS IS HOW YOU REPAY ME FOR SAVING YOUR FAMILY?
GACKKK!
YOU SAID IT YOURSELF-- YOU EXPECTED ME TO BETRAY YOU.
HOW SHOULD I KILL THEM? SHOULD I LET THE BIOWEAPON WIPE THEM OUT? OR SAVE THEM FROM IT AND TORTURE THEM TO DEATH LATER?
HMM. I THINK YOU'LL COME TO SEE THINGS MY WAY--
--OR NOT AT ALL.
AAAAAAHHH!

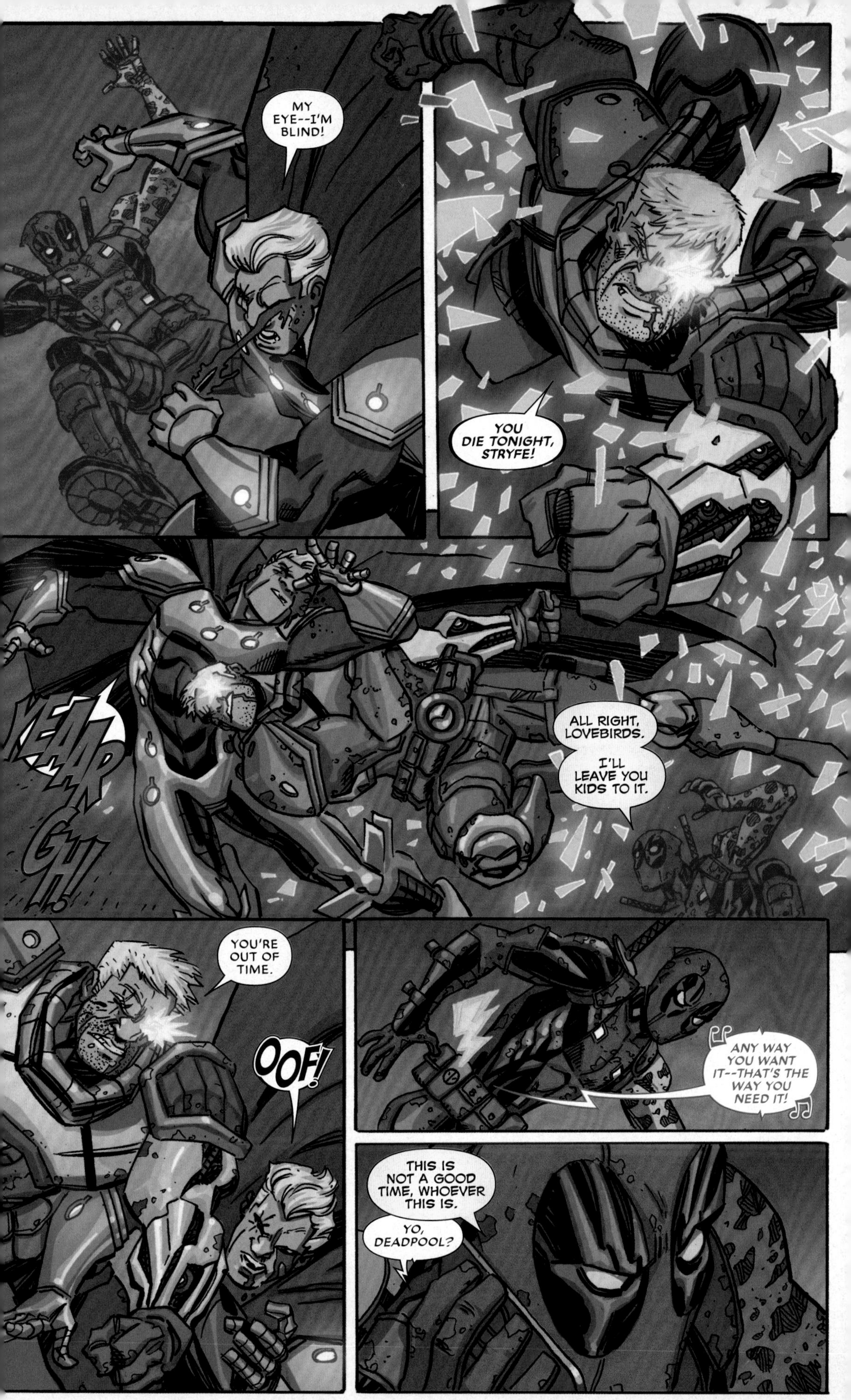

MY EYE--I'M BLIND!
YOU DIE TONIGHT, STRYFE!
YEAARGH!
ALL RIGHT, LOVEBIRDS.
I'LL LEAVE YOU KIDS TO IT.
YOU'RE OUT OF TIME.
OOF!
ANY WAY YOU WANT IT--THAT'S THE WAY YOU NEED IT!
THIS IS NOT A GOOD TIME, WHOEVER THIS IS.
YO, DEADPOOL?

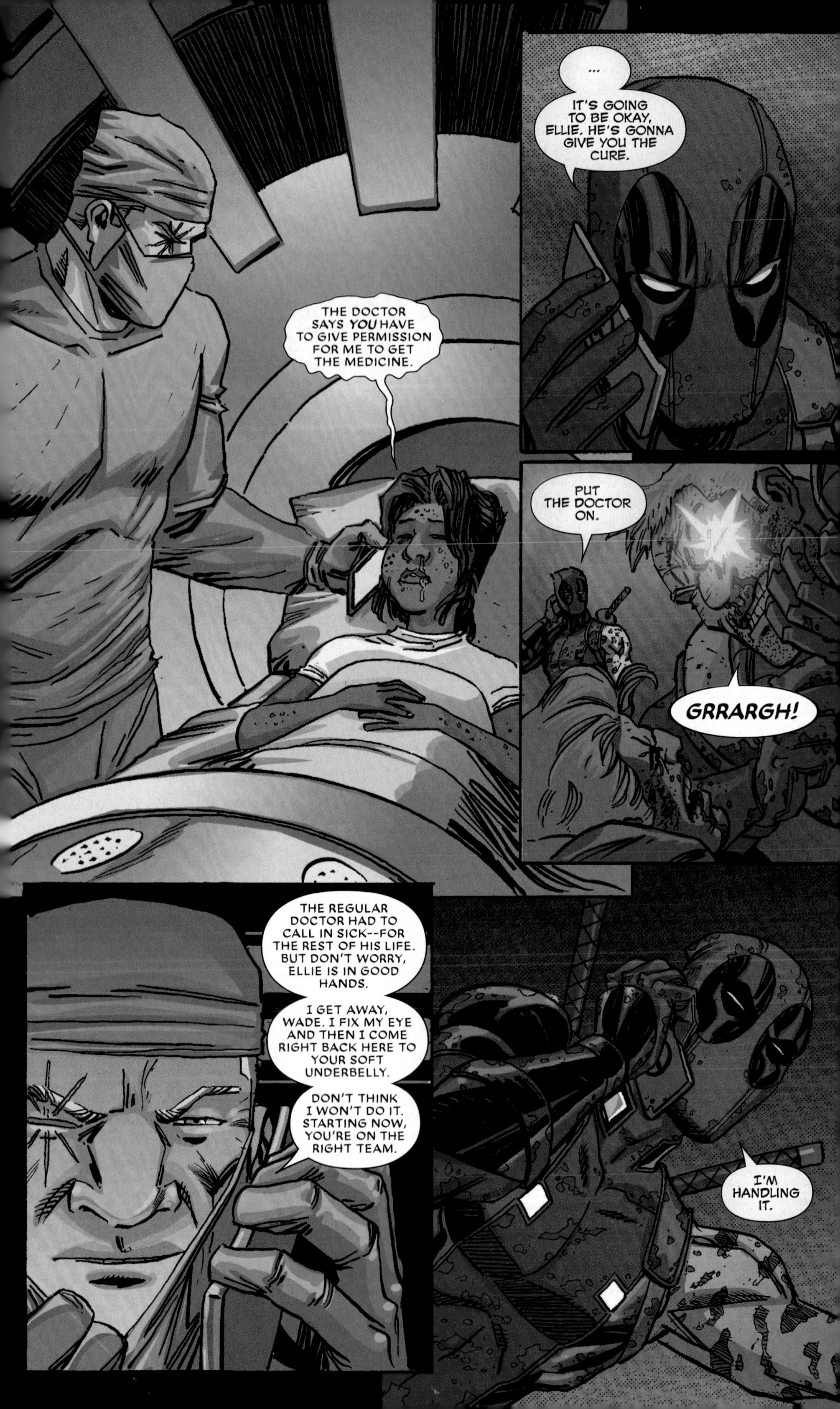
THE DOCTOR SAYS YOU HAVE TO GIVE PERMISSION FOR ME TO GET THE MEDICINE.
...
IT'S GOING TO BE OKAY, ELLIE. HE'S GONNA GIVE YOU THE CURE.
PUT THE DOCTOR ON.
GRRARGH!
THE REGULAR DOCTOR HAD TO CALL IN SICK--FOR THE REST OF HIS LIFE. BUT DON'T WORRY, ELLIE IS IN GOOD HANDS.
I GET AWAY, WADE. I FIX MY EYE AND THEN I COME RIGHT BACK HERE TO YOUR SOFT UNDERBELLY.
DON'T THINK I WON'T DO IT. STARTING NOW, YOU'RE ON THE RIGHT TEAM.
I'M HANDLING IT.

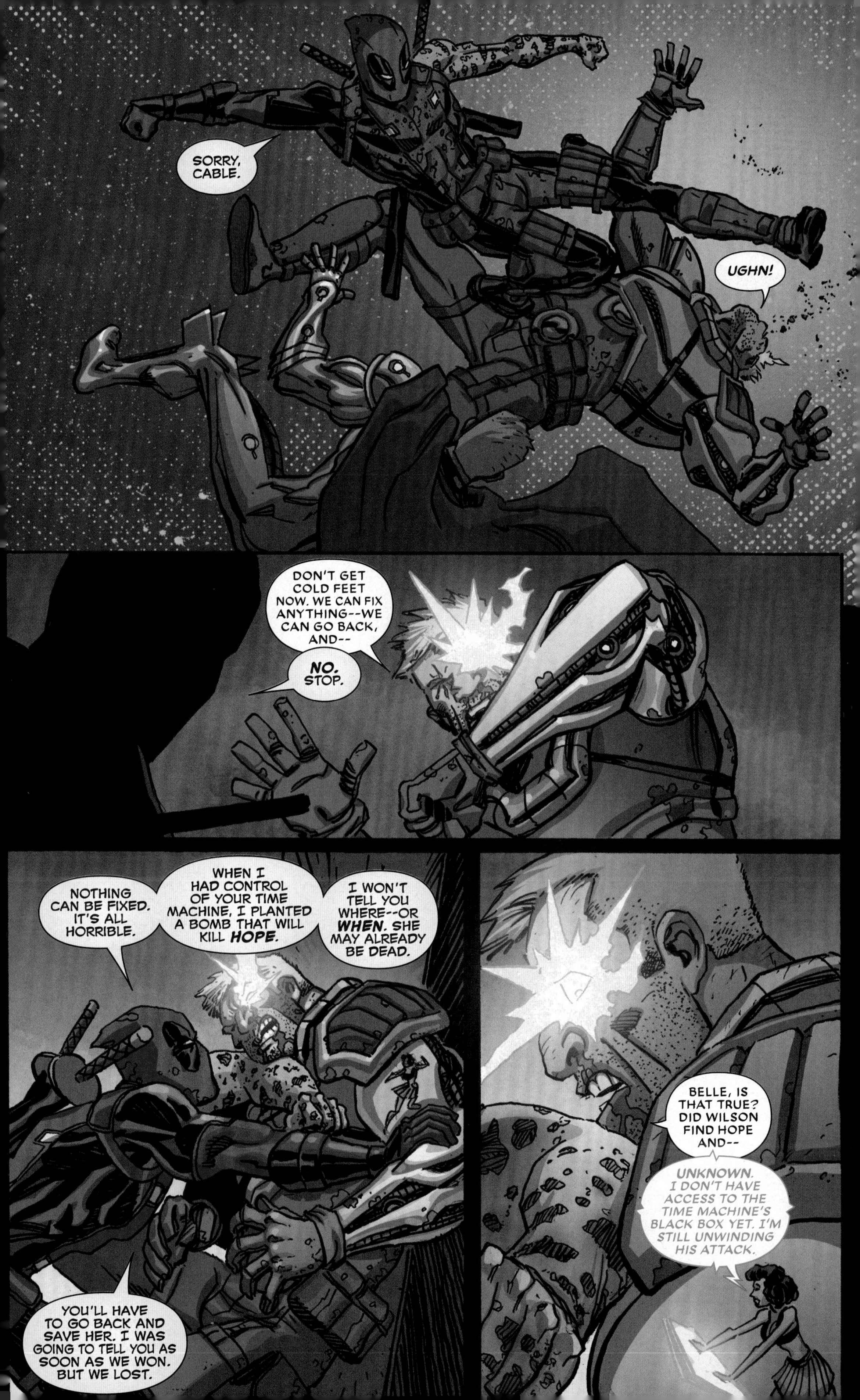

SORRY, CABLE.
UGHN!
DON'T GET COLD FEET NOW. WE CAN FIX ANYTHING--WE CAN GO BACK, AND--
NO. STOP.
NOTHING CAN BE FIXED. IT'S ALL HORRIBLE.
WHEN I HAD CONTROL OF YOUR TIME MACHINE, I PLANTED A BOMB THAT WILL KILL HOPE.
I WON'T TELL YOU WHERE--OR WHEN. SHE MAY ALREADY BE DEAD.
YOU'LL HAVE TO GO BACK AND SAVE HER. I WAS GOING TO TELL YOU AS SOON AS WE WON. BUT WE LOST.
BELLE, IS THAT TRUE? DID WILSON FIND HOPE AND--
UNKNOWN. I DON'T HAVE ACCESS TO THE TIME MACHINE'S BLACK BOX YET. I'M STILL UNWINDING HIS ATTACK.

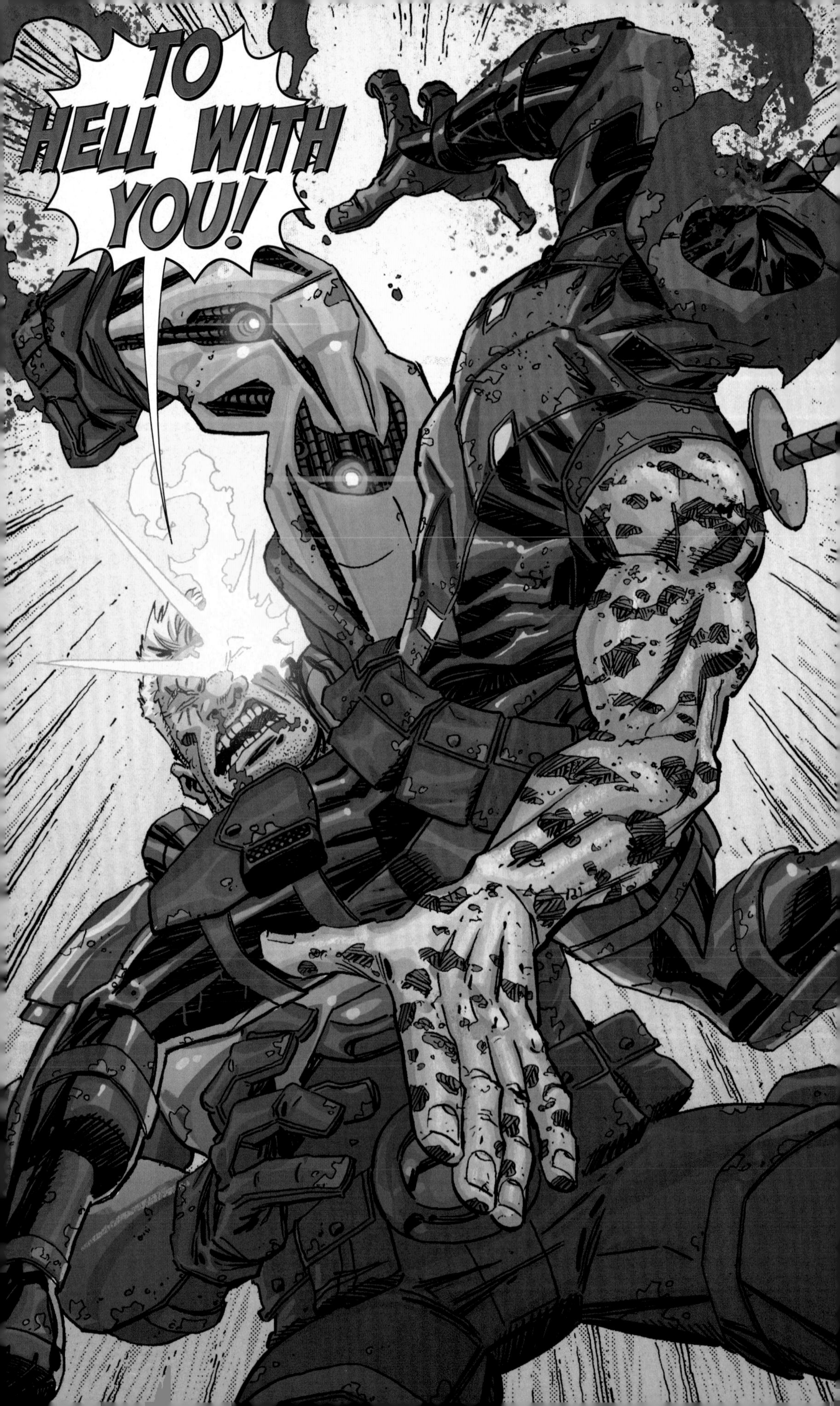
TO HELL WITH YOU!

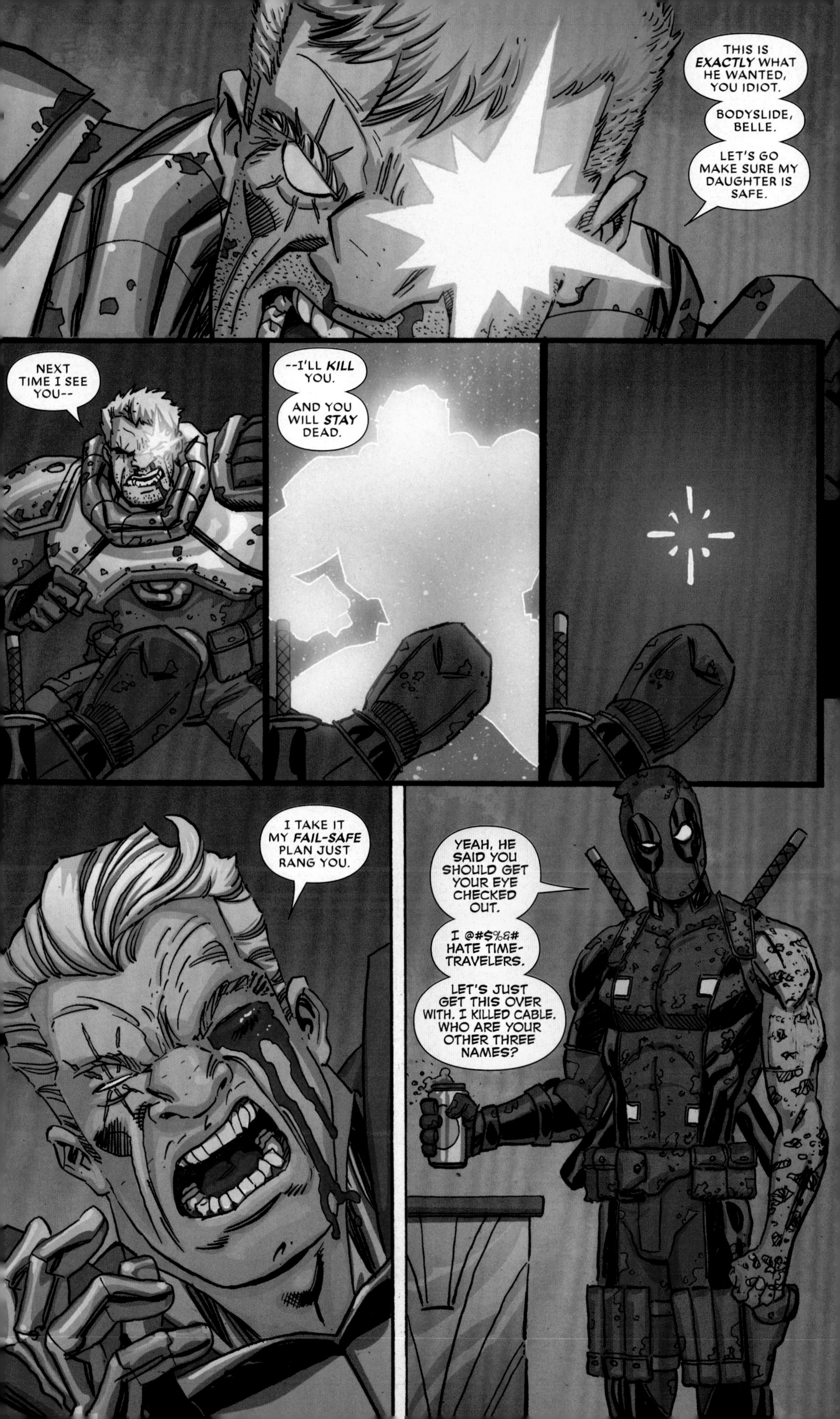
THIS IS EXACTLY WHAT HE WANTED, YOU IDIOT.
BODYSLIDE, BELLE.
LET'S GO MAKE SURE MY DAUGHTER IS SAFE.
NEXT TIME I SEE YOU--
--I'LL KILL YOU.
AND YOU WILL STAY DEAD.
I TAKE IT MY FAIL-SAFE PLAN JUST RANG YOU.
YEAH, HE SAID YOU SHOULD GET YOUR EYE CHECKED OUT.
I @#$%&# HATE TIME-TRAVELERS.
LET'S JUST GET THIS OVER WITH. I KILLED CABLE. WHO ARE YOUR OTHER THREE NAMES?

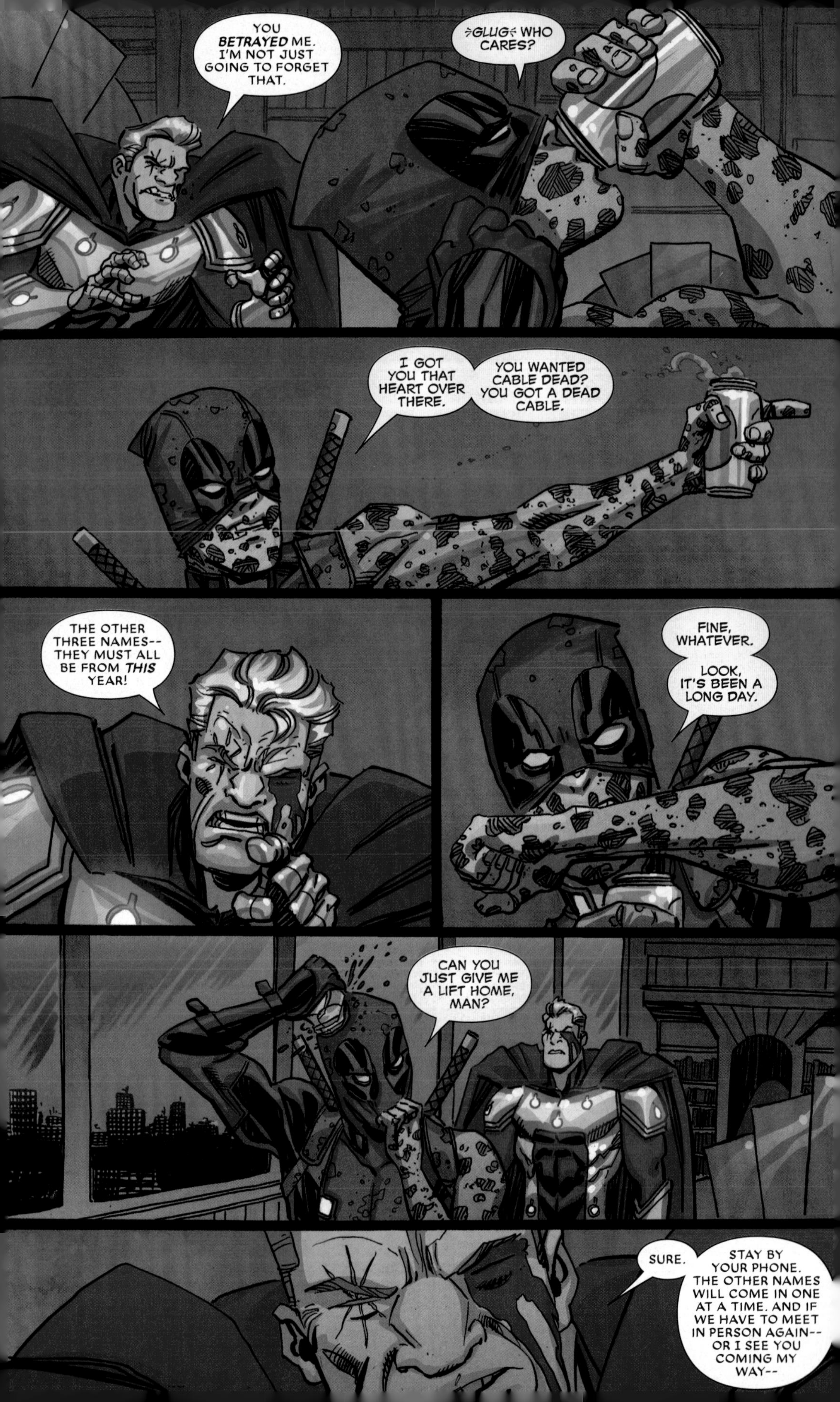
YOU BETRAYED ME. I'M NOT JUST GOING TO FORGET THAT.
>GLUG< WHO CARES?
I GOT YOU THAT HEART OVER THERE.
YOU WANTED CABLE DEAD? YOU GOT A DEAD CABLE.
THE OTHER THREE NAMES--THEY MUST ALL BE FROM THIS YEAR!
FINE, WHATEVER.
LOOK, IT'S BEEN A LONG DAY.
CAN YOU JUST GIVE ME A LIFT HOME, MAN?
SURE.
STAY BY YOUR PHONE. THE OTHER NAMES WILL COME IN ONE AT A TIME. AND IF WE HAVE TO MEET IN PERSON AGAIN--OR I SEE YOU COMING MY WAY--

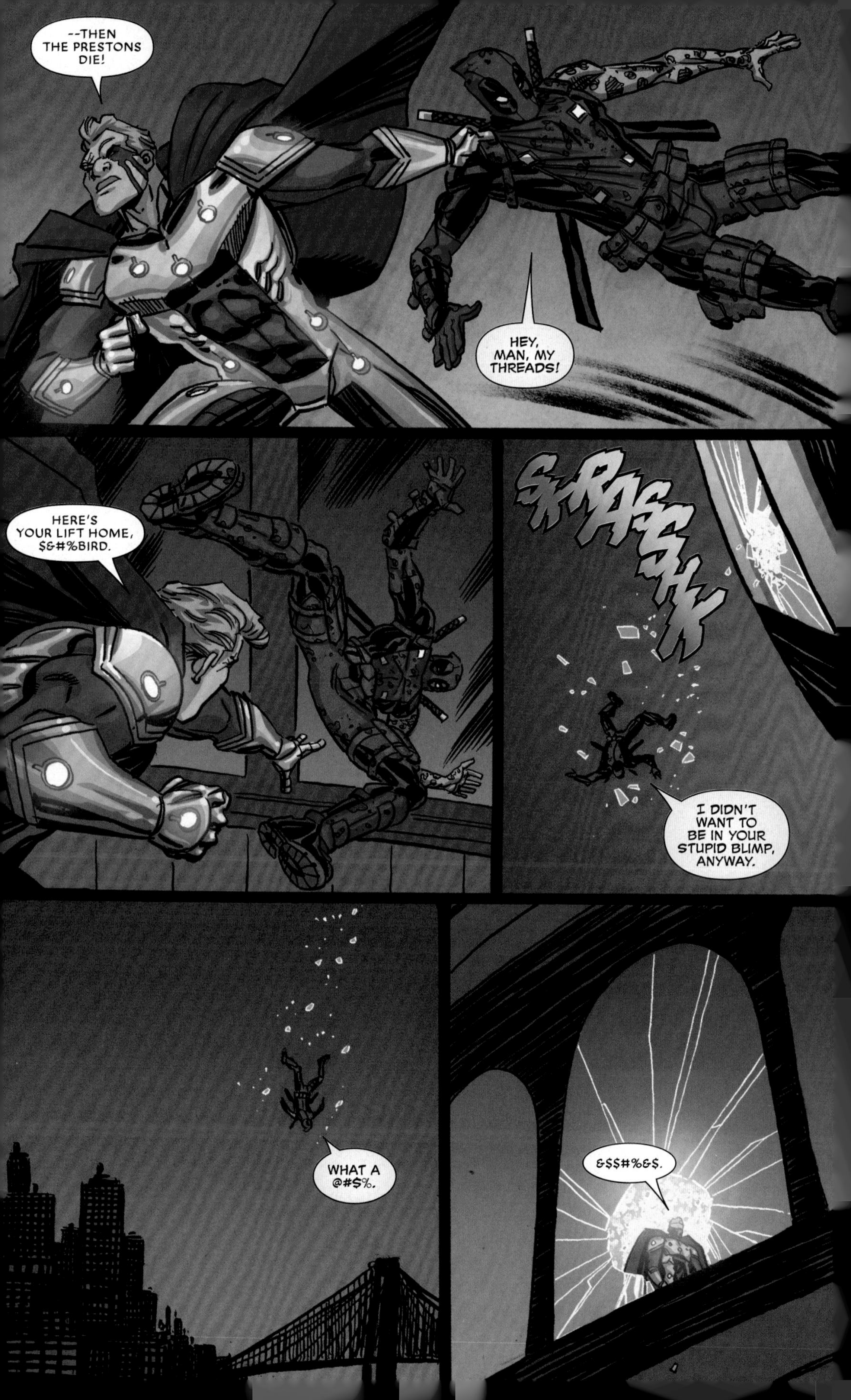
--THEN THE PRESTONS DIE!
HEY, MAN, MY THREADS!
HERE'S YOUR LIFT HOME, $&#%BIRD.
SKRASHK
I DIDN'T WANT TO BE IN YOUR STUPID BLIMP, ANYWAY.
WHAT A @#$%.
&$$#%&$.

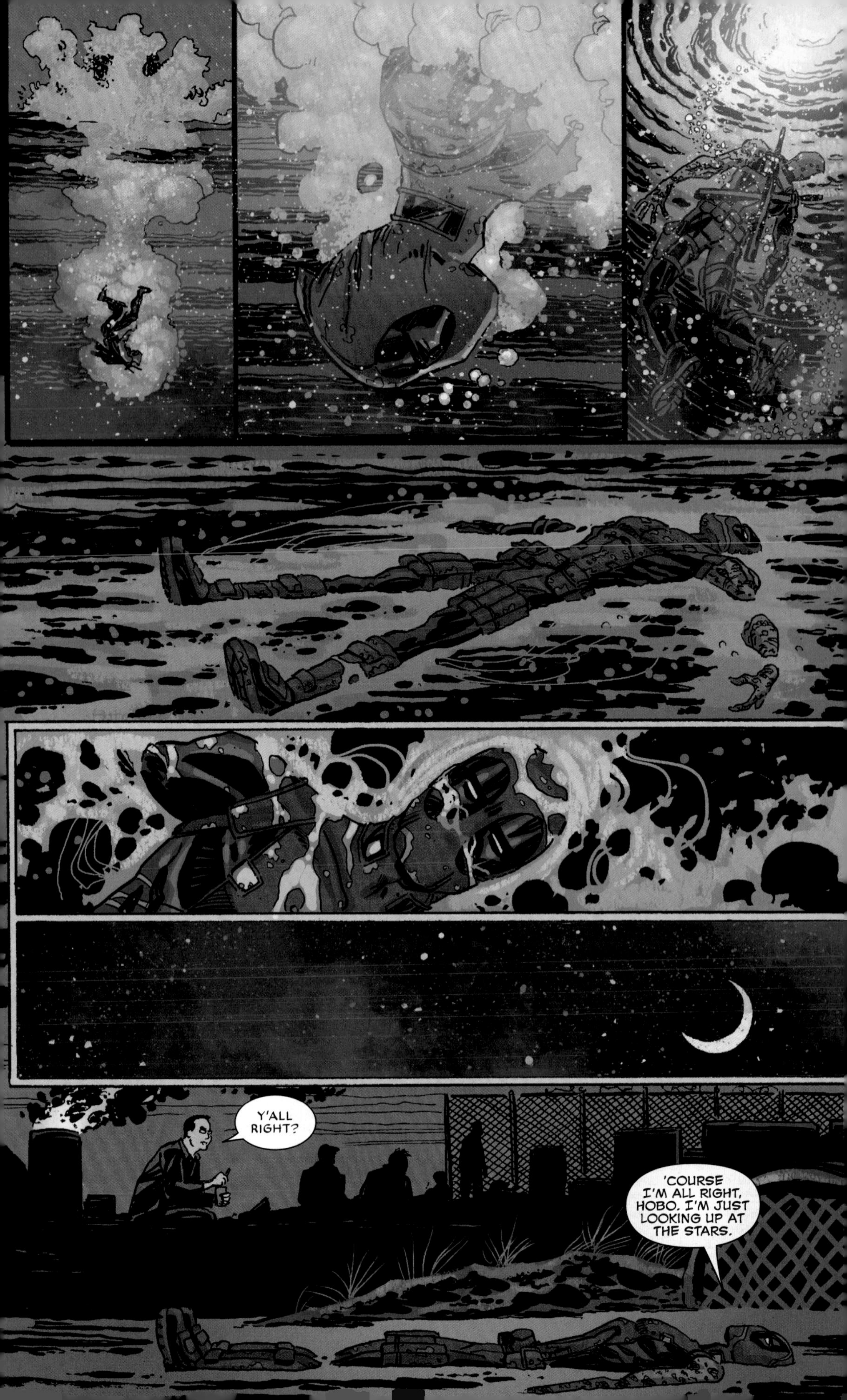
Y'ALL RIGHT?
'COURSE I'M ALL RIGHT, HOBO. I'M JUST LOOKING UP AT THE STARS.

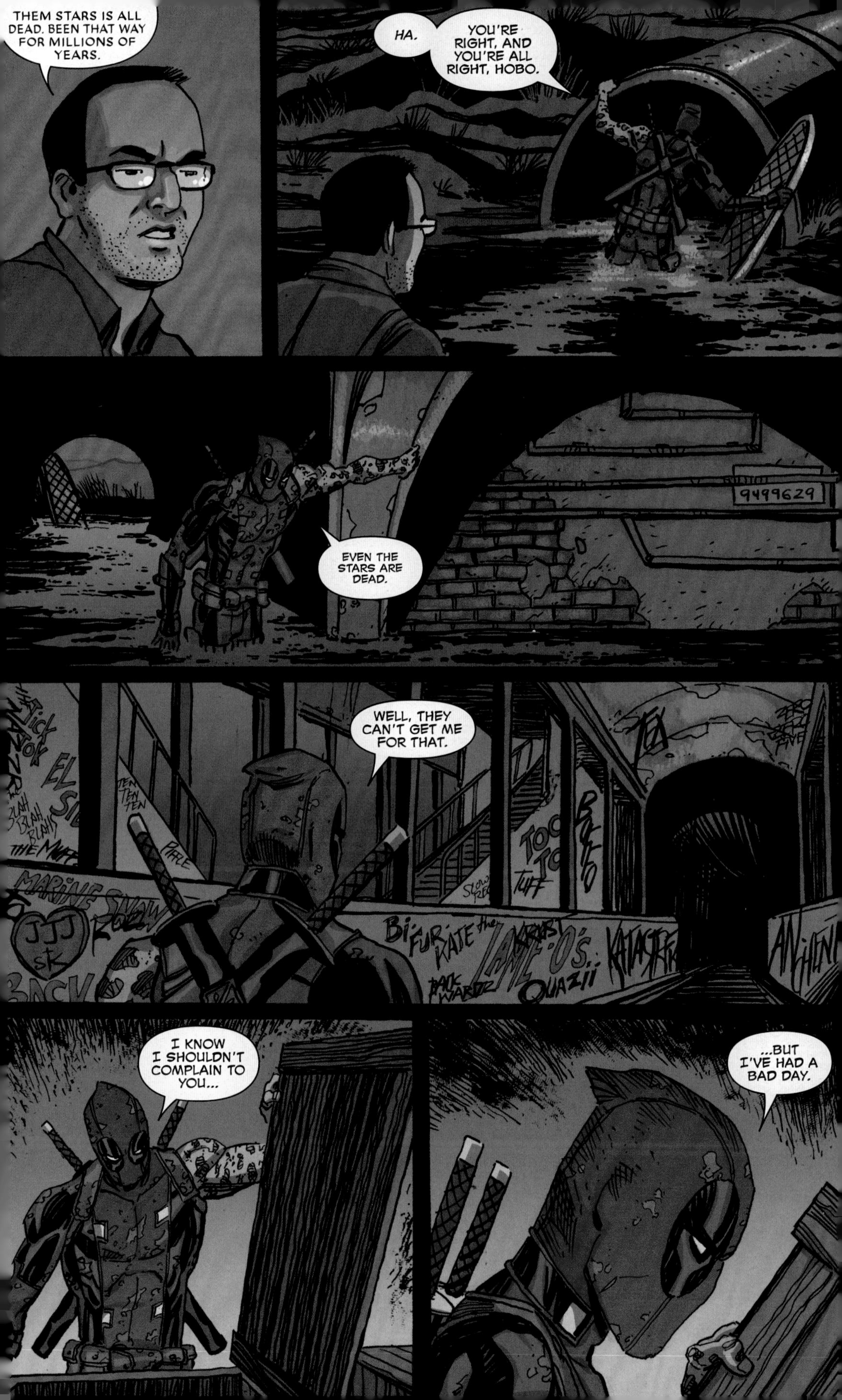
THEM STARS IS ALL DEAD. BEEN THAT WAY FOR MILLIONS OF YEARS.
HA.
YOU'RE RIGHT, AND YOU'RE ALL RIGHT, HOBO.
9499629
EVEN THE STARS ARE DEAD.
WELL, THEY CAN'T GET ME FOR THAT.
I KNOW I SHOULDN'T COMPLAIN TO YOU...
...BUT I'VE HAD A BAD DAY.

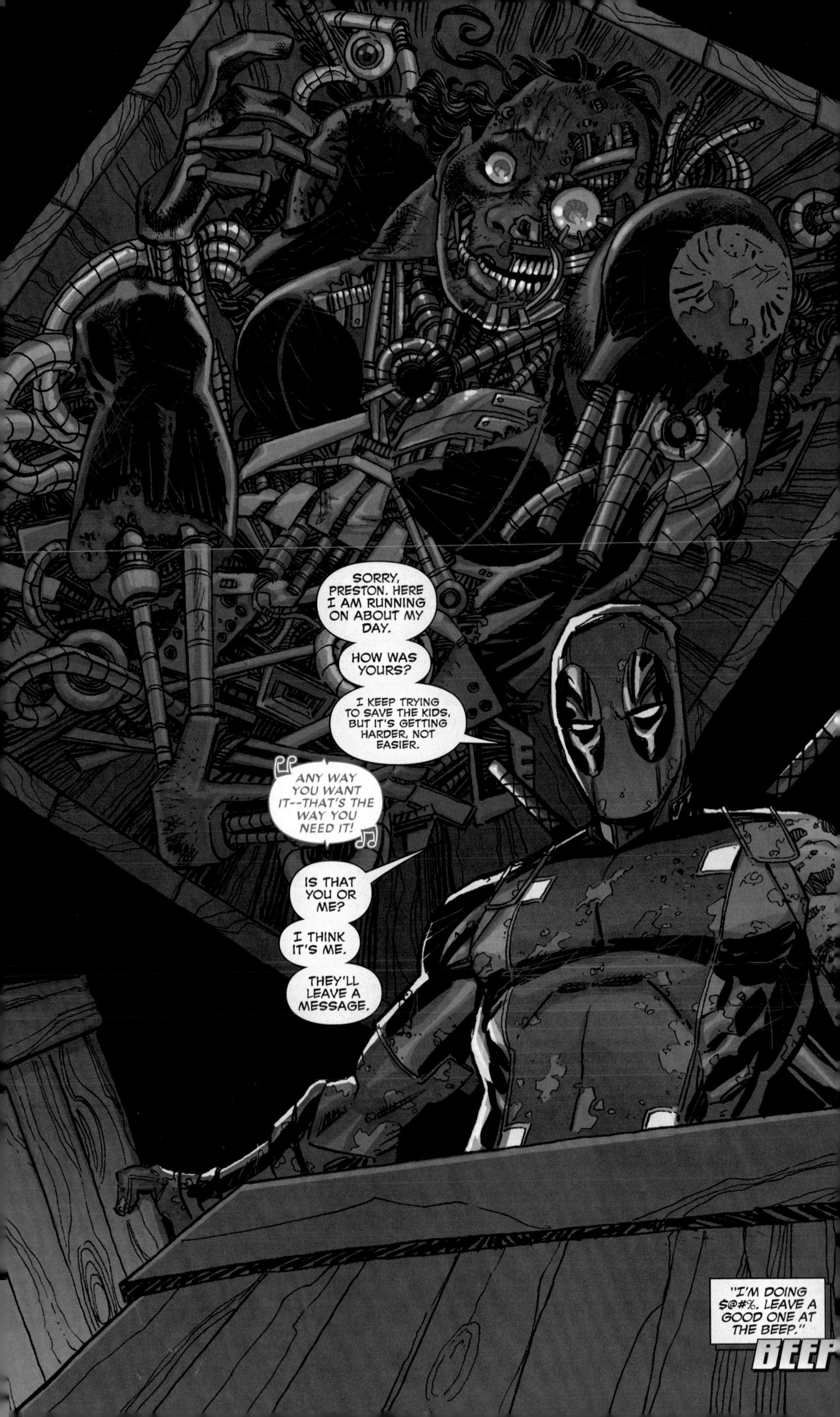

SORRY, PRESTON. HERE I AM RUNNING ON ABOUT MY DAY.
HOW WAS YOURS?
I KEEP TRYING TO SAVE THE KIDS, BUT IT'S GETTING HARDER, NOT EASIER.
ANY WAY YOU WANT IT--THAT'S THE WAY YOU NEED IT!
IS THAT YOU OR ME?
I THINK IT'S ME.
THEY'LL LEAVE A MESSAGE.
"I'M DOING $@#%. LEAVE A GOOD ONE AT THE BEEP."
BEEP

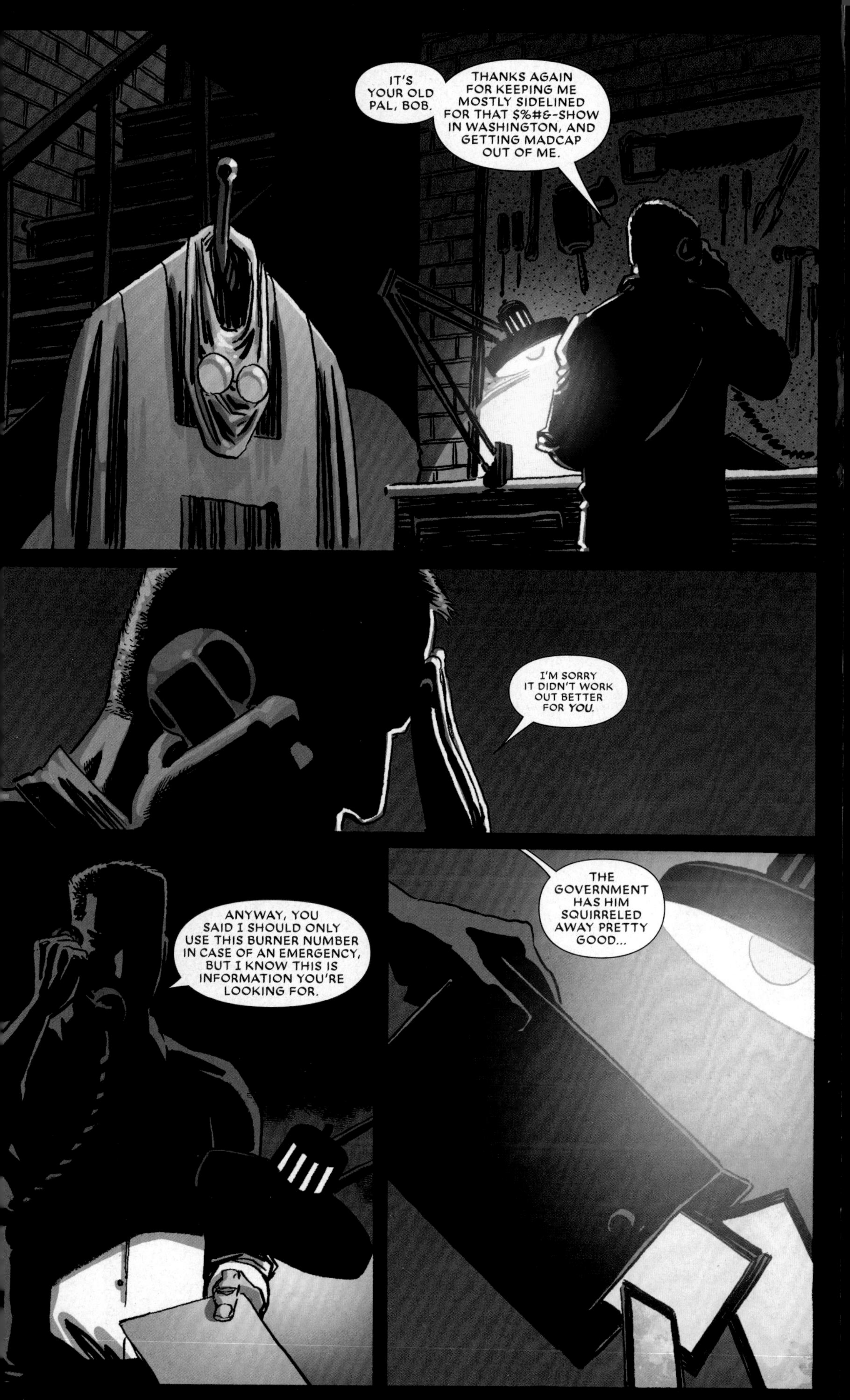

IT'S YOUR OLD PAL, BOB.
THANKS AGAIN FOR KEEPING ME MOSTLY SIDELINED FOR THAT $%#&-SHOW IN WASHINGTON, AND GETTING MADCAP OUT OF ME.
I'M SORRY IT DIDN'T WORK OUT BETTER FOR YOU.
ANYWAY, YOU SAID I SHOULD ONLY USE THIS BURNER NUMBER IN CASE OF AN EMERGENCY, BUT I KNOW THIS IS INFORMATION YOU'RE LOOKING FOR.
THE GOVERNMENT HAS HIM SQUIRRELED AWAY PRETTY GOOD...

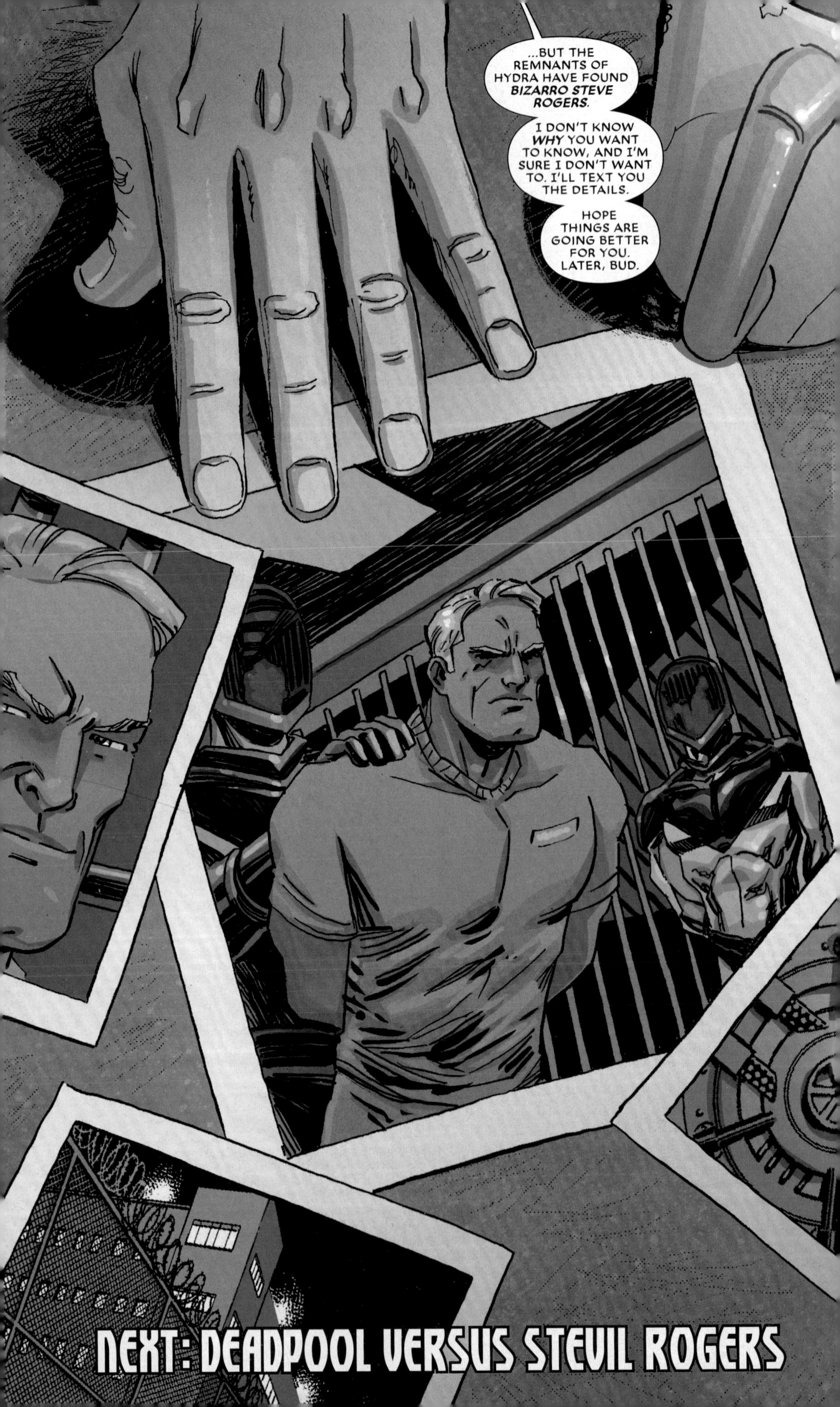
...BUT THE REMNANTS OF HYDRA HAVE FOUND BIZARRO STEVE ROGERS.
I DON'T KNOW WHY YOU WANT TO KNOW, AND I'M SURE I DON'T WANT TO. I'LL TEXT YOU THE DETAILS.
HOPE THINGS ARE GOING BETTER FOR YOU. LATER, BUD.
NEXT: DEADPOOL VERSUS STEVIL ROGERS